Spiritual Power

This selection from the rich heritage of nineteenth-century Christian writing has been specially chosen to represent material that was popular in its day and offers spiritual challenge to the twentieth-century reader. It includes both well-known authors and those who are less well-known. *Spiritual Power* includes excerpts from:

- *God is Love,* by Dwight L. Moody
- *Songs in the Night,* by Charles Haddon Spurgeon
- *The Christ-Life for the Self-Life,* by F.B. Meyer
- *Little Way,* by Thérèse of Lisieux
- *The Key to Prayer,* by Dora Greenwell
- *The Busybody,* by T. De Witt Talmage
- *My Life and Travels,* by Hans Nielsen Hauge

Spiritual Power is the third volume of the Christian Heritage Classics series, following *Exploring the Spiritual Life,* a compilation of seventeenth-century devotional writing, and *Spiritual Awakening,* a selection of classic devotional writings of the eighteenth century. Sherwood Eliot Wirt, the compiler and editor, is the author of a dozen or so other books, including *The Confessions of Augustine* in modern English

SPIRITUAL POWER

Classic writings of nineteenth-century spirituality to inspire and help the twentieth-century reader

Editor Sherwood Eliot Wirt

A LION PAPERBACK
Oxford · Batavia · Sydney

To my wife
Ruth Evelyn Love Wirt

Nunc scio quid sit Amor!

First published by Crossway Books,
a division of Good News Publishers, Westchester, Illinois 60153, USA
First UK edition 1989
published by arrangement with Good News Publishers

Published by
Lion Publishing plc
Sandy Lane West, Littlemore, Oxford, England
ISBN 0 7459 1799 2
Albatross Books Pty Ltd
PO Box 320, Sutherland, NSW 2232, Australia
ISBN 0 7324 0059 7

Printed and bound in Great Britain
by Cox & Wyman Ltd, Reading

CONTENTS

Foreword

In the summer of 1978, at a writers' conference, publisher Jan Dennis and I first discussed the plan of the Christian Heritage Classics series. Our hope was to provide modern readers with some of the fine Christian literature of the earlier centuries. With the help of five able advisers, Geoffrey W. Bromiley, Calvin D. Linton, Helga Bender Henry, D. Bruce Lockerbie, and the late Frank E. Gaebelein, the first volume, *Spiritual Disciplines*, appeared in 1983, covering the seventeenth century. The eighteenth century volume, *Spiritual Awakening*, appeared in 1986, and won an award as the finest entry in the classics field that year.

The present volume, third in the series, draws on nineteenth-century writings. Once again we tried to reach beyond the borders of any one country. Represented are six American authors, four English, one French, one Norwegian, one Danish and one German. As previously, the aim has been to look not primarily for masterpieces (although some certainly fit that description), but rather for material that was popular in its day, is still highly interesting to read, and offers valid spiritual challenge.

For their wise counsel I again thank my five advisers, and acknowledge with thanks the help of my editors.

Since the nineteenth century is so close to our own, readers might wonder why some obscure names are included in this volume, while others more prominent and better-known are not. Perhaps in my opinion the writings of those selected better reflect the mind of Christ, or perhaps they seem to read better, or are more spiritual? Please make no such assumptions. I am well aware of the risks involved in making comparisons. If you look for a reason for the selections, I will just say that the compilation represents the editor's choices and the advisers' agreement. I hope you like them.

S.E.W

Dwight L. Moody

God, the late evangelist Joe Blinco remarked, has a strange way of laying his hands on the wrong man. To some contemporary observers Dwight Lyman Moody (1837-1899) must have seemed such a man. The only water baptism he received was at the hands of a Unitarian minister. He never went to college, was never ordained. I once heard his voice on an early recording: it seemed high and rather thin. His grammar, it was said, made people wince. His figure was overweight and unprepossessing.

Yet this is the man God used to bring hundreds of thousands of people to Jesus Christ, to revitalize churches all across America and Britain, to found some of the great Christian institutions of our day, and to pioneer soul-winning through mass evangelism. Among Christian leaders he was a superb activist. He communicated to his generation by word and deed, and God has given the increase.

Moody was born in Northfield, Massachusetts, and attended school there until he was thirteen. His father had died when he was four. At age seventeen he set out for Boston, where his uncle hired him as a shoe salesman. Converted through the witness of a Sunday school teacher, Moody left Boston after two years for Chicago, where he found employment and began recruiting children for Sunday schools. In time he resigned his business connections and gave himself fully to YMCA and church work.

The story of Moody's dramatic rise to prominence as an evangelist, of his precedent-shattering trips to Britain with song leader Ira Sankey, of his historic campaigns for souls in New York, Boston, Philadelphia, Chicago, Baltimore, Cleveland, and San Francisco, cannot here be fully recounted. His marriage to Emma Revell, a printer's daughter, led to a tract ministry that also produced millions of low-cost Christian books for mass distribution and consumption.

Yet it was not so much Moody the builder, publisher or administrator who touched his generation as Moody the evangelist. His folksy sermons, sprinkled with sentimental anecdotes that touched people where they lived, were in marked contrast to the flowery rhetoric that characterized nineteenth-century preaching. People tolerated such pulpit elegance, but they flocked to hear Moody. His message was amazingly simple: Jesus Christ bore our sins on the cross of Calvary so we could become forgiven and restored children of the loving Heavenly Father who made us. Compassion, grace, repentance, salvation, holiness—Moody preached a Spirit-filled message, and preached it from a full heart. His words conveyed warmth, humor, profound belief in homely virtues (today we would call them "traditional values") and lots and lots of Bible teaching:

In a day when Biblical criticism was spreading rapidly through America's educational institutions, Moody remained a stout champion of God's authoritative written Word. On one occasion when critics downgraded a well-known Old Testament prophet as myth, Moody declared, "I stand by Jonah!" During his worldwide travels to preach the gospel he addressed more than one hundred million people—without electronic aid! While conducting a campaign in Kansas City in 1899 he became ill, and died shortly thereafter.

For all the solidity of his convictions, Moody was a gentle, loving man. It is safe to say that no evangelical leader of his day was so deeply mourned in Britain and America as was Moody when word of his death was flashed by telegraph and cable. Today, nearly a century later, the very name Moody stands for persuasive, oaklike Biblical Christianity. The following sermon is taken from the fifteenth edition of an 1879 volume published in Chicago by J. Fairbanks, titled, The Gospel Awakening, comprising the sermons and addresses . . . of the great revival meetings conducted by Moody and Sankey in the cities of Philadelphia, New York, etc. . . . from verbatim reports by our own phonographer and those of the New York Tribune.

ONE

GOD IS LOVE
by Dwight L. Moody

My text, "God is love," is taken from the first epistle of John,[1] and it is one of those texts the world does not believe. If I could make everyone in this building believe this text, I would not preach a sermon. If we all believed it, we would not need a sermon. If I thought I could make the world believe that God is love, I would take this text and go up and down the earth trying to counteract what Satan has been telling them so effectually, that God is not love. This is one of the texts Satan would like to blot out of the Bible. If you can only make [people] believe God is love, it would not take twenty-four hours to make the world come to God.

Love begets love, and hate begets hate. If you can really make a man believe you love him, you have won him. Let me report to you that I heard a man say this week that you were one of the meanest men in town, and you will conclude that the man who said that was the meanest man you ever heard of. Let me tell you I heard a man say he thought more of you than of any other man in the city, and your love will spring up and you will say, "I think a great deal of that man."

If I could only make people really believe that God loves them, what a rush we would see for the Kingdom of God! Oh, how they would rush in! But man has a false idea about God, and he will not believe that God loves him. It is because he doesn't know Him that he believes the Devil's lies.

In Paul's second letter to the Corinthians, chapter 13, he writes, "Finally, brethren, farewell. Be of one mind. Live in peace, and the God of love"—he calls Him the God of love—"and peace shall be with you."[2] Then John, who was better acquainted with Christ, writes in the evening of his life these words: "Beloved, let us love one another, for love is of God, and everyone that loves is born of God and knows God, and he that loves not knows not God, for God is love."[3]

A few years ago we built a church in Chicago, and we were so anxious to make people believe that God is love, that if we could not preach it into their hearts, we would burn it in. A friend put up over the pulpit in gas-jets the words, "God is love." Every night we had it lit there, and one night a man going along glanced in through the door and saw the text. As he walked away he said to himself, "God is love? No. God is not love. He does not love me. If God was love, He would love me." Yet there the text was, burning down into his soul. He went a little further, and turned around and came back into the meeting, to see the text as it was burning there upon the wall. He did not hear what the sermon was, but the arrow reached its mark. He went into the inquiry meeting. I asked him what it was impressed him. He said it was not the sermon, it was those words that had burned into his soul. He was weeping, and wanted to know what he should do to be saved. I unfolded the Scripture, and told him how God had loved him from his earliest childhood all along. The light of the gospel broke into his mind, and he went away rejoicing.

I hope this text will find its way into every heart here. I want to prove it from Scripture. The great trouble with men is, they are all the time trying to measure God by their own rule, and from their own standpoint. A man is apt to judge others from his own standard. If a man is covetous, he thinks everyone else is covetous. If he is a selfish man, he thinks everyone else is selfish. If a man is guilty of adultery, he thinks every other man is. If a man is dishonest, he thinks every other man is.

Many are trying to bring God down to their own level. They don't know that between human love and divine love there is as much difference as there is between darkness and light. God's love is deep and high; Paul says it passes knowledge. We are all the time measuring God's love by ours. We love a man as long as he is worthy, and then we cast him off; but that is not divine love. We don't find in the Word of God that God casts off those who are not worthy of His love. If He did, there would be no one in the Kingdom of God except Jesus Himself. There would be no hope for any of us if the Lord did that.

I have the idea that our mothers are to blame for a good deal of that in their teaching during our childhood. They tell their children that the Lord loves them when they are good children, and when they are bad children the Lord does not love them. That is false teaching. God loves them all the time, just the same as you love your children. Suppose a mother should come in here with a little child, and after she has been here a while the child begins to cry, and she says, "Keep still." But the child keeps on crying, and so she turns him over to the police and says, "Take that child, I don't want him." What would you say of such a mother as that? Teach a child that God loves him only so long as he is good, and you will find that when he grows up, if he has a bad temper, he will have the idea that God hates him. Now God hates sin, but He loves the sinner, and there is a great difference between the love of God and our love—all the difference in the world between human and divine love.

Turn to the thirteenth chapter of John, at the first verse: "Now, before the feast of the Passover, when Jesus knew that His hour was come that He should depart out of this world to the Father, having loved His own which were in the world, He loved them unto the end." We find His love is unchangeable. Jesus knew His disciples were to forsake Him and leave Him. Peter was to deny Him with a curse. Judas was that night to betray Him with a kiss. Yet it is said, He loved them right through it all. I should have thought that love would have broken the heart of Judas. If there is a soul goes down to Hell, it must go over God's love. You have to trample that love under your feet. It is said in Jeremiah 31:3, "I have loved you with an everlasting love." That means love without end. The only way you can get into the pit of Hell is to go right over the love of God; you cannot get there in any other way. God so loved the world that He gave His Son to die for you. That is what will make Hell so terrible.

Look at John 16:27—"For the Father Himself loves you because you have loved Me and have believed that I came from God." For the first few years after I was converted I had a good deal more love for Christ than for God the Father, whom I looked upon as the stern Judge. I regarded Christ as the Mediator who had come between me and that stern Judge, and had appeased His wrath; but when I got a little better acquainted with my Bible all those views fled. After I became a father, and woke up to the realization of what it cost God to have His Son die, I began to see that God was to be loved just as much as His Son was. Why, it took more love for God to give His Son to die than it would to die Himself. You would a thousand times sooner die yourself in your son's place than have him taken away.

Think of the love God must have had for this world, that he gave His only begotten Son to die for it. This is what I want you to understand: "The Father Himself loves you because you have loved Me."⁴ If a man has loved Christ, God will set His love upon him. When it is said that God loves us as He loved His own Son, it used to seem downright blasphemy to me, until I found it was in the Word of God.⁵ That was the wonderful prayer He made on the night of His betrayal. Is there any love in the world like that? Is there anything to be compared to the love of God? Well may Paul say, "It passes knowledge!"⁶

Some people say, "I like some proof of love." If a man told me he loved me, and never gave me any token, and never showed his love by any act, it would not be long before I would doubt his love. There is love by the tongue, that does not strike down into the heart, but that is not worth much. God does not say He loves us without giving us some proof of His love. The prophet Isaiah says in 63:9, "In all their affliction He was afflicted." You cannot afflict one of God's own without afflicting Him. He takes the place of a loving father. That is what He wants you to believe, that He loves you, and is in sympathy with you. If a man has loved Christ, God will set His love upon him.

Not only that, but in Isaiah 38:17 it is said, "You have cast all my sins behind Your back." Out of love for his soul, says the prophet, God has taken all his sins—not a part of them—and has cast them behind His back. Now tell me, how is Satan going to get at our sins if God has put them behind His back? If God has washed us, how is Satan going to find anything against us? Who shall say anything against God's elect? Satan could get behind my back, but he cannot pass the Lord God Almighty. I like that little word "all"—"all my sins." Suppose my little boy had committed ten sins, and he came to me and confessed and wanted me to forgive him, and I said, "I will forgive you nine of them, but one is such a big one I will not forgive that." That would not do him any good. Is it not a proof of His love that He forgives us freely? If I attempt to cover my sins, they will find me out. If I dig a grave, I cannot bury them so deep but they will have a resurrection. But the Lord takes them away. Not one of them shall ever be mentioned. They are gone for time and eternity. Is not that a proof of God's love, that He has taken all our sins out of the way, and put them behind His back forever?

I can imagine some of you saying, "Well, He loved His disciples and He loves those who serve Him faithfully, but then, I have been untrue." I may be speaking now to some backsliders, but if I am, I want to say to everyone here, "The Lord loves you." A backslider came into the inquiry room night before last, and I was trying to tell him God loved him, and he would hardly believe me. He thought because he had not kept up his love and faithfulness to God and to his own vows, that God had stopped loving him. Remember John 13, "He loved them unto the end."[7] You may have forgotten Him and betrayed Him and denied Him, but nevertheless He loves you. There is not a person here that has wandered from God and betrayed Him but what the Lord Jesus loves him and wants him to come back.

In the fourteenth chapter of Hosea God says, "I will heal their backsliding. I will love them freely."[8] So the Lord tells the backsliders, "If you will only come back to Me, I will forgive you." It was thus with Peter who denied his Lord. The Savior forgave him and sent him to preach His glorious gospel on the Day of Pentecost, when three thousand were won to Christ under one sermon of a backslider. Don't let a backslider go out of this hall this evening with that hard talk about the Lord. No backslider can say God has left him. He may think so, but it is one of the Devil's lies. The Lord never left a man yet.

I can imagine some of you saying, "If God has loved us with an everlasting love, why does it say that God is angry with the sinner every day?"[9] Why, dear friends, that very word "anger" in the Scriptures is one of the very strongest evidences and expressions of God's love. Suppose I have two boys, and one of them goes out and lies and swears and steals and gets drunk. If I have no love for him, I don't care what he does; but just because I do love him, it makes me angry to see him take that course. It is because God loves the sinner that He gets angry with him. That very passage shows how strong God's love is. Let me tell you, dear friends, God loves you in all your backslidings and wanderings. You may despise His love and trample it under your feet and go down to ruin, but it won't be because God doesn't love you.

I heard of a father who had a prodigal boy, and the boy had sent his mother down to the grave with a broken heart. One evening the boy started out as usual to spend the night in drinking and gambling. As he was leaving, his old father said, "My son, I want to ask a favor of you tonight. You have not spent an evening with me since your mother died, and now I want you to spend this night at home. I have been very lonely since your mother died. Won't you gratify your old father by staying at home with him?"

"No," said the young man, "it's lonely here, and there's nothing to interest me, and I am going out."

The old man prayed and wept and at last he said, "My boy,

you are just killing me as you have killed your mother. These hairs are growing whiter, and you are sending me, too, to the grave." Still the boy would not stay, and the old man then said, "If you are determined to go to ruin, you must go over this old body tonight. I cannot resist you. You are stronger than I, but if you go out you must go over this body." And he laid himself down before the door, and that son walked over the form of his father, trampled the love of his father underfoot, and went out.

That is the way with sinners. You have got to trample the blood of God's Son under your feet if you go down to death, to despise and make light of the wonderful love of God. But whether you do or not, He loves you still.

You say, why does He not show His love to us? Why, how can it be any further shown than it is? You won't read His Word and find out how much He loves you. If anyone will take a concordance and run through the Scriptures with the one word *love*, he will find out how much He loves you. He will find out that it is all one great assurance of His love. God is continually trying to teach you this one lesson, and to win you to Himself by a cross of love. All the burdens He has placed upon the sons of men have been out of pure love, to bring them to Himself.

Those who do not believe that God is love are under the power of the evil one. He has blinded you, and you have been deceived by his lies. God's dealing has been all love, love, love, from the fall of Adam to the present hour. Adam's calamity brought down God's love. No sooner did the news reach Heaven than God came down after Adam with His love. The voice that rang through Eden was the voice of love, hunting after the fallen one—"Adam, where are you?"[10] For all these thousand years that voice of love has been sounding down the ages. Out of His love he made a way of escape for Adam. God saved him out of His pity and love.

I do not see how any man with an open Bible before him can get up and say to me that he does not see how God is love. "Greater love has no man than this, that a man will lay down his life for his friend."[11] Christ laid down His life on the cross, and cried in His agony, "Father, forgive them, they know not what they do."[12] That was wonderful love. You and I would have called fire down from Heaven to consume them. We would have sent them all down into the hot pavement of Hell. But not the Son of God.

What more proof do you want that God loves you? It's true that we are not worthy to be loved. I will admit that. And God does not love you because you deserve it. Take a mother with nine children, and they are all good children save one. That mother will probably love that prodigal boy as much or more than all the rest. A friend of mine was visiting some time ago at a house where quite a company were assembled and were talking pleasantly together. He noticed that the mother seemed agitated, and was all the while going out and coming in. He took her aside and asked what troubled her, and she took him into another room and introduced him to her boy. There he was, a poor wretched boy, all mangled and bruised with the fall of sin. She said, "I have much more trouble with him than with all the rest. He has wandered far, but he is my boy yet." She loved him still. So God loves you still.

People think that if they could get rid of their sins, God would love them. In Revelation 1:5 is an ascription, "Unto Him that loved us and washed us from our sins in His own blood." It does not say He washed us from our sins and then loved us. He loved us first, and then washed us clean. How can you get rid of it until you come to Him? He takes us into His own bosom and then He cleanses us from sin. He has shed His blood for you and wants you, and He will redeem you today if you will.

An Englishman told me a story that may serve to illustrate this truth that God loves men in their sin. He does not love sin, but He loves men even in their sin and seeks to save them from sin. A great many years ago a boy was stolen in London. Long months and years passed away, and the mother prayed and prayed, and all her efforts failed. The others had given up all hope, but the mother did not quite give up her hope. One day a little boy was sent up into the neighboring house to sweep the chimney, and by some mistake he came down through the wrong chimney. When he got down, he came in by the sitting-room chimney.

His memory began at once to travel back through the years that had passed. He thought that things looked strangely familiar. The scenes of the early days of his youth were dawning upon him; and as he stood there surveying the place, his mother came into the room. He stood there covered with rags and soot. Did she wait until she had sent him to be washed before she rushed and took him in her arms? No, indeed. It was her own boy. She took him to her arms, all black and smoke, and hugged him to her bosom, and shed tears of joy upon his head.

You have wandered very far from God. There may not be a sound spot on you, but if you will just come to God, He will forgive and receive you. "You have in love to my soul delivered it from the pit of corruption, for You have cast all my sins behind Your back."[13] Mark you, the love comes first. He did not say that He had taken away sins and cast them behind Him. He loved us first, and then He took our sins away. I like that little word "my." The reason we do not get any benefit from Scripture is because we are always talking about generalizations. We say God loves nations, God loves churches, and loves certain classes of people. But He has taken all *my* sins, Isaiah says; and I will defy any fiend from Hell to find them. Satan can torment me with them no more.

Paul says, "He loved me, and gave Himself for me,"[14] as if there was not another person in the wide, wide world that the Lord Jesus Christ loved but Paul. He took the benefit of what Christ had done, and in order to get the benefit from Christ we must appropriate Him to ourselves. "He loved me, and gave Himself for me." Is not that a proof of His love? To think He loved us so that He gave Himself for us, should make us love Him.

Some people say, "Oh, yes, I love God," and never do it. You never see it in their lives or in their actions; you never see it in anything they do. Let me tell you, you may deceive your neighbors or yourself; you may join some church and profess to love God, you may make a great profession of religion, you may be a teacher in some Sunday school, but the Lord God looks into the heart to see if there is some love. Many a man is resting his hope upon having joined some church. What God wants is love. If love does not prompt us to work for God, it is all abomination to him. He cannot want sacrifice; it is love in the heart he wants.

In 1 Corinthians 8:3 we read, "If any man love God, the same is known of Him." God knows all about him. God measures his love, and He knows how deep and how broad it is. God knows the street you live on and the number of your house. He knows all about you. He said there was not a sparrow that fell to the ground without His notice. He knows all about the sparrows; He hears the young ravens when they cry. He says the very hairs of our heads are numbered. I see mothers who think a great deal of their babes, but I never heard of a mother who loved her babe so much that she numbered the hairs on its head. God is looking down to see how many are loving Him tonight. He knows your heart; you cannot conceal it. If you love Him, He will make His abode with you; but if your heart is full of malice and bitterness, the Lord cannot dwell with you. If you only love Him, then He comes.

There are some people who love God, and yet get into darkness because things go against them. They get almost to doubting God's love. I want to call your attention to Romans 8:28. It reads, "And we know that all things work together for good to them that love God." Again, put in that little word "all." A great many drop that "all." They say some things work together for good to them that love the Lord. If you do a good stroke in business, you say that is one of the things that work for good; but if you lose a great deal, you do not think it is.

Now, it may be that the losses will work more for your good than your successes. Let a man have prosperity, and how he turns away from God! It was when Jeshurun waxed fat that he kicked against God.[15] See how this nation [America] has been sinking into iniquity since the [Civil] War. Men turn their influence against God and His cause. You need not go out of Philadelphia to see that; you need not go out of your own acquaintance. People want prosperity, and that often turns them against God. Paul says, "All things work together for good to them that love God." Do you love Him?

I had a little girl taken down a few years ago with scarlet fever. I was very anxious about her, and I went to a physician with whom I was well acquainted. He wrote a prescription, and I took it to one of the leading druggists and said, "I want you to fill this with great care." I watched him as he went to a shelf and took down a great many different kinds of bottles, and he poured some out of each of them, and put it all in one and mixed it up. Then he put it in another bottle and stamped it, and gave it to me. Perhaps the medicine from any one of those bottles would have been rank poison, and would have killed the child, but they, being all mixed together, were just the medicine the child needed, and it worked for good and saved the child.

So it is that all things work together for good to them that love God. It is a little affliction here, a little trouble, and a little persecution—all working together for good. Some of you may have lost a little child a while ago; but perhaps you had no thoughts of Heaven until God took that child. A lady came into the inquiry room this afternoon and she had had no thought of Heaven for a long time, until death came and took two of her lambs.

I was told a story by a man who had been in Palestine. He saw a shepherd coming down to a stream with his flock. The shepherd tried to get them into the water, but they would not follow him. He took a little lamb and put it in his bosom, and plunged into the river and took it to the other side. The old sheep looked up at him and began to bleat. In a few minutes the whole flock went over, and he then put the lamb down and led the flock away into the pasture. Out of love to you the Great Shepherd has brought you into affliction. "All things work together for good to them that love God." If any of you are under the afflicting rod, don't complain. You will find, when you get yonder, that it was pure love that prompted Him to afflict you.

The Apostle Paul prayed that we might be able to comprehend what is the breadth and length and depth and height of God's love.[16] If we only knew that love, how much more we would be with Him and love Him. The only way for us to comprehend the love of God is to survey the wondrous cross at Calvary, on which the Prince of Glory died. Christ laid down His life not just for His friends, but for His enemies. It is the cross that speaks of His love. Do you think God would have given up His Son if He had not loved you? Was it not pure love in Him?

A story is told of the Roman Catholic Archbishop of Paris who, when France was at war with Prussia in 1871, was thrown into prison by the commune. It seemed he had been to Calvary and knew something of this wondrous love of God. Before he was executed he wrote on the top of a little window in his prison, which was in the shape of a cross, the word "height"; at the bottom, "depth"; and at the end of each arm of the cross, "length" and "breadth." Ah, that man had been to Calvary. He had surveyed the cross, had drank in its truth, and had laid hold of its power. He saw its height reached to the throne of God, its depth to the borders of Hell, and its length and breadth to the corners of the earth.

Oh, that this love might sink down deep into every heart! Some may say, "God loves Christians, but I am a sinner, and I have rebelled against Him all my life." He is wrong; God loves sinners. The Bible says so. It teaches another thing: that God loves you in your sin. If you could get rid of your sin, you would not need a Savior. If He does not love us until we are free from sin, there is no hope for any of us. To be sure, He saves us from sin, but it was while we were yet in our sin that Christ loved us and died for us.

A poor woman came into the inquiry room and said she had no strength. I said, "Thank God for that; Christ died for us when we were without strength."[17] He died for the ungodly. There was a time when I preached that God hated the sinner, that God was after every poor sinner with a double-edged sword. Many a time have I represented that God was after every poor sinner, ready to hew him down. But I have changed my ideas upon this point. I will tell you how.

In 1867, when I was preaching in a large hall in Dublin, Ireland, a young man who did not look over seventeen, though he was older, came up to me at the close of the service and said he would like to go back to America with me and preach the gospel.[18] I thought he could not preach it, and said I was undecided when I could go back. He asked me if I would write to him when I went, and he would come with me. When I did return I thought I would not write to him, as I did not know whether I wanted him or not.

After I arrived in Chicago I received a letter saying he had just arrived in New York and he would come preach. I wrote him a cold letter, asking him to call on me if he came west. After a few days I got a letter stating he would be in Chicago next Thursday. I didn't know what to do with him. I said to the officers of the church, "There is a man coming from England and he wants to preach. I am going to be absent on Thursday and Friday. If you will let him preach on those days, I will be back on Saturday and take him off your hands." They did not care about him preaching, being a stranger; but at my request they let him preach.

On my return on Saturday I was anxious to hear how the people liked him, and I asked my wife how that young Englishman got along. She said, "They liked him very much. He preaches a little different from what you do. He tells people God loves them. I think you will like him." I said he was wrong. I thought I could not like a man who preached contrary to what I was preaching. I went down Saturday night to hear him, but I had made up my mind not to like him. He took his text, and I saw everybody had brought their Bibles with them. "Now," he says, "if you will turn to the third chapter of John and the sixteenth verse, you will find my text."

He preached a wonderful sermon from that text, "For God so loved the world that He gave His only begotten Son, that whosoever believes in Him should not perish, but have everlasting life." My wife had told me he had preached the two previous sermons from that text, and I noticed there was a smile over the house when he took the same text. Instead of preaching that God was behind them with a double-edged sword to hew them down, he told them God wanted every sinner to be saved, and He loved them. I could not keep back the tears. I didn't know God thought so much of me. He went from Genesis to Revelation, and preached that in all ages God loved the sinner.

On Sunday night a great crowd came to hear him. He took the same text, and preached his fourth sermon from it, to show it was love, love, love that brought Christ from Heaven, that made Him step from the throne to lift up this poor fallen world. He struck a higher chord that night, and it was glorious. The next evening there was an immense crowd, and he preached his fifth sermon from that wonderful text. He did not divide it into firstly, secondly, and thirdly, but he took the whole text and threw it at them. I thought that sermon was better than ever. I got so full of love that I got up and told my friends how much God loved them. The whole church was on fire before the week was over.

I have never forgotten those nights. I have preached a different gospel since, and I have had more power with God and man from that time.

Do not believe that God does not love you. He loves you with an everlasting love. Here is a verse from the Song of Solomon: "He brought me to the banqueting house, and his banner over me was love."[19] A story is told of a young man who came to this country from England, became a naturalized citizen and went to Cuba, and lived there some time. When civil war broke out in Cuba in 1867, he was arrested as a spy, taken before the Spanish military court and ordered to be shot. He sent for the two consuls, American and British, and told them his case. He was neither a spy nor a politician. They went to the officers of the Spanish government and said, "This man is innocent; he had nothing to do with the war, and is not guilty of what he is accused."

They were told, "He was found guilty by our government and he must die." There was no time for appeal. A detail of soldiers was lined up, the man was brought before them and the black cap was drawn over him. But just before the troops received the command to fire, the American and British consuls rushed up and wrapped the Stars and Stripes and the Union Jack around him. Then they said, "Fire on these flags if you dare." But the Spanish militia did not dare to fire, because behind those flags were two powerful nations.

Think of the flag of Heaven! God says, "My banner over you shall be love." Come under the banner of Heaven tonight. Do not go out of this building until you are sheltered under this precious banner. If you are under His blood, you are saved for time and eternity.

There are four expressions wherein God puts our sins away.

The first is, He has blotted out our sins like a thick cloud.[20] You remember, don't you, how in the morning we wake and sometimes find the sky covered with clouds, but by the afternoon there is not a cloud to be seen? Can anyone tell where the clouds go to? They vanish and we see them no more, and no one can tell what has become of them. God has blotted out our sins like these clouds.

Another verse is, "I will remove them as far as the east is from the west."[21] Still another is, "I will roll them into the depths of the sea."[22] And then there is this one which reads, "who will take them out of love to my soul and cast them behind His back."[23] They are gone through time and eternity.

Bear in mind, it is out of love God does it, not out of justice. It is not justice we want, but mercy. God feels wonderful love, which it ought to break every heart here to contemplate, and the love of God ought to sweep over this audience and bow every head here tonight, and fill our hearts full of gratitude and praise that God so loved us and gave Himself for us. Christ shed every drop of His precious blood for sinners. Some people say, "Only one single drop of Christ's blood is enough to cleanse you from sin." It is not true. If one drop would have done it, He would have shed but one drop; but it took every drop of blood that His life had, and He gave it all up to save us. Paul says, "He loved me and gave Himself for me,"[24] and so Paul loved Him in return. If you could but get that thought in your mind that Christ has loved you so much as to give Himself for you, you could not help loving Him in return.

If you just take your Bibles you will find that God loves you. There is no one in this wide world that loves you as God loves you. You may think your father loves you, or your mother, or a brother or a sister, but let me tell you, you can multiply it by ten thousand times ten thousand before it will equal God's love. How a man with an open Bible can say that God doesn't love him is more than I can understand. But the Devil is deceitful and puts that into people's heads. Let me beg you, go to Calvary and there you may, just for a moment, catch a glimpse of God's love.

You ask me why God loves. You might as well ask me why the sun shines. It can't help shining, and neither can He help loving, because He is Love Himself, and anyone who says He is not Love does not himself know anything about love. If we have got the true love of God shed abroad in our hearts, we will show it in our life. We will not have to go up and down the earth proclaiming it. We will show it in everything we say or do.

I met a lady in the inquiry room today, and I could not convince her that God loved her, for she said if He did love her, He would not treat her as He had. And I believe people are all the time measuring God with their own rule, and we are not sincere in our love, and we very often profess something we don't really possess. Very often we profess to have love for a person when we do not, and we think God is like us. Now God is just what He says He is, and He wants His children to be sincere in love—not to love just merely in word and in tongue, but to love in earnest. That is what God does.

We won't win the world to Christ if we are cold and luke-warm; but if the love of God beats in warm pulsations in our hearts, and we show people we are full of love and sympathy for them, how easy it will be to win souls to Christ! I like to see in a Christian's face the light that comes down from the celestial hills of glory. To love those that abuse Him—that is what the Master did; and if we have His Spirit, we will certainly love those that don't love us.

I am tired of the word *duty;* tired of hearing duty, duty, duty. Men go to church because it is their duty. You can never reach a man's heart if you talk to him because it is your duty. Let us strike for a higher plane. God loved the world when it was full of sinners and those who broke His law. If He did so, can't we do it and love our fellowmen? If the Savior could die for the world, can't we work for it? The churches would soon be filled if outsiders could find that people in them loved them when they came. Actions like these speak louder than words.

Three thoughts I have tried to bring out: that God is love; that His love is unchangeable; that His love is everlasting. The fourth thought is this: His love is unfailing. Your love is not. His is. When people come to me and talk about their love for God, it chills me through and through; the thermometer goes down fifty degrees. But when they talk about God's love for them, I know what they mean.

Is there a poor wanderer tonight who has wandered far from Christ? He sends me to invite you to come to Him again. Let this text sink deep into your soul: "God is love." If you want to find out God's love, take this last will and testament of Jesus Christ. He showed His love by going to Calvary, by His death agony there. He loves you with an everlasting love. He doesn't want you to perish. O, may you love Him in return!

NOTES

1. 1 John 4:16.
2. 2 Corinthians 13:11.
3. 1 John 4:7, 8.
4. Cf. John 17:23.
5. John 17:26.
6. Ephesians 3:19.
7. John 13:1.
8. Hosea 14:4.
9. Psalm 7:11.
10. Genesis 3:9.
11. John 15:13.
12. Luke 23:24.
13. Isaiah 38:17.
14. Galatians 2:20.
15. Deuteronomy 32:15.
16. Ephesians 3:18, 19.
17. Cf. Romans 5:6.
18. The young man was evangelist Henry Morehouse of Manchester, England, who frequently joined with Moody in evangelistic campaigns in later years, both in America and England.
19. Song of Solomon 2:4.
20. Isaiah 44:22.
21. Psalm 103:12.
22. Cf. Micah 7:19.
23. Isaiah 38:17.
24. Galatians 2:20.

Charles Haddon Spurgeon

Of the many eloquent voices that proclaimed the gospel to an expanding world in the nineteenth century, none had nobler appeal or wider influence than the voice of the British Baptist preacher Charles Haddon Spurgeon (1834-1892).

With his clear tones, his masterful use of Anglo-Saxon, his grasp of Holy Scripture, his deep love for Christ, and his sharp, spontaneous and unconventional sense of humor, this prince of the sacred desk produced some of the finest gospel messages of any age. His life and labors, and especially his Lectures to My Students, *are required subjects of study in evangelical schools everywhere.*

In his History of Preaching *Edwin Dargan wrote, "What were the elements of [Spurgeon's] power? The natural man was well endowed. While he had a homely face and a stocky figure, he had a fine expression, and was gifted with a voice of great sweetness, smoothness, compass and delivery. In intellect he was alert, clever, sound, and strong, with fine imagination, large and shrewd observation, and wide reading with retentive memory. In temperament he was genial, winsome, hearty. Candor and sincerity were evident traits, with simplicity and strength of character.*

"The Christian showed in all his work. To his pious upbringing was added the deep experience of a definite and decisive conversion, and the joy of his salvation by grace resounded in no uncertain tones throughout his whole ministry. He was a mighty man in prayer. The pastor's heart was his; he kept in personal touch with his great flock in many telling ways, and his leadership was wise, loving, progressive and masterful. The preacher, however, was ever preeminent. He was an old-fashioned evangelical Calvinist from beginning to end. His delivery was without notes, free, easy and natural. The glory of God in saving men was his ruling motive. Great was his work and great his reward."

Spurgeon was born into a preacher's family in Essex, England, and was converted at age sixteen while listening to a sermon in a Primitive Methodist chapel in Colchester, where he had sought shelter during a snowstorm. That same year he preached his first sermon, and in 1851 was called to the pulpit of Waterbeach Baptist Chapel. His youthful popularity was such that in 1854 (now aged twenty) he was called to New Park Street Chapel in London's Southwark, where crowds soon overflowed the building.

In 1856 Spurgeon married Susanna Thompson, who became the mother of twin sons. He launched a "pastor's college" to train young men for the ministry and supported it himself. He also started an orphanage, a clothing society, and a colportage association, among other charities and good works. Meanwhile, increasing attendance at worship necessitated the erection of the London Metropolitan Tabernacle in 1859, where he preached Sundays and Thursdays. His congregation increased to six thousand persons, and his sermons were reprinted weekly and shipped to missionaries all over the world, as well as being printed in the London papers and sold throughout England (to quote the Encyclopedia Britannica) *"by the ton."*

Spurgeon's last years were marred by theological controversy and ill health. By steering a path between liberalizing trends among his fellow Baptists and reactionary Calvinists who looked with disfavor upon all evangelism, he came under siege from both sides. "Lord," he would pray, "save all the elect, and then elect some more!" Seeking physical relief in a better climate, he went to Mentone, France, where he became ill and died in January 1892.

It was Professor Andrew Blackwood who, while I was a graduate student at Princeton Theological Seminary in 1943, introduced me to this sermon. "Songs in the Night" has remained a favorite of mine ever since, and I marvel that Spurgeon preached it when only twenty-two years of age. It may be found in many anthologies, including Fish, Masterpieces of Pulpit Eloquence, XIX Century.

SONGS IN THE NIGHT
by Charles Haddon Spurgeon

Then Elihu said [to Job]: "I would like to reply to you and
to your friends with you. . . . Men cry out under a load
of oppression; they plead for relief from the arm of the
powerful. But no one says, 'Where is God my Maker, who
gives songs in the night, who teaches more to us than to
the beasts of the earth and makes us wiser than the birds
of the air?' " (Job 35:1, 4, 10, 11)

Elihu was a wise man, exceedingly wise, though not as wise
as the all-wise Jehovah, who sees light in the clouds, and finds
order in confusion. Being much puzzled at beholding Job [so]
afflicted, Elihu cast about him to find the cause of it, and very
wisely hit upon one of the most likely reasons, although it did not
happen to be the right one in Job's case.

Elihu said within himself, "Surely, if men be tried and troubled, it is because while they think about their troubles and distress themselves about their fears, they do not say, 'Where is God
my Maker, who gives songs in the night'?" Elihu's reason was right
in the majority of cases. The great cause of the Christian's distress,
the reason for the depth of sorrow into which many believers are
plunged, is this: while they are looking about on the right hand
and the left to see how they may escape their troubles, they forget
to look to the hills whence all real help comes.[1] They do not say,
"Where is God my Maker, who gives songs in the night?" We shall
dwell on those sweet words.

The world has its night. It seems necessary that it should
have one. The sun shines by day and men go forth to their labors;
but they grow weary, and nightfall comes like a sweet boon from
Heaven. The darkness draws the curtains and shuts out the light,
which might prevent our eyes from slumber; while the sweet, calm
stillness of the night permits us to rest upon the lap of ease, and

there forget a while our cares until the morning sun appears. [Then] an angel puts his hand upon the curtain, and draws it back, touches our eyelids, and bids us rise and proceed to the labors of the day.

Night is one of the greatest blessings men enjoy; we have many reasons to thank God for it. Yet night is to many a gloomy season. There is the "pestilence that walks in darkness," there is the "terror by night,"[2] there is the dread of robbers and of fell disease, with all those fears that the timorous know when they have no light by which they can discern objects. It is then they fancy that spiritual creatures walk the earth, though if they knew rightly, they would find it to be true that

> Millions of spiritual creatures walk this earth
> Unseen, both when we sleep and when we wake,[3]

and that at all times they are round about us—not more by night than by day.

Night is the season of terror and alarm to most men. Yet even night has its songs. Have you never stood by the seaside at night, and heard the pebbles sing, and the waves chant God's glories? Or have you never risen from your couch, and thrown up the window of your chamber, and listened there? Listened to what? Silence—save now and then a murmuring sound, which seems sweet music then. And have you not fancied that you heard the harp of God playing in Heaven? Did you not conceive that those stars, those eyes of God looking down on you, were also mouths of song? That every star was singing God's glory, singing as it shone, its mighty Maker and His lawful, well-deserved praise?[4]

Night has its songs. We need not much poetry in our spirit to catch the song of night, and hear the spheres as they chant praises which are loud to the heart, though they be silent to the ear: the praises of the mighty God who bears up the unpillared arch of Heaven, and moves the stars in their courses.

Man, too, like the great world in which he lives, must have his night. For it is true that man is like the world around him. He is a little world. He resembles the world in almost everything; and if the world has its night, so has man. And many a night do we have—nights of sorrow, nights of persecution, nights of doubt, nights of bewilderment, nights of anxiety, nights of oppression, nights of ignorance—nights of all kinds, which possess our spirits and terrify our souls. But blessed be God, the Christian can say, "My God gives me songs in the night."

It is not necessary, I take it, to prove to you that Christians have [their] nights; for if you are Christians you will find that you have them, and you will not want any proof, for nights will come quite often enough. I will, therefore, proceed at once to the subject; and I will speak this evening upon songs in the night, their matter—what do we sing about in the night? Songs in the night, their excellence—they are hearty songs, and they are sweet ones; songs in the night, their uses—their benefits to ourselves and others.

First, songs in the night—who is the author of them? "God," says the text, our "Maker": He gives songs in the night.

Any fool can sing in the day. When the cup is full, man draws inspiration from it. When wealth rolls in abundance round about him, any man can sing to the praise of a God who gives a plenteous harvest, or sends home a loaded argosy. It is easy enough for an Aeolian harp to whisper music when the winds blow; the difficulty is for music to come when no wind is blowing. It is easy to sing when we can read the notes by daylight; but the skillful singer is he who can sing when there is not a ray of light to read by. [Such a man] sings from his heart, and not from a book that he can see, because he has no means of reading, save from that inward book in his own living spirit, from which notes of gratitude pour out in songs of praise.

No man can make a song in the night by himself. He may attempt it, but he will feel how difficult it is. Let all things go as I please—I will weave songs, weave them wherever I go, with the flowers that grow upon my path. But put me in a desert, where no flowers are, and wherewith shall I weave a chorus of praise to God? How shall I make a crown for Him? Let this voice be free, and this body full of health, and I can sing God's praise; but stop this tongue, lay me upon the bed of languishing, and it is not easy to sing from the bed and chant high praises in the fires. Give me the bliss of spiritual liberty, and let me mount up to my God [and] get near the throne, and I will sing, aye, sing as sweet as seraphs. But confine me, fetter my spirit, clip my wings, make me exceeding sad, so that I become old like the eagle—ah! then it is hard to sing.

It is not natural to sing when in trouble, "Bless the Lord, O my soul, and all that is within me bless his holy name," for that is a daylight song. But it was a divine song that Habakkuk sang when in the night he said, "Though the fig tree shall not blossom . . . yet will I trust in the Lord, and stay myself in the God of Jacob."[5] [Safely across] the Red Sea, any man could have made a song like that of Moses,[6] "The horse and his rider He has hurled into the sea."[7] The difficulty would have been to compose a song before the Red Sea had been divided and to sing it before Pharaoh's hosts had been drowned, while yet the darkness of doubt and fear was resting on Israel's hosts. Songs in the night come only from God; they are not in the power of men.

But what does the text mean when it asserts that God gives songs in the night? We think we can find two answers to the question. The first is that usually in the night of a Christian's experience, God is his only song. If it be daylight in my heart, I can sing songs touching my graces—songs touching my sweet experience—songs touching my duties—songs touching my labors; but let the night come—my graces appear to have withered. My evidences, though they are there, are hidden. I cannot

> . . . read my title clear
> To mansions in the skies.

And now I have nothing left to sing of but my God. It is strange that when God gives His children mercies, they generally set their hearts more on the mercies than on the Giver of them. But when the night comes, and He sweeps all the mercies away, then at once they say, "Now, my God, I have nothing to sing of but You. I must come to You and to You only. I had cisterns once; they were full of water; I drank from them then; but now the created streams are dry. Sweet Lord, I quaff no stream but Your own self. I drink from no fount but from You."

Aye, child of God, you know what I say. Or if you don't understand it yet, you will do so by-and-by. It is in the night we sing of God, and of God alone. Every string is tuned, and every power has its attribute to sing, while we praise God, and nothing else. We can sacrifice to ourselves in daylight—we sacrifice to God only by night. We can sing high praises to our dear selves when all is joyful, but we cannot sing praise to any save our God when circumstances are untoward, and providences appear adverse. God alone can furnish us with songs in the night.

And yet again, not only does God give the song in the night because He is the only subject upon which we can sing then, but because He is the only one who inspires songs in the night. Bring me a poor, melancholy, distressed child of God. I come into the pulpit. I seek to tell him sweet promises, and whisper to him sweet words of comfort. He listens not to me. He is like the deaf adder; he listens not to the voice of the charmer, charm he never so wisely.

Send him around to all the comforting divines, and all the holy Barnabases that ever preached, and they will do very little. They will not be able to squeeze a song out of him, do what they may. He is drinking the gall of wormwood. He says, "O Lord, You have made me drunk with weeping. I have eaten ashes like bread."[8] Comfort him as you may, it will be only a woeful note or two of mournful resignation you will get from him. You will get no psalms of praise, no hallelujahs, no sonnets. But let God come to His child in the night, let Him whisper in his ear as he lies on his bed, and how you see his eye flash fire in the night! Do you not hear him say,

> Tis paradise, if thou art here,
> If thou depart, 'tis hell.

I could not have cheered him; it is God who has done it, and God gives songs in the night. It is marvelous, brethren, how one sweet word of God will make whole songs for Christians. One word of God is like a piece of gold, and the Christian is the goldbeater, and he can hammer that promise for whole weeks. I can say myself, I have lived on one promise for weeks and want no other. I want just simply to hammer that promise out into gold leaf, and plate my whole existence with joy from it. The Christian gets his songs from God. God gives him inspiration and teaches him how to sing: "God my Maker, who gives songs in the night."

So then, poor Christian, you need not go pumping up your poor heart to make it glad. Go to your Maker and ask Him to give you a song in the night. You are a poor dry well. You have heard it said that when a pump is dry, you must pour water down it first of all, and then you will get some up. And so, Christian, when you are dry, go to God, ask Him to pour some joy down you, and then you will get some joy up from your own heart. Don't go to this comforter or that, for you will make them Job's comforters, after all. Go first and foremost to your Maker, for He is the great composer of songs and teacher of music. He it is who can teach you how to sing, "God my Maker, who gives me songs in the night."

Thus we have dwelt upon the first point. Now the second. What is generally the matter contained in a song in the night? What do we sing about?

Why, I think, when we sing at night, there are three things we sing about. Either we sing about the yesterday that is over, or else about the night itself, or else about the morrow that is to come. Each of these is a sweet theme when God our Maker gives us songs in the night.

In the midst of the night the most unusual method for Christians is to sing about the day that is over. "Well," they say, "the night is now, but I can remember when it was daylight. Neither moon nor stars appear at present, but I remember when I saw the sun. I have no evidence just now, but there was a time when I could say, 'I know that my Redeemer lives.'[9] I have my doubts and fears at this present moment, but it is not long since I could say with full assurance, 'I know that He shed His blood for me; I know that my Redeemer lives, and when He shall stand a second time upon the earth, though the worms devour this body, yet in my flesh I shall see God.'[10] It may be darkness now, but I know the promises were sweet. I know I had blessed seasons in His house. I am quite sure of this. I used to enjoy myself in the ways of the Lord, and though now my paths are strewn with thorns, I know it is the King's highway. It was a way of pleasantness once; it will be a way of pleasantness again. 'I will remember the days of old. I will meditate upon the years of the right hand of the Most High.' "[11]

Christian, perhaps the best song you can sing to cheer you in the night is the song of yesterday. Remember, it was not always night with you. Night is a new thing to you. Once you had a glad heart, a buoyant spirit. Once your eye was full of fire. Once your foot was light. Once you could sing for very joy and ecstasy of heart. Well, then, remember that God, who made you sing yesterday, has not left you in the night. He is not a daylight God who cannot know His children in darkness, but He loves you now as much as ever. Though He has left you [for] a little, it is to prove you, to make you trust Him better and serve Him more.

Let me tell you some of the sweet things of which a Christian may make a song when he is in the night.

If we are going to sing of the things of yesterday, let us begin with what God did for us in past times. My beloved brethren, you will find it a sweet subject for song at times to begin to sing of electing love and covenanted mercies. When you yourself are low, it is well to sing of the Fountainhead of mercy; of that blessed decree that ordained you to eternal life, and of that glorious Man who undertook your redemption. Of that everlasting love which, before the mountains were begotten, or the aged hills were children, chose you, loved you firmly, loved you fast, loved you well, and loved you eternally.

I tell you, believer, if you can go back to the years of eternity; if you can in your mind run back to that period before the everlasting hills were fashioned, or the fountains of the great deep were scooped out; and if you can see your God inscribing your name in His eternal book—if you can see in His loving heart eternal thoughts of love to you, you will find this a charming means of giving you songs in the night. No songs [compare with] those which come from electing love; no sonnets [are] like those that are dictated by meditations on discriminating mercy.

Some, indeed, cannot sing of election: the Lord open their mouths a little wider! Some there are that are afraid of the very term; but we [can] only despise men who are afraid of what they believe, afraid of what God has taught them in His Bible. No, in our darker hours it is our joy to sing:

> Sons we are through God's election
>   Who in Jesus Christ believe;
> By eternal destination,
>   Sovereign grace we now receive.
> Lord, thy favor
>   Shall both grace and glory give.

Think, Christian, of yesterday, I say, and you will get a song in the night. But if you do not have a voice tuned to so high a key as that, let me suggest some other mercies you may sing of. They are the mercies you have experienced. What! man, can you not sing a little of that blessed hour when Jesus met you; when, a blind slave, you were sporting with death, and He saw you, and said, "Come, poor slave, come with me"?

Can you not sing of that rapturous moment when He snapped your fetters, dashed your chains to the earth, and said, "I am the Breaker; I came to break your chains and set you free"? What though you are ever so gloomy now, can you forget that happy morning when, in the house of God, your voice was almost as loud as a seraph's voice in praise? For you could sing, "I am forgiven! I am forgiven!"

> A monument of grace,
> A sinner saved by blood.

Go back, man! Sing of that moment, and then you will have a song in the night. Or if you have almost forgotten that, then surely you have some precious milestone along the road of life that is not quite grown over with moss, on which you can read some happy inspiration of His mercy toward you. What! Did you never have a sickness like that which you are suffering now, and did He not raise you up from that? Were you never poor before, and did He not supply your wants? Were you never in straits before, and did He not deliver you?

Come, man! I beseech you, go to the river of your experience, and pull up a few bulrushes, and weave them into an ark on which your infant faith may float safely on the stream. I bid you not forget what God has done. What! Have you buried your own diary? I beseech you, man, turn over the book of your remembrance. Can you not see some sweet hill Mizar?[12] Can you not think of some blessed hour when the Lord met with you at Mount Hermon? Have you never been on the Delectable Mountains? Have you never been fetched from the den of lions? Have you never escaped the jaw of the lion and the paw of the bear? Listen, man, I know you have. Go back, then, a little way, and take the mercies of yesterday; and though it is dark now, light up the lamps of yesterday, and they shall glitter through the darkness, and you shall find that God has given you a song in the night.

And I think, beloved, there is never so dark a night, but there is something to sing about, even concerning that night. For there is one thing I am sure we can sing about, let the night be ever so dark, and that is, "It is of the Lord's mercies that we are not consumed, because His compassions fail not."[13] If we cannot sing very loud, yet we can sing a little low tune, something like this: "He has not dealt with us after our sins, nor rewarded us according to our iniquities."[14]

"Oh," says one, "I do not know where to get my dinner from tomorrow [on]. I am a poor wretch." So you may be, my dear friend, but you are not so poor as you deserve to be. Do not be mightily offended about that; if you are, you are no child of God, for the child of God acknowledges that he has no right to the least of God's mercies, but that they come through the channel of grace alone.

As long as I am out of Hell, I have no right to grumble; and if I were in Hell, I should have no right to complain. For I feel, when convinced of sin, that never creature deserved to go there more than I do. We have no cause to murmur. We can lift up our hands and say, "Night! You are dark, but you might have been darker. I am poor, but if I could not have been poorer, I might have been sick. I am poor and sick—well, I have some friends left. My lot cannot be so bad, but it might have been worse." And therefore, Christian, you will always have one thing to sing about: "Lord, I thank You, it is not all darkness!"

Besides, Christian, however dark the night is, there is always a star or moon. There is scarce ever a night that we have, but there are just one or two little lamps burning up there. However dark it may be, I think you may find some little comfort, some little joy, some little mercy left, and some little promise to cheer your spirit. The stars are not put out, are they? Even if you cannot see them, they are there, and I believe one or two must be shining on you. Therefore give God a song in the night. If you have only one star, bless God for that one. Perhaps He will make it two; and if you have only two stars, bless God for the two stars, and perhaps He will make them four. Try, then, [and see] if you cannot find a song in the night.

But, beloved, there is another thing of which we can sing yet more sweetly, and that is, we can sing of the day that is to come. I am preaching tonight for the poor weavers of Spitalfields.[15] Perhaps there are not to be found a class of men in London who are suffering a darker night than they are. For while many classes have been befriended and defended, there are few who speak up for them, and (if I am rightly informed) they are generally ground down within an inch of their lives. I suppose that their masters intend that their bread shall be very sweet, on the principle that the nearer the ground, the sweeter the grass; for I should think that no people have their grass so near the ground as the weavers of Spitalfields.

In an inquiry by the House of Commons last week, it was given in evidence that their average wages amount to seven or eight shillings a week, and that they have to furnish themselves with a room, and work at expensive articles, which my friends and ladies are wearing now, and which they buy as cheaply as possible; but perhaps they do not know that they are made with the blood

and bones and marrow of the Spitalfield weavers who, many of
them, work for less than man ought to have to subsist upon.

Some of them waited upon me the other day; I was exceedingly pleased with one of them. He said, "Well, sir, it is very hard,
but I hope there is better times coming for us."

"Well, my friend," I said, "I am afraid you cannot hope for
much better times, unless the Lord Jesus Christ comes a second
time."

"That is just what we hope for," said he. "We do not see there
is any chance for deliverance, unless the Lord Jesus Christ comes
to establish His Kingdom upon the earth; and then He will judge
the oppressed, and break the oppressors in pieces with an iron rod,
and dash them in pieces like a potter's vessel."[16]

I was glad my friend had got a song in the night, and was
singing about the morning that was coming. Often do I cheer
myself with the thought of the coming of the Lord. We preach
now, perhaps, with little success. "The kingdoms of this world" are
not "become the Kingdom of our Lord and of His Christ."[17] We
send out missionaries; they are for the most part unsuccessful. We
are laboring, but we do not see the fruits of our labors. Well, what
then? [Wait] a little while. We shall not always labor in vain, or
spend our strength for naught. A day is coming, and now is, when
every minister of Christ shall speak with unction, when all the
servants of God shall preach with power, and when colossal systems of heathenism shall be scattered to the winds.

The shout shall be heard, "Alleluia! Alleluia! the Lord God
Omnipotent reigns!" For that day do I look. It is to the bright
horizon of that Second Coming that I turn my eyes. My anxious
expectation is that the sweet Sun of righteousness will arise with
healing beneath his wings;[18] that the oppressed shall be righted;
that despotisms shall be cut down; that liberty shall be established;
that peace shall be made lasting, and that the glorious liberty of
the gospel shall be extended throughout the known world. Christian! If you are in a night, think of tomorrow. Cheer up your heart
with the thought of the coming of your Lord.

There is another sweet tomorrow of which we hope to sing
in the night. Soon, beloved, you and I shall lie on our dying bed,
and we shall want a song in the night then. I do not know where
we shall get it, if we do not get it from the tomorrow. Kneeling last
night by the bed of an apparently dying saint, I said, "Well, sister,
He has been precious to you. You can rejoice in His covenant
mercies, and His past lovingkindnesses."

She put out her hand and said, "Ah, sir, do not talk about them now. I want the sinner's Savior as much now as ever. It is not a saint's I want; it is still a sinner's Savior that I am in need of, for I am a sinner still." I found that I could not comfort her with the past, so I reminded her of the golden streets, of the gates of pearl, of the walls of jasper, of the harps of gold, of the songs of bliss; and then her eyes glistened. "Yes," she said, "I shall be there soon. I shall meet them by-and-by." And then she seemed so glad!

Ah, believer, you may always cheer yourself with that thought. Your head may be crowned with thorny troubles now, but it shall wear a starry crown directly. Your hand may be filled with cares, but it shall grasp a harp soon, a harp full of music. Your garments may be soiled with dust now, but they shall be white by-and-by. Wait a little longer. How despicable our troubles and trials will seem when we look back upon them! In prospect they seem immense; but when we get to Heaven, we shall then,

> With transporting joys recount
> The labors of our feet.

Our trials will seem to us nothing at all. We shall talk to one another about them in Heaven, and find all the more to converse about, according as we have suffered more here below. Let us go on, therefore; and if the night be ever so dark, remember there is not a night that shall not have a morning; and that morning is to come by-and-by.

And now I want to tell you, very briefly, what are the excellences of songs in the night above all other songs.

In the first place, when you hear a man singing a song in the night—I mean in the night of trouble—you may be quite sure it is a hearty one. Many of you sang very prettily just now, didn't you? I wonder whether you would sing very prettily if there was a stake or two in Smithfield[19] for all of you who dared to do it? If you sang under pain and penalty, that would show your heart to be in your song. We can all sing very nicely indeed when everybody else sings. It is the easiest thing in the world to open your mouth and let the words come out; but when the Devil puts his hand over your mouth, can you sing then? Can you say, "Though he slay me, yet will I trust in him"?[20]

That is hearty singing. That is real song that springs up in the night. The nightingale sings most sweetly because she sings in the night. A poet has said that, if she sang by day, she might be

thought to sing no more sweetly than the wren.[21] It is the stillness
of the night that makes her song sweet. And so does a Christian's
song become sweet and hearty, because it is in the night.

Again: the songs we sing in the night will be lasting. Many
songs we hear our fellow-creatures singing in the streets will not
do to sing by-and-by. I guess they will sing a different kind of tune
soon! They can sing nowadays any rollicking drinking song; but
they will not sing them when they come to die. They are not
exactly the songs with which to cross Jordan's billows. It will not
do to sing one of those light songs when death and you are having
the last tug. It will not do to enter Heaven singing one of those
unchaste, unholy sonnets.

No; but the Christian who can sing in the night will not have
to leave off his song. He may keep on singing it forever. He may
put his foot in Jordan's stream, and continue his melody. He may
wade through it, and keep on singing still, and land himself safe in
Heaven. And when he is there, there need not be a gap in his
strain, but in a nobler, sweeter strain he may still continue singing
His power to save.

There are a great many of you that think Christian people
are a very miserable set, don't you? You say, "Let me sing my
song." Aye, but, my dear friends, we like to sing a song that will
last. We don't like your songs. They are all froth, like bubbles on
the beaker, and they will soon die away and be lost. Give me a
song that will last. Give me one that will not melt. Don't give me
the dreamer's gold! He hoards it up and says, "I'm rich," and when
he wakes, his gold is gone. But give me songs in the night, for they
are songs I sing forever.

Again: the songs we warble in the night are those that show
we have real faith in God. Many men have just enough faith to
trust God as far as they can see Him, and they always sing as far as
they can see Providence go right. But true faith can sing when its
possessors cannot see. It can take hold of God when they cannot
discern Him.

Songs in the night prove that we have true courage. Many
sing by day who are silent by night. They are afraid of thieves and
robbers. But the Christian who sings in the night proves himself to
be a courageous character. It is the bold Christian who can sing
God's sonnets in the darkness.

He who can sing songs in the night, too, proves that he has
true love to Christ. It is not love to Christ to praise Him while

everybody else praises Him; to walk arm in arm with Him when He has the crown on His head is no great deed, I wot; [but] to walk with Christ in rags is something. To believe in Christ when He is shrouded in darkness, to stick hard and fast by the Savior when all men speak ill of Him and forsake Him—that is true faith. He who sings a song to Christ in the night, sings the best song in all the world, for he sings from the heart.

I am afraid of wearying you, therefore I shall not dwell [further] on the excellences of night songs, but just, in the last place, show you their use.

It is very useful to sing in the night of our troubles, first, because it will cheer ourselves. When you were boys living in the country, and had some distance to go alone at night, don't you remember how you whistled and sang to keep your courage up? Well, what we do in the natural world we ought to do in the spiritual. There is nothing like singing to keep your spirits alive. When we have been in trouble, we have often thought ourselves to be well-nigh overwhelmed with difficulty; and we have said, "Let us have a song." We have begun to sing; and Martin Luther says, "The Devil cannot bear singing." That is about the truth; he does not like music. It was so in [King] Saul's days. An evil spirit rested on Saul, but when David played on his harp, the evil spirit went away from him.[22]

This is usually the case; if we can begin to sing we shall remove our fears. I like to hear servants sometimes humming a tune at their work. I love to hear a plowman in the country singing as he goes along with his horses. Why not? You say he has no time to praise God, but he can sing a song—surely he can sing a Psalm, it will take no more time. Singing is the best thing to purge ourselves of evil thoughts. Keep your mouth full of songs, and you will often keep your heart full of praises. Keep on singing as long as you can; you will find it a good method of driving away your fears.

Sing for another reason: because it will cheer your companions. If any of them are in the valley and in the darkness with you, it will be a great help to comfort them. John Bunyan tells us that as Christian was going through the valley he found it a dreadful dark place, and terrible demons and goblins were all about him. Poor Christian thought he must perish for certain; but just when his doubts were the strongest, he heard a sweet voice. He listened to it, and heard a man in front of him saying, "Yea, when I pass through the valley of the shadow of death, I will fear no evil."[23]

Now, that man did not know who was near him, but he was unwittingly singing to cheer a man behind. Christian, when you are in trouble, sing; you do not know who is near you. Sing, perhaps you will get a companion by it. Sing! Perhaps there will be many a heart cheered by your song. There is some broken spirit, it may be, that will be bound up by your sonnets. Sing! There is some poor distressed brother, perhaps, shut up in the Castle of Despair, who, like King Richard, will hear your song inside the walls, and sing to you again, and you may be the means of getting him a ransom.[24] Sing, Christian, wherever you go. Try if you can to wash your face every morning in a bath of praise. When you go down from your chamber, never go to look on man till you have first looked on your God. And when you have looked on Him, seek to come down with a face beaming with joy. Carry a smile, for you will cheer up many a poor wayworn pilgrim by it.

One more reason, and I know it will be a good one for you. Try and sing in the night, Christian, for that is one of the best arguments in all the world in favor of your [Christianity]. Our divines [ministers] nowadays spend a great deal of time in trying to prove Christianity against those who disbelieve it. I should like to have seen [the Apostle] Paul trying that! Elymas the sorcerer withstood him; how did our friend Paul treat him? He said, "Oh, full of all guile and all craft, [you] son of the Devil [and] enemy of all righteousness, will you not cease perverting the right ways of the Lord?"[25] That is about the politeness such men ought to have who deny God's truth.

We start with this assumption: we will prove that the Bible is God's Word, but we are not going to prove God's Word. If you do not like to believe it, we will shake hands and bid you good-bye; we will not argue with you. The gospel has gained little by discussion. The greatest piece of folly on earth has been to send a man round the country to follow up another, who has been lecturing on infidelity just to make himself notorious.

Why, let them lecture on. This is a free country. Why should we follow them about? The truth will win the day. Christianity need not wish for controversy; it is strong enough for it, if it wishes it; but that is not God's way.

God's direction is, "Preach, teach, dogmatize." Do not stand disputing. Claim a divine mission, tell men that God says it, and there leave it. Say to them, "He that believes . . . shall be saved, and he that disbelieves shall be condemned";[26] and when you have done that, you have done enough. For what reason should our missionaries stand disputing with Brahmins? Why should they be wasting their time attempting to refute first this dogma, and then another, of heathenism? Why not just go and say, "The God whom you ignorantly worship, I declare unto you; believe me and you will be saved; believe me not, and the Bible says you are lost."[27] And then, having thus asserted God's Word, say, "I leave it, I declare it unto you; it is a thing for you to believe, not a thing for you to reason about."

Religion is not a thing merely for your intellect, a thing to prove your own talent upon, by making a syllogism on it. It is a thing that demands your faith. As a messenger of Heaven, I demand that faith. If you do not choose to give it, on your own head be the doom, if there be such. If there be not, you are prepared to risk it. But I have done my duty. I have told you the truth. That is the truth, that is enough, and there I leave it.

Oh, Christian, instead of disputing, let me tell you how to prove your [faith]. Live it out! Live it out! Give the external as well as the internal evidence. Give the external evidence of your own life. You are sick. There is your neighbor who laughs at religion. Let him come into your house. When he was sick, he said, "Oh, send for the doctor," and there he was fretting and fuming and whining and making all manner of noises. When you are sick, send for him, tell him that you are resigned to the Lord's will; that you will kiss the chastening rod; that you will take the cup and drink it, because your Father gives it.

You do not need to make a boast of this, or it will lose all its power; but do it because you cannot help doing it. Your neighbor will say, "There is something in that." And when you come to the borders of the grave—he was there once, and you heard how he shrieked, and how frightened he was—give him your hand and say to him, "Ah! I have a Christ that will do to die by. I have a [faith] that will make me sing in the night."

Let me hear how you can sing, "Victory, victory, victory!" through Him that loved you. I tell you, we may preach fifty thousand sermons to prove the gospel, but we shall not prove it half so well as you will through singing in the night. Keep a cheerful frame. Keep a happy heart. Keep a contented spirit. Keep your eye up, and your heart aloft, and you prove Christianity better than all the Butlers,[28] and all the wise men that ever lived. Give them the analogy of a holy life, and then you will prove religion to them. Give them the evidence of internal piety, developed externally, and you will give the best possible proof of Christianity.

NOTES

1. Psalm 121:1.
2. Psalm 91:5, 6.
3. John Milton, *Paradise Lost*.
4. Cf. Job 38:7.
5. Habakkuk 3:17, 18.
6. It is also the song of Miriam.
7. Exodus 15:1, 21.
8. Psalm 102:9.
9. Job 19:25.
10. Job 19:26.
11. Cf. Psalm 77:5, 10, 11.
12. Psalm 42:6.
13. Lamentations 3:22.
14. Cf. Psalm 103:10.
15. In the nineteenth century Spitalfields, a district of east London, was a center of the silk weaving trade. The term "Spital" is a corruption of *hospital;* St. Mary Without Bishopsgate Hospital was founded there in 1197.
16. Cf. Psalm 2:9.
17. Cf. Revelation 11:15.
18. Cf. Malachi 4:2.
19. Queen Mary Tudor ("Bloody Mary") made Smithfield infamous as a site of executions. During her reign (1553-1558) some three hundred Protestants and Jews were burned at the stake there. Today Smithfield is a cattle market in London.
20. Job 13:15.
21. William Shakespeare, *The Merchant of Venice*.
22. Cf. 1 Samuel 16:23.
23. Psalm 23:4. Cf. John Bunyan, *Pilgrim's Progress*.
24. According to tradition, King Richard I (Coeur de Lion), returning from the Crusades, was secretly captured and imprisoned by King Leopold of Austria in Dürenstein castle on the Danube. His presence was discovered in 1192 by his faithful servant Blondel, by means of a song they had jointly composed, Blondel singing a verse under the castle wall and Richard answering from his prison window. Richard was later ransomed and returned to England.
25. Acts 13:10.
26. Mark 16:16.
27. Acts 16:31; 17:23.
28. Joseph Butler, dean of St. Paul's Cathedral, London, and later bishop of Bristol and Durham, wrote *The Analogy of Religion* in 1736 to discredit deism. A high churchman, he opposed the field preaching in Bristol by George Whitefield and John Wesley.

Samuel P. Jones

Had I been admonished, when compiling this nineteenth century volume of the Christian Heritage Classics, not to include the name of Samuel Porter Jones (1847-1906), I would never have attempted the project. Over many years I have read Jones' sermons for sheer enjoyment. He belongs to a very select company of preachers who have mastered the art of humor in speech—Thomas Fuller and John Bunyan in the seventeenth century, Rowland Hill in the eighteenth, Charles Spurgeon in the nineteenth, Halford Luccock and Grady Wilson in the twentieth.

Yet to call Jones a humorist would be a travesty, for in his day he was the greatest soul-winner the southern United States produced. Eighteen times the city of Nashville, Tennessee, bent its knees under the man's preaching. By actual count, he closed down twenty-seven bars in the city. During one great campaign he addressed crowds of five thousand three times a day, and saw ten thousand respond to his invitation to give their lives to Christ. In Chicago, Brooklyn, Cincinnati, Baltimore, St. Louis, St. Joseph, Missouri, and all through the southland from the Carolinas to Texas, people flocked to hear this highly appealing, articulate son of the Methodist Episcopal Church South. On the closing day of his campaign in Cincinnati's music hall, forty thousand came to hear him speak—without benefit of amplification.

What Sam Jones said was orthodox and Biblical, but the way he said it was pure Jones. "The Lord always fishes on the bottom. . . . Many a man is praying for rain with his tub the wrong side up. . . . When I was a pastor, some fellows would growl because I didn't go to see them. What do I want to go to see you for? The Bible tells me to keep out of bad company."

Born at Oak Bowery, Alabama, Jones came from a devout Methodist family. His mother died when he was seven, and his father, a lawyer and Civil War veteran, moved the family to Cartersville, Georgia. There Sam was graduated from high school, but dyspepsia and chronic indigestion kept him from going on to college, where he had hoped to pursue the study of law. While studying at home, he sought relief in drink. He managed to be admitted to the bar at age twenty-one, but was forced to give up his practice because of alcoholism. Moving to Alabama, he taught school, and in 1869 married Laura McElwain. Efforts at reform failed, and his dissipation soon made a shambles of his life.

At the age of twenty-four Sam returned home to visit his dying father, to whom he promised, "I'll quit! I'll quit!"—and he did. He was converted to Christ, and at once applied to the Methodist headquarters for a license to preach. His wife and family bitterly objected to this course of action, since he was heavily in debt. But Sam took counsel of no one around him. In 1872 he was licensed and thereupon assigned to Bartow and Polk Counties, where he was to ride one of the poorest circuits in the North Georgia conference. After serving as an itinerant preacher for eight years, he was assigned to raising funds for a church orphanage. But he was becoming increasingly known as an evangelist, and calls came to him from all over Georgia.

What served to make Jones famous was now quite apparent. His denunciations of vice and sin, and his scathing rebukes of hypocritical church members, brought down wrath—but also stirred up revival. By 1884 he was so well-known that he entered large-scale evangelistic work. The city of Nashville even offered him $25,000 to move there, but he declined, preferring to stay in Cartersville. De Witt Talmage traveled a hundred miles to hear Sam preach, and invited him to his Brooklyn pulpit. At home, liquor interests dynamited the floor of Sam's buggy-house, but his reaction was simply, "I would as soon go to Heaven by the dynamite route as by any other." He turned back a $600 offering in Murfreesboro, Tennessee, asking that it be used for the families of converted saloon keepers until the fathers could find other work.

At the time of his death Sam Jones was still preaching to overflow crowds. The following message is from a series of sermons preached in a gospel tent at Nashville in May 1885. The series was issued that year as Sermons and Sayings, by the Rev. Sam P. Jones, and was edited by W. M. Leftwich, D.D., for the Southern Methodist Publishing House, Nashville.

THREE

WAITING AND HOPING
by Samuel P. Jones

There are a thousand persons here tonight who would like to know the way to God, who long for and aspire to a better life. Now, you pray as Christians while I talk. We invite your attention to these words of the Psalmist: "What am I waiting for? My hope is in You."[1] Here is a question and a statement. I want every one of you to transfer that question from the utterance of David in this book to your own heart. Let us give our hearts a chance tonight.

A man doesn't go head foremost toward God, he goes heart foremost. The great trouble with sinners is that they put the head before the heart. "What am I waiting for?" We see that most of the questions in the Bible are preeminently personal: "What must I do to be saved?"[2] "What am I waiting for?" Personal in the highest and most important sense.

Now, we will go down on your side and look at it [that is, at the first half of the text] a moment. When a man says, "I tell you what I am waiting for—the Lord's good time, the Lord's own time," is that a fact? Well, you can't say that any longer. That good time has come at last. I am so glad that what you have been waiting for until you are gray-headed has come at last. That time was the day when you were five years old, and every breathing day of your life since; from the time your mother kissed you as a little child up to this hour.

These revival services are to get men willing to be saved, not to get God willing to save them. You understand that. It is God's accepted time. "Now is the accepted time, today is the day of salvation."[3] Every moment that you are a sinner: that is the moment God is ready to save you. You will never see the gates wider open than they are now. You may get in after a while, but if you don't go in now the chances are against you. In Hell you will carry the recollection that you stood once in this city right before the open gates of God's mercy and grace and would not enter.

"Ah, but I am waiting for God's good time to save sinners." I want to say a thing or two to you men about waiting. I knew a man in Knoxville who was a moral, upright fellow (you have not many of that kind in this city). I said to him, "Brother, do you know you are the hardest case in Knoxville?"

"Why, no, sir," he said, "I am not the hardest case."

"Well," I said, "we got the hardest case in the city, a gambler, and we have not got you yet!"

In this city we have got some of the hardest cases up to this time. Did you know that you are a harder case? We have them, and we have not got you. "Waiting on God's good time!" Let me say to you tonight, with my Bible in my hand, and with love toward you in my heart, that that time has come at last in all its fullness and power.

But one says, "I am not waiting for God's time, I am waiting for better terms." Let me tell you about that "terms" business. Down in Georgia they have a stock law. No fences at all down there. All the county is thrown into one field. I want no fences in farming and politics, but in religion I want the Devil's goats fenced out. I will not let the fences down for you, but I will help you over them. There are plenty of people that want to go to Heaven on their own schedule. They want to drink a little, lie a little, and gamble occasionally.

Everybody in this country has an old aching tooth, and the first dentist that won't hurt them, they are going to have pull it out. I have been hunting a painless dentist for a long time, but they don't live in this country. They might fill you with laughing-gas and pull your head off. A great many people object to pointed preaching because they say it pains them. This suggests the story of the old lady whose daughter's tooth ached. She sent for a dentist. He came, and pulled out a pair of big, old-fashioned forceps. The old lady screamed, "Don't put them things in my daughter's mouth. Pull it with your fingers!"

That would be mighty nice, if it could be done. God bless you all! If you will let me get the old gospel forceps and take hold of those teeth, I will bring them out; but I cannot pull them with my fingers. I want that understood.

Brethren, some of you have been trying the finger business. But hear me, hear me! "Better terms, better terms!" Do you know the terms on which God will take hold of you and carry you through this world and safely up to Heaven? You just lay down those things that are hurting you, and take up those other things that will help you, and you will have His help in time and eternity. Why will a man ask better terms than that he quit those things that damage him on earth and in Heaven?

I am so glad that God would not let me go on and drink. I would have been in a drunkard's grave years ago, if He had; I would have been ruined. Many a fellow is out in the goat-yard, and thinks he is in the house. It is disgusting to have an elder rear back on his dignity and defend his drinking. You old demijohn, you![4] All you lack of being a demijohn is a few willows. He is an elder and a deacon too! His wife has to run her arm into the handle of a demijohn when she goes to church. How many demijohns have you, Brother Witherspoon?[5] How many have you, Brother Strickland?

Hear me tonight! Never, never do I want God to lower the standard. I am so glad He holds up the standard that we must live righteous and godly lives in this world. Bless God, when I have climbed the steepest hills, what a view I have! I have faltered many a time, and said I could not pull another foot. Then the Lord came down and backed my shoulders and said, "Go on." When I shall stand on the mount of God forever I will say, "Thank God this old Heaven is as high as it is!" There is no sickness, sorrow, pain, disease or death in Heaven. We won't let the standard down, but we will go up to it.

There is something very precious about the cross. When a man gets squarely under it, denying himself and bearing his burdens, and falls under the load, God will pull him up on the cross and make it tote him. No, sir. We won't let down the standard. Blessed be God, we will keep it up! Here is light and love and purity and salvation to make you fit and meet for God's use in Heaven and the companionship of angels by-and-by. I never want to see the day in the history of the cross when a man can be saved on any lower plane than that he quits his meanness and goes to doing right.

"I am not waiting for any better terms," says [another] sinner. "I know that right is right and wrong is wrong. I am waiting for the church to get right." You will be in Hell a million years before that happens. Mark what I tell you. A man is in mighty poor business haggling around at these members of the church. They are good-hearted fellows. They go off into devilment, but if you check them up they will come back. There are many members on the road tonight, coming back. They did not know how low down they were. There are hundreds of these men—Methodists, Baptists, and Presbyterians—in all the churches in this town. You will never see them doing as they have been doing. You try next year to run a bar-room, and want these men to help you, and you will get a fuss on your hands.

We are going to do better, and we call on men and angels to witness what we say. We preachers are going to do better. The good women are going to do better. God help the mothers to be all that mothers ought to be, and the wives to be all that wives ought to be. You men of this city[6] are going to have better wives. I want every wife who will say, "My husband shall have a more consecrated wife," to stand up. I want every mother who says, "God helping me, I will be a better mother" to stand up. You who are as good as you are going to be, keep your seats. Will you members of the church, both male and female, who will say, "God helping me, I am going to do better," stand up?

You old sinners are going to feel mighty lonesome about this time. You are kind-hearted men, but the Devil has had you off juggling with you. Let us quit him now. I tell you what tickles me: to see an old sinner come in and pull out an old, lame, dwarfed[7] member of the church, and lay him down and measure by him: "Look here, boys, I am as long and broad and good as this member of the church!" I would die, if I was a decent man, to lay myself down by the side of such a man. Why don't you go and pick out one of these grand old Christians? You would look like a rat-terrier lying beside an elephant. You quit measuring by these dwarfs. We got them from you, and you can have them back.

"Waiting for the church to get right!" Let the church do and be as it will, I am going to so live that my life will be consecrated to God. Don't stay out because of the hypocrites, but come in and help crowd them out. A fellow says he can't live with these trifling church members. Is it not better to come in and live with them and go to Heaven than to go to Hell living without them? That is a heap worse, ain't it? "Waiting for the church to get right!" In all my experience, I never saw churches respond as readily as they do here. They are about as near right as you will ever see them.

"I am waiting for feeling," says some fellow. You look at me. You are an honest, sensible citizen of this town. What are your feelings? What do you mean by feeling? Do you mean serious thought? If you don't mean that, you don't mean anything. If serious thought is not feeling, there is no serious thought in repentance. If serious thought is not repentance, there is no feeling in religion. I recollect once I went down into the congregation and said to an old sinner, "Come up, and give your heart to God."

He said, "Mr. Jones, I have not got a bit of feeling." And he could hardly stand on his feet, he had so much. When a man sees he ought to do right and quit the wrong, that is the only feeling there is on the subject. Do you think that you ought to be a Christian, and ought to start tonight? If you do, you have got feeling enough to sweep you right under the cross, if you will start now.

Another fellow says, "I am not waiting for feeling; I am waiting until I am fit." Yes, you take the most intelligent lawyer out of Christ in this town, and the most ignorant man, and say to the ignorant one, "Tom, do you belong to the church?"

"No, sir, 'cause I ain't fitten."

Then you meet the lawyer and ask the same question, and he will reply, "Why I am not fit, sir, to be a member of the church."

Is it not astonishing that they meet on precisely the same ground? "I am waiting until I am fit." I tell you, brethren, when you analyze that thing in the light of the gospel, it is the most ridiculous position a man can put himself in. Here is a fellow starving to death; there is a richly-loaded table.

"Are you hungry?"

"Yes, I am just as hungry as I can be, but I can't go to that table; my hands ain't fitten."

"Here are soap and water and towels."

He says, "I ain't fitten to wash."

You come up and join the church. Don't hang back because "I am not fitten." Come up here and get fitten. He says, "I ain't fitten to get fitten." What are you going to do with that sort of man? Let me tell you, my congregation, that the very fact that you don't feel fit is the very thing that commends you to God. Jesus Christ came into the world to save good people? Oh no, but to save sinners. If you are a sinner you are a man; now, understand that. I have had such a sense of unworthiness from the day I started until this hour. It grows with me. I have never felt worthy of membership in the church of Jesus Christ. I started well, but I am climbing still, ascending all the time. If you wait till you are worthy to join the church, you will wait until millions of years shall have rolled away.

Another says, "I know Christ died to save me, but I am waiting to try myself a while." I have seen many a fellow come up and resolve to be a good man. "I ain't going to do anything, but I am going to try myself." The Devil doesn't want any better joke on a fellow than to get him out trying himself. A great big lump of drunk trying to walk a straight line. Watch him! "I will walk here. I want to see if I can hold out." That is just like a fellow saying, "I am going to sit out under this tree to see if I can't go to town sitting here." Trying himself! I tell you, I like to see a man just walk up and get his ticket, jump on the train and move off. That's the sort! The difficulty with some of us is, we buy our tickets to way-stations and never get through.

Coming through from Atlanta I noticed when the conductor came around and took the tickets, he gave checks and put marks on the checks. He gave some red checks. I noticed that these red-checked fellows came through to Chattanooga, and the other fellows got off at the different way-places. Many a fellow buys his ticket to conviction; he will land off right there. Another fellow will buy his ticket up to the penitent's altar; another will go as far as church membership, and he will get off there. Another will buy to obedience, and another up to family prayer, or the station just this side of that. Hundreds of them have not gone up that high yet, but buy to the little station just this side of family prayer. They will be put off at that little flag-station in a swamp, and no hotel for a man to stop at, and the whole region infested with mosquitoes.

All of you who have gone that far know that family-prayer town is a delightful place. I am glad I have got my wife and children off at that town. Let us get a limited ticket clear through to the next world, have our baggage checked through, and into Heaven we will ride. Don't trouble yourself about the destination. Stick to the train, and you will land in Heaven.

Don't act like that fellow who said, "I want to go to Chattanooga, but I am afraid I can't get through."

"This is the train," said the conductor. "We are going that way now."

As the train pulled out of the station the fellow said, "I wouldn't miss it for all the world."

"Keep your seat," said the conductor, "and we'll take you to Chattanooga."

When they reached Stevenson he said, "I am so afraid we won't get to Chattanooga."

"Keep your seat," repeated the conductor.

At Bridgeport the man said, "I am troubled a good deal about getting to Chattanooga."

"Keep your seat."

As the whistle blew for Chattanooga he said, "I am afraid I will miss it."

"Keep your seat."

At last the train rolled into the car shed at Chattanooga, and he was still giving vent to his fear about missing the place.

An old church member says, "I have so many dark days. I do want to get to Heaven."

Keep your seat! The train goes through. If you want to get to the good world, get on God's excursion train, and you will run in under the old car shed of heaven. Some of you will have children there to take hold of your hand and welcome you to the city of God. We will get there, thank God! Sister, keep your seat, it will go through. Brother, keep your head in at the window; the train is in safe hands. I have quit troubling myself. I have turned it all over to God.

Another says, "I am waiting for faith." Yes, you have been waiting forty years for faith. How much have you saved up? Like the fellow who had ten bushels of wheat, and was waiting till more grew before he would sow what he had. Sow it, and you will have a hundredfold. By keeping it, you will not get any more, but the rats will eat up what you have.

[It's as if a man said] "I want to be a blacksmith as soon as I get muscle." Why don't you go at it? There he stands until at last he has not muscle enough to lift the hammer. He is "getting it" with a vengeance. How did you get faith? By using what you had. I tell you what tickles me—to hear a fellow down praying for faith. "Lord, give me faith." The next time you get any in that way, bring it over and let me see it. That ain't Scriptural, that talk you are doing now. Christ rebuked those who prayed for faith. The trouble with you is not that you need more faith. You use the faith you have, and then you will get more. I would as soon pray for sweet potatoes as for faith.

Let me tell you, my congregation, there is not a man in this tent who has not got faith enough ultimately to save his soul if he will use what he has; and the way to get more is to use what you have. I don't know how this idea fits theology. Does it suit theology? You, my [ministerial] brethren, may take care of theology, and I will take care of these sinners and the Bible. Don't you let theology get hurt! If you do, we are all gone! Lord, Lord, help me to use the faith I have, and then I know it will increase.

Have you got faith enough to believe that there is a better

life? I tell you that is just about enough to start with. You believe you are wrong, and you believe you ought to get right. It will not be a week until you believe some other things that are mighty grand.

"I am not waiting for faith," says another. "That ain't my trouble. Nor [am I] waiting for salvation, nor better terms, for I know I have enough to start with." What then? Waiting for the church to get right? "No, I believe any church member is better than I am." I have taken in a few of your sort. They are of no more account than the others. It will be about all you can do to keep up with the rear rank. If a fellow can get a good look at himself it will cure him of his conceit, and he can be a first-class member. Mark what I tell you, this is the human side in all its fullness.

Now, let us look at the other side a moment. "My hope is in God." Here you have struck the keynote on which we believe for eternal life. My hope is not in my friends, for the day may come when my friends will turn their backs upon me; nor in riches, for riches may take to themselves wings and fly away. My hope is not in my pastor, for the day may come when he will spurn me from his presence. My hope is not in the church, for the time might come when she would turn me out. My hope is not in my father and mother; if it was, my hope would be gone, for father and mother are both, in this life, gone from me forever. My hope is not in my wife, with all her fondness and love for me, for the day will come (but may I never live to see it!) when she shall be buried under the sod for all time. I am so glad our text doesn't say that our hope is in our children, for we might bury them too—forever.

My hope, my friends, is not in riches, pastor, church, friends, father and mother, or children; my hope is in God. Will you start tonight? You may say, "I am mighty weak." I know that; but your hope is in God. You may add, "Yes, but I am a poor sinner." Listen! My hope is in God, it is not in myself. I know I am a sinner. [The enemy tells me] "Yes, you are very, very weak; you are as frail as a bruised reed." Yes, but my hope is in God. "You have an appetite that will crush you in a week." My hope is in God, and He is stronger than appetite.

Let us make a start. The question is not, "Have I got enough religion to take me to Heaven?" The question is, "Have I got enough to start?" Enough to make me say, "Right is right, and I am going to do it. Wrong is wrong, and I am going to quit it"?

When traveling by train in Georgia I frequently ride on the engine. Once while in the cab, admiring the locomotive that was to draw our train from Atlanta to Chattanooga, I heard the engineer ask his fireman, "Have we steam enough to start with?"

The reply was, "Yes, sir."

On looking at the steam-gauge, I observed that the register was but sixty pounds, and that the capacity of the boiler was one hundred and forty pounds. I wondered why so light a pressure was deemed sufficient; but the train had not reached the Chattahoochee River, less than seven miles away, before I saw the engine blowing off steam; it already had too much. And so it was at intervals all along the route. I found that the locomotive generated steam faster when running than when stationary. Mark you, that engineer did not ask, "Have we steam enough to run to the river, or to Chattanooga?" but, "Have we steam enough to *start* with?"

Glory to God! We generate power while in motion faster than when standing still. Lord Jesus Christ, let men see that all they need is to step out in the right direction! Oh, how I want to see men make this start! Success for both worlds depends upon this start. Where the road is rough the [repair] shops are thick, and just as sure as you live, they hold out to the next world.

The gospel of the Son of God is nothing more or less than a line of wagon-shops on the way to Heaven to mend your vehicle and start you on the road again. I rolled my old broken-down humanity under the wagon-shop of the cross. In a few minutes it was fixed from tongue to coupling-pole. I was fixed up for time and eternity, and I started; but sir, I didn't get a mile until down came a wheel. I said, "I will give it up; I am gone."

I looked up the roadside, and the wagon-maker said, "Just bring that wagon here, and I will fix it up."

When the repairs were made I said, "How much do I owe you?"

"Nothing. Only promise to stop at the next shop if you break down."

I didn't go two miles till smash came down one of the axles. I said, "I am breaking down every mile. I might as well quit."

"Bring that axle up here; I am fixing axles. I charge you nothing; only be sure and stop at the next shop if you break again."

Further down the road I made a quick turn, and pop went the tongue, and I was about to give it up forever, when another wagon-maker said, "Bring it up here; I am working in the interest of wagons going in the right direction."

You know, I don't believe I have got the linch-pin of the old wagon I started with, it has broken down so many times; but if the [repair] shops hold out, I am going through.

I was talking about this with an old soldier who had been traveling all his life. I said, "Brother, do the shops hold out?"

He answered, "They do. It is not half a year since I was in a shop myself." Thank God, no man ever broke down out of sight of a shop!

The fact is, a man gets religion a good deal like he gets the measles. Religion is catching. A fellow goes and gets tangled up with the measles, and in about ten days he says, "Wife, you can send for the doctor; I feel bad; I ache from head to foot." She sends for a doctor, and he comes and examines the case.

He asks, "Have you been exposed to measles? That is what you have got." He gives him a cup of good hot tea, and says, "You keep on drinking that until you get it broke out on you, and then you will be all right."

Now, some of you have got tangled up in this meeting, and you never felt so mean in your life. You have caught religion. I will just give you two or three cups of gospel tea, and break it out on you; then keep it broke out, and you are elected. If you will walk right up and take two or three cups of this sort of tea—"Ask, and ye shall receive; seek, and ye shall find; knock, and it shall be opened unto you"[8]—take two or three cups of this warm tea, and then you shall be saved. Break it out, and keep it broke out. Religion is like measles; if it goes in on you, it will kill you. The trouble with a great many Christians in this city is, religion has gone in on them. Wrap up and keep warm, and keep it broke out on hands, feet, and tongue.

I don't underrate a man's religious experience because he can't give place or date. Some of the best men I ever saw could not give the place and time when this miracle of grace occurred; but they could say, "I love God." I don't underrate a man's religious experience because he did not have it like somebody else. But I say this much: I want a fellow to feel awful mean.

This is a common feeling, and it is a very natural one. Sister, if you never felt mean, then you never felt natural; and brother, if you never felt mean, then you never came within half a mile of feeling natural. Like that fellow up at Lebanon; he said he felt mean, and I told him he felt natural for one time in his life. I like to see a fellow so low down that he doesn't ask any questions. The best repentance you can do is to quit your meanness.

What is repentance? It is quitting my devilment. If my boy

does any devilment, the best repentance he can do is to quit. What sort of repentance do I want? I want quitting repentance. That is what we call evangelical repentance. You will have to explain legal repentance. This evangelical repentance—that is the sort these sinners want. They don't want legal repentance. They are like the Irishman who said about justice, "Faith, that is just what I *don't* want!" Evangelical repentance is quitting. I am done. I won't do it any more. That is the best proof in the world that a fellow is sorry for his meanness—that he quits. The law of God will show me how mean I am, but it is only the grace of God that can save me from that meanness. That goes for every fellow in this tent.

Repentance is the first conscious movement of the soul from sin toward God. Many a fellow is praying for rain with his tub the wrong side up. God cannot fill a tub when it is wrong side up without inverting the law of gravity. God is holding up His clouds for you while you are holding your tub the wrong side up.

There is but one road. Heaven is at one end and Hell at the other end. The road to Hell is the road to Heaven. The only difference is in the way you are going. It is not so much what road you are on, but which way you are going. The meanest sinner only has to turn round and face the other way, and he is on the way to Heaven.

It is not asking much of you to ask you to believe on the Lord Jesus Christ. I believed on Him for twenty-five years; but I did not believe on Him as much as the Devil did. He believed and trembled; I believed and went on drinking. Now I believe on the Lord Jesus Christ in the sense that I will follow Him. I am not running on understanding. I could not get to my front gate on understanding. I love Him.

If you will open your heart when He knocks, He will save you. He that worships God, let him do it in spirit and in truth. "What must I do to be saved?" Open your heart and let the heavenly guest come in. A stranger knocks at the door. Will you admit this guest and say, "Abide forever"? Christ always lives where there is room for Him. If there is room in your heart for Christ, He lives there. If there is room in a law office for Christ, He lives there. If there is room in your store for Christ, He lives there. If there is room on a locomotive engine, He will be there. If there is room in your baggage car, He will be there. Everywhere there is room for Him, He will come into our homes, and into our stores, and into our shops, and on our engines, and in our cars— that is, if we will provide room for Him.

And it is Christ, *Christ*, CHRIST; and it is not getting religion. When it comes to the understanding of the thing, I don't understand it, but I know that twelve years ago there was a knock at my heart, and I know I got the doors open. It took me a week. How I pried and dug! But my trouble was not getting Christ in, but getting the doors open. As soon as the doors flew open He came in, and brought salvation with Him.

"If we confess our sins, He is faithful and just to forgive us."[9] A man is never ready to confess his sins until he has quit his sins. You let an old drunkard get religion and join the church, and you will hear him say he was the biggest old drunkard this country ever saw; but you tackle that red-nosed fellow before he repents, and he will say that he does not know how liquor tastes. He hasn't quit.

The best man I ever knew in my life came to the altar so drunk he didn't know who he was. If you are drunk tonight I don't care, [just] so you are sober tomorrow. There are some men in this city who will have to get religion drunk if they get it at all, for they never draw a sober breath. I do believe God will save a man when he is drunk.

Old Uncle Jimmy Payne, the most saintly man we ever had, stopped at the corner grocery while his wife went to meeting. One night meeting held a little longer than usual, and he went down to church. He was so drunk he did not know his identity. When the call was made for persons wishing to join the church, he walked right up the aisle and gave the preacher his hand, to the disgust of everybody. His wife was shamed almost to death, but she got him home and put him to bed.

In the morning she told him what he had done. She said, "Don't you know you joined the church last night?"

"No."

"Yes, you are a church member."

He said he was not.

"Yes, you are."

He said, "Did I join?"

She told him he did.

He lay perfectly still a minute, and then said, "If I did, I will stick to it." And he did stick until God called him higher. I like that—I mean the sticking part. I reckon he must have got Presbyterian religion, but he made a good Methodist. I declare to you he was one of the most saintly men I ever saw, and that was the way he started. It is not what you are when you set out, but will you stick to it?

Let me tell you how to get religion. A man who lived down in middle Georgia a number of years ago, a very intelligent man, young and married, went to church one day. His wife didn't go with him. When he came home his wife said, "What sort of meeting had you today?"

"A pretty good meeting. I joined the church today."

"Have you got religion?"

"No."

"What did you do that for, if you haven't got religion?"

"The preacher said if I would do before I got religion as I would do after I got religion, I would get religion."

"Well," said she, "if that doesn't head me. You joined the church, and haven't got relgion!"

That night just before they retired, he said, "Wife, get down that old Bible; I am going to pray at home."

"Are you going to pray when you haven't got religion?"

"Yes."

In the morning he said, "Get that Bible, wife; I am going to pray again."

"What do you pray for without religion?"

Wednesday night he went to prayer meeting in the country, and they called on him to pray. He got down and did his best; and his wife said, when he told her he had prayed at the meeting, "You pray in public, sir, and got no religion! What did you do that for?"

But he moved along on that line about three weeks, and the first thing you know religion broke out on him all over, from head to foot. Just as certain as that passenger train will carry a man to Chattanooga, just so certainly will the means of grace take a man to God.

A man is just a strong as the thing he commits himself to, and no stronger. If you commit yourself to a little [floating] box in the Atlantic, you and the box will go down together. If you get on board a grand ocean steamer, then all the comfort and strength and safety of the steamer are yours. If I commit myself to myself, then I am no stronger than this arm of flesh. If I commit myself to God, I will never go down; I will stay up as long as God stays up. I put my hand in the hand of God, and commit it all to Him tonight. Won't you do it?

Let me tell you, God will hear a man pray from any point,

and answer him. A child will put its hand on the place where it hurts, and cry. If you want to get to Heaven, put your hand on that desire and pray. If you want to be saved from sin, put your hand on that desire and pray to God, and He will save you. If you are ready to say, "Oh, God, I want to be a good man!," lay your hand on that desire and God will hear you. Yes; have hope in God, and all the trials, temptations, dark days, heavy hearts, and all that sort of thing will disappear.

I have not a word to say in palliation. This journey we are on ends well. I never think much about the road, but much about where I am going. People whose friends move out west go to the Post Office daily looking for letters. They want to hear about Texas. The letters say that Texas has the most fertile soil and the most magnificent climate you ever saw. They speak in glowing terms of that great western country. But every letter has a post-script: "There are graveyards and coffins and sickbeds and death out here."

The Bible tells me of a country where there is no more sickness, sorrow, pain, or death forever and ever. I want to get to that country where I shall never see my wife's cheek pale any more. I want to see eternal health on the faces of my wife and children. I have made a start on that journey, and am going on. God help you men tonight! God help me tonight! Whatever other men may do, I start tonight.

The train is here; the bell is ringing to start; I step aboard, and move out for the good world tonight. Will you go? There are five hundred persons here tonight whom I want to see on these front pews. Some of you are already on them. It is a quarter past eight o'clock. We have plenty of time here tonight. I want to see every man who has no religion here tonight. I want to take your hand, and help you to start to Heaven. Will you believe tonight? Will you confess tonight? Will you say, "I consecrate my life to Christ. I make him my Savior, and will do His will from this time on and forever"? I want every man in this tent tonight who feels as if he wants to take every essential step that will bring him to God, to rise up, and we will pray for him.

NOTES

1. Psalm 39:7.
2. Acts 16:30.
3. 2 Corinthians 6:2.

4. A demijohn, sold by liquor merchants, was a narrow-necked glass bottle enclosed in wickerwork, and holding from one to ten gallons. It had one or two wicker handles.
5. The evangelist is addressing ministers on his platform.
6. The city was Chattanooga, Tennessee, where the evangelist often spoke and was highly popular.
7. The evangelist is speaking in spiritual terms.
8. Matthew 7:7.
9. 1 John 1:9.

F. B. Meyer

He closed down five hundred English houses of prostitution. He raised such a protest over the scheduled heavyweight boxing match between the American Jack Johnson and the Englishman Bombardier Wells that the event was canceled. He went into the window-washing business and the lumber business to provide work for unemployed laborers. He formed a prison aid society that fed breakfast to thousands of just-released prisoners who had no place to go but the nearest tavern. He established a savings bank for ex-convicts and erected a Provident House to provide them with living quarters. He actively supported the temperance movement, and traveled on missionary journeys to South Africa and inland China.

Yet all this activity was peripheral to the underlying gospel ministry of Frederick Brotherton Meyer (1847-1929)—better known as F. B. Meyer, pastor, author, Bible teacher and evangelist. Even today his devotional books are found on ministers' shelves throughout the English-speaking world. A warmhearted, modest, saintly, charming English gentleman, Meyer in his day attracted thousands of listeners on both sides of the Atlantic. He was a popular speaker at deeper life conferences: Keswick in England, Northfield in New England, and the Stony Brook Assembly on Long Island. He brought an untold number of seekers into the Kingdom of God.

Two of the most prominent preachers of their day, Charles Spurgeon, the Englishman, and J. Wilbur Chapman, the American, were powerfully influenced by Meyer. Dwight L. Moody, who has been called the greatest evangelist of his century, owed his first recognition to the support Meyer gave him in York, England, where Meyer was then a young pastor.

Born in London into a wealthy family of German ancestry, Meyer enjoyed a fine Christian upbringing. This background proved useful when his father's business suffered a reverse and the family home in Brighton had to be sold. A year later, at age sixteen, Meyer decided to enter the ministry. On his pastor's advice, before enrolling in London University he joined a tea firm for two years. After graduation he completed his theological training at Regent's Park (Baptist) College.

In 1871 Meyer married and accepted a call to Priory Street Baptist Church in York as his first full-time charge. It was at York that the Moody and Sankey team from America was just beginning its evangelistic tour of England. Crowds were small, however, both at the York Independent Chapel and at Moody's noontime prayer meetings. Meyer was among those who heard Moody preach on the Holy Spirit, and he received a genuine touch from God. He thereupon opened his own chapel to the Americans and for the first time all seats were filled.

In 1874 Meyer accepted a call from the Victoria Road Baptist Church of Leicester. But here his new zeal ran into trouble: a wealthy deacon informed him, "This is not a gospel shop!" After attending a convention at Keswick, Meyer tells us, he was led of the Holy Spirit to resign from his church. A group of merchants induced him to form a new local church, and so in 1881 Melbourne Hall came into being. It proved to be not only a church, but also a rescue mission, social center, Sunday school, and Bible institute and was, says Arthur Clarke, Meyer's "abiding memorial."

After seven years at Melbourne Hall, Meyer heeded the call to London, first to Regent's Park Chapel, then to Christ Church, Westminster Bridge Road, where he served for fifteen years. Concurrently he wrote devotional books by the bushel. In response to invitations, he preached frequently in American pulpits, notably in Boston, New York, Philadelphia and Chicago. He preached his last sermon in February 1929 in London, and died the following month.

Meyer's natural ease of delivery he attributed to the example of D. L. Moody in the early days at York. The following message is taken from one of his fifty books titled A Castaway and Other Addresses. It was preached during a week's series of meetings at Carnegie Hall, New York City, and was published in 1897 by Fleming H. Revell, Chicago.

FOUR

THE CHRIST-LIFE FOR THE SELF-LIFE
by F. B. Meyer

I would almost shrink from speaking about the profound philosophy wherewith the Apostle Paul deals with the self-life; but I believe that God's Spirit will take my broken words and speak to each of you. Will you turn to 1 Corinthians 2:14? "The natural man receiveth not the things of the Spirit of God, for they are foolishness to him; neither can he know them, because they are spiritually discerned."

"The natural man." The Greek is the "psychical man," the man in whom the soul is all, and the spirit is like a dark, untenanted chamber. The temple of old was constituted thus: outer court, holy place, holy of holies. The outer court corresponds to our body, the holy place to our soul, the holy of holies or the most holy place to our spirit. In the regenerate man the most holy place is tenanted by the Spirit of God, but in the unregenerate man it is untenanted and dark, waiting for its occupant. The natural man is the man whose spirit is empty of God.

In the fifteenth verse of the same chapter we read: "But he that is spiritual judgeth all things, yet he himself is judged of no man." Here we have the "spiritual" man, the man whose spirit is quick with the Spirit of God, who speaks and wills and lives beneath the impulse of the Holy Spirit Himself. Oh, that every believer were to become truly spiritual, with the Spirit of God (written with a large S) dominating the spirit of man.

In the third chapter of the same epistle, Paul begins, "And I, brethren, could not speak to you as unto spiritual, but as unto carnal, even as unto babes in Christ." Now, the "carnal" man is a Christian, a babe in Christ. We might think that the carnal man is unregenerate, but it is not so. He is regenerate, he is in Christ, and Christ is in him; but instead of Christ being predominant, the

65

carnal element is predominant. I believe there are hundreds of people who are in Christ, but they are babes in Christ. Christ is in them, but He is overcrowded by the superiority of their self-life. Their self-life was once clothed in rags; now it is clothed in the externals of religion, but it is still the self-life, and in the Christian it may predominate over the Christ-life, and be the cause of unutterable darkness and sorrow.

May God help us now to reverse it, so that the carnal element shall be crowded out, shall be crucified, and the Christ element shall become the pivot of your life.

In order that you may know what the carnal element is, let me say that that word also stands for "flesh." The apostle uses the word in a very special form. He does not mean the natural body, but he means the element of self. In Romans 7:18 he says, "In me (that is, in my flesh) dwelleth no good thing." My flesh is "me." Some spell it with a tiny m, some with a capital M, but the "me" in each person is the flesh. Spell "flesh" backward, drop the h, as we are apt to do in London, and you get s-e-l-f. Flesh is self and self is flesh. It is "me," and as long as "me" is first and Christ second, I am living a carnal life though I am in Christ and a saved man.

Now, the carnal life is a *babe life*. What is sweeter than a babe? So wee, so beautiful! But what is tender and beautiful in a babe for a few months is [unless there is growth] terrible at the end of twelve months, or ten years. And what is lovely in a young convert is terrible in a man of ten or twenty years of Christian life. If you are still living in the elementary stage of experience and feeling and prayer, and do not grow, do not know God better, do not know the Bible better, do not know yourself better, do not know Christ better, you are a little babe, you are carnal.

The carnal man *lives on milk*. Paul said, "I have fed you with milk, and not with meat; for hitherto you were not able to bear it, nor are you yet able."[1] Milk is food which has passed through the digestion of another. The babe cannot take meat, so the mother takes meat and breaks it down, and the child takes milk. So many Christians cannot read the Bible, cannot get any good out of the Bible. It must be broken down by their minister, and they are fed with a spoon. Ministers become nurses. They have to spend their time wheeling the converts about, comforting them, putting them to sleep, waking them up and feeding them; and if they are not fed with a spoon three or four times a week, there is no knowing what will happen. And if you are in that state that you must take spiritual truth through the digestion of another, you are a babe.

A carnal Christian is also *sectarian*. "I am of Paul, and I am
of Apollos, and I of Cephas."[2] Oh, how much we make of the fold,
and how little of the flock! How much we think of the hurdles,
and how little of the sheep! One man says, "I am a Baptist," and
another, "I am a Presbyterian"; a third says, "I am a Roman
Catholic," and a fourth, "I am evangelical." Half the time we are
worrying about the sect to which we belong. Directly a man begins
in that course, and forgets the Church with a large C—the Church
of Christ—he is a carnal Christian and a babe.

I would lead you one step further. In Hebrews 5:14 we read,
"Strong meat belongs to them that are of full age, even those who
by reason of use have their senses exercised to discern both good
and evil." Here we have a fourth characteristic of the carnal
Christian: such a one is *unable to exercise his senses to discern good
and evil*. When I returned to England from one of my Atlantic
voyages, my nose was very sensitive; the pure air of the Atlantic
had made me keen to discern impurity. I went to stay with some
friends in the country, and all that time I was haunted by noxious
effluvia. I asked, "What is the matter?"

"Oh," they said, "there is nothing wrong."

I said, "I am sure there is," and after investigating, we discovered about a mile off a sewage farm which infected the air. My
friends who had not been on the Atlantic were unable to detect it.
So there are those who take up a book full of impure thought and
read it and do not feel hurt, though the hurt has certainly been
received. There are men and women who listen to uncharitable
talk, without detecting its undertone; men and women who go in
and out in the world and mix in its pleasure and sin, and still call
themselves Christians, but they cannot discern good and evil.

I am here as a surgeon, to help you to anatomize yourself and
know where you are. Are you growing? Are you living on the
strong meat of the Bible? Are you a sectary? Have you the power to
discriminate between good and evil? By these four tests you may
know whether the Christ-life or the flesh-life is predominant in
you.

Let us go deeper. When God created man, He gave all
intelligent beings a selfhood, a power of self-determination. He
gave it to angels. Demons have it, because they were angels. Men
have it. The Creator meant this selfhood to be dependent upon
Himself, so that a Christian might turn to his Creator and say,
"Lord, live in Your will through me." When Jesus Christ, the
perfect man, came among us, during all His earthly life He said

and willed nothing from Himself. He lived a truly dependent life.

The vegetable creation—flowers, trees—depend on God absolutely, and that makes them so beautiful. Consider the lilies and the cedars, how they grow! And the angels who have kept their first estate live on God. God wills, thinks, acts, energizes through them. Satan was once an archangel dependent on God, but something passed over him and he caught the fever of independence, and began to make himself his own pivot; and so he began to be in Hell. Because Hell is the assertion of self to the exclusion of God, and Heaven is the assertion of God to the exclusion of self. The Devil fell, and all his crew that leaned on him instead of on God fell also.

Then when man was made, Satan traversed the abyss and whispered to man, "Be God, be independent, take your own way, do your own will."

Man in his fall withdrew his nature from dependence upon God, and made himself a center of his own life and activity. And this world is cursed today because men and women are living for self and the flesh-life. The carnal mind is enmity against God, and is darkness and despair.

Christianity is a deep science which seeks to do away with the evil or the fall into selfishness by substituting for self the Son of God, which is Christ. Is it not wonderful that Hinduism and Christianity are each intended to deal with the same root of evil? But the Hindu tries to exterminate the self-life by absorption into eternity until Nirvana sets in, while the Christian, who also sees that the self-life is accursed, eliminates it by the philosophy and the action which I am now going to describe.

Paul writes, "Now the works of the flesh are manifest, which are these: adultery, fornication, uncleanness, lasciviousness, idolatry, sorcery, enmities, strife, jealousy, indignations, contentions, divisions, sects, envyings, murders, drunkennesses, revels, and such like."[3] There you have the passion of the self-life, trying to perfect itself. "Are you so foolish?" Paul asks the Galatians. "Having begun in the Spirit, are you now made perfect by the flesh?"[4] There was a school of perfection in Galatia; they sought to perfect themselves in their own energy; and there have been schools of perfection ever since, which have tried to be good in the energy of the flesh.

Paul wrote the Colossians, "Let no one defraud you of the prize by doing his will in humility and worship of angels, intruding into things which he has not seen, vainly puffed up by the mind of his flesh."[5] There you have intellectualism prying into the things of God, but not submitting to the will of God and the teaching of God. There you have the self-life planning, scheming and arranging for itself; but the apostle says, "I am not going to plan after the flesh."

We see then that we are always in danger of doing good things from the self pivot. That is our curse. I hear of a man who has consecrated himself to God, and I say to myself, "I will do the same." I hear of a man who has attracted crowds by some special lantern, or by some other new equipment, and I say, "I too will do the same." I learn of a school which is teaching a certain line of doctrine, and because it will pay, and get me prestige and popularity, I adopt it. But not until I begin to notice the working of my own life, shall I have any conception how perpetually the self-life is underlying all.

The same principle of self-life which is working unrestrained and unbridled in man's [unregenerate] nature is working also in the heart of the regenerate man, the church member. He gives to the collection, to the subscription list, that men may see how much he gives. He seeks to please God by prayer, by the communion, by ritualistic observances. He will even try to be perfect. There is many a person who goes to Keswick and to Northfield, trying to pile up his religious life in the energy of his religious-looking self. Self is our pivot. It is because Satan made self his pivot that he became a Devil. Take Heaven from its center in God, and try to center it in self, and you transform Heaven into Hell. Hell is selfishness, and selfishness is Hell.

When I am dealing with a drunkard I am inclined to say to him, "Be a man."

What a fool I am! Trying to cast out the evil of drink by the evil of self-esteem. If I want to save a man, I must cast out the spirit of self, and substitute the Lord Jesus Christ. But how? How? I will show you. There are *three steps:* the cross, the Spirit, and the contemplation of the risen Christ. May we take them now, and may the Spirit of God reveal to each of us this blessed secret.

On the cross Jesus Christ offered a substitutionary sacrifice for the sins of the whole world. But there is a second, significant meaning in the cross. Paul writes to the Roman Christians, "What the law could not do in that it was weak through the flesh, God sending His own Son in the likeness of sinful flesh, and for sin, condemned sin in the flesh, that the righteousness of the law might be fulfilled in us, who walk not after the flesh but after the

Spirit."⁶ Now please understand. "For sin" is substitutionary. "In the likeness of sinful flesh" is a reference to sanctification. On the cross God nailed in the person of Christ the likeness of our sinful flesh. I cannot explain it to you more than that; but I know this—that next to seeing Jesus as my sacrifice, nothing has revolutionized my life like seeing the effigy of my sinful self in the sinless, dying Savior.

I say to myself, "God has nailed the likeness of my self-life to the cross. The cross is the symbol of degradation and curse. If then God has treated the likeness of my sinful self, when borne by the sinless Christ, as worthy of His curse, how terrible in God's sight it must be for myself to hug it and embrace it and live in it!"

In Galatians 2:20 Paul writes, "I have been crucified with Christ." God demands that every man and woman should unite with the cross and (so to speak) kill the self-life, the egotism, the personal element which has been so strong in each one. Not your individuality, however! Isaiah will still be Isaiah, and Malachi Malachi. But the proud, fussy self-esteem, yourself, ego, the flesh, must be crucified. Christ denied His divine self, and you and I must deny our fallen self. Christ's temptation was to use His divine attribute; your temptation is that you should use your human attribute. We are to put it to the cross, and believe that from this moment it shall be crucified to us and we to it. Barabbas to the cross, to the cross! Christ, come down from the cross and live in us!

This wonderful Epistle to the Galatians speaks of the cross as between me and Egypt, between me and the wilderness, between me and my past, my wanderings; and now the cross is my Jordan River by which I pass through death into the land where Joshua leads, the land that flows with milk and honey.

O wondrous cross! But that is not all. Christ and I are one. In Him I hung there. I came to an end of myself in Christ, and kneeling at His cross I took the position of union with Him in His death, and I consigned my self-life to the cross. It was as though I took my self-life with its passions, its choices, its yearnings after perfection, its wallowing, its fickleness, its judgment of others, its uncharity, as a felon, and said, "You shall die. My God nailed you to that cross. I put you there by my choice, by my will, by my faith. Hang there."

After that moment, I have ever reckoned that my self-life is on the cross, and that the death of Christ lies between me and it. Let me make that clear. Suppose a woman has been married to a man who turns out to be a felon, a drunkard, a libertine. After years of sorrow there comes a moment of liberty when she seeks and obtains a divorce. She now enters into union with a perfectly lovely blessed man who becomes to her everything. Whenever her former husband reels along the street and seeks again to get her back in his power, she points to a moment when the divorce was granted and says, "From that moment I became divorced from you. Touch me if you dare."

If he comes across the street, she only clutches closer the arm of the true man she loves, and puts him on the other side between the sot and herself. She counts from the moment of deliverance.

Now think about it, pray about it. Realize why your Christian life has been a failure. The cause of your darkness and sorrow and desertion is to be found here: you have never consigned the self-life where God consigned it. In your will, unite yourself with the death of Christ.

Doing so, remember that you will do what Jesus said Peter must do. Peter said, "You are the Christ."[7]

"Well and good," Jesus replied. "I am going to die."

Peter said, "You must not think of it. Spare Yourself."[8] And that is what you will hear said to you a thousand times—spare yourself!

Jesus said, "Get behind Me. That is Satan. It is the spirit of the pit. If a man will come after Me, let him deny himself, and take up his cross and follow Me."

You may say what you like about Christianity, but I undertake to affirm that it has been shamefully misrepresented, both by Protestants and any other class of Christians. They have thought that Christianity depended upon the objective, whereas it is equally and largely subjective. They have thought that it depended upon trusting Christ to put away your sin, whereas it also consists in trusting Christ to deliver you from yourselves, who are the center and curse of your life.

Whenever the self obtrudes, reckon yourself dead to it. Reckon that the cross stands between you and it.

But you say, "Sir, I do not see how I am to live like that. I shall always be on pins and needles, always in agony whether this is self or not, and I do not see how I am to live."

Ah, I thought you would say that! I said it myself, and here comes the second point: The Holy Spirit. Paul writes, "If through the Spirit you mortify the deeds of the body, you shall live."[9] I reckon that my self-life is on the cross, but only the Holy Spirit can make my reckoning true. We choose the cross, but the Holy Spirit as it were mortifies, makes dead, makes real. You reckon, He makes real your reckoning.

In Galatians we read, "The flesh lusts against the Spirit, and the Spirit against the flesh, and these are contrary the one to the other, so that you cannot do the things that you would."[10] Listen: If you choose the cross, if you live in the Spirit, the Spirit lusts (always the present tense) against the flesh. I don't know how your Bible reads, but some Bibles are printed wrongly. "Spirit" is spelled with a small s. Take some ink and alter that. It is not "spirit" with a small s; it is "Spirit" with a capital S, the Holy Spirit. And while we walk in the Spirit (Galatians 5:16), and are led of the Spirit (5:18), and live in the Spirit (5:25), the Holy Spirit will go on lusting and agonizing and making real to you your reckoning of death.

We are not therefore to worry about the death side; think about the life side. Do not live looking at the corpse, but live looking to the Holy Spirit. As you trust Him for every movement, as you breathe in the Holy Spirit moment by moment as you breathe in air, in the depth of your heart He will draw you away from the flesh, the self, the world, the Devil; and insensibly, unconsciously, exquisitely He will bring you into life. And the more you live on the life side, the more, without knowing much of it, you will live on the death side. For while you are engrossing with the Holy Spirit, the Holy Spirit in the depth of your being is carrying the sentence of death deeper, deeper, deeper down, and things are being mortified of which you once had no conception.

Paul tells the Galatians, "It pleased God . . . to reveal His Son in me, that I might preach Him among the heathen."[11] Now to "reveal" means to undrape. There is a statue. It is covered with a veil. The statue is there, but hidden. I take off the veil, and you see it. When you were unregenerate, Christ came to you; that is what regeneration means—Christ born into your spirit. But perhaps Christ came in as a veiled figure. You have Christ in you, but He is veiled. Now, mark. When Jesus died, the veil of the Temple was rent in twain from the top to the bottom; and when the soul appreciates the death of Christ as its own death to sin, the veil is rent from top to bottom, and the Holy Spirit reveals Jesus as the substitute for the self-life.

A friend of mine was staying near Mont Blanc. In a fortnight he had not seen the "monarch of the Alps." As he was preparing to leave, he went up to dress for dinner and passing a window, saw that the mountain was still veiled in mist. Having dressed, he came downstairs and passed the window again. Every vestige of mist had now parted, and Mont Blanc stood revealed from base to snow-clad peak. So there shall come upon you a breath of the Holy Spirit, and God will reveal His Son in you as the center of your life.

A woman sits alone. Twenty years ago her son ran away to sea, leaving her a widow, poor and lonely. One day a mysterious bronzed stranger knocks at the door. "Can I sleep in your spare room?"

"I have a room to let, so you can stay."

It is her son, but he comes in disguise so that she cannot see him clearly. He is there, but she knows him not. But as they sit together at dinner and there is a gesture, she says, "John!"

"My mother!"

"My boy!"

After dinner he tells her, "Mother, here is gold. You shall never lack again. I am going to live with you, never to go away again." That is what Paul means when he writes the Colossians that "God would make known what is the riches of the glory of this mystery among the Gentiles, which is Christ in you, the hope of glory."[12]

Jesus has come, but He is a mystery. Now we have come to the cross, and mystery is gone. The riches of the glory of the mystery is Christ in us, and He will do for us better than ever we could have done for ourselves.

Some young men belonging to the Salvation Army came to old Andrew Bonar and said, "Dr. Bonar, we have been all night with God. Can't you see our faces shine?"

The old man said, "Moses wist not that his face shone."[13]

When you have the real article you do not need to advertise it. The public will come for it. But the man who has got what we call in England Brummagem ware, a sham, must puff it. If you have Christ in you, people will not glorify you, they will glorify Christ in you, and they will say, "Teach us about Christ."

Paul told the Galatians, "They glorified God in me."[14] Dear brother ministers, when you get this, they will not glorify your sermons, they will not glorify your intellect, and they will not glorify your eloquence, but they will glorify God who shines through you as the Shekinah shone through the Temple of old.

Hudson Taylor told me that on the threshold of his great lifework, God said to him, "My child, I am going to evangelize inland China, and if you would like to walk with Me I will do it through you."

Paul said, "He was mighty in me."[15] I cannot take that Bible class, but Christ is in me, and He can. I cannot conduct that mission, but Christ is in me, and He can. I cannot assume these responsibilities, but hallelujah! It does not mater. A copper wire has only to convey the message; it is for the battery to send it. You may be forevermore like the wire which connects you with cities, the wire along which the [message] passes without fret, without anxiety, without care, a mighty force conveyed in the wire. When it is not self but Christ, it is "mighty in me."

One day when traveling by train, I found a young man seated opposite me reading Thomas à Kempis' *Imitation of Christ*. I knew the book, and seating myself beside him I said, "A grand book."

"Yes," he said.

Said I, "I have found something better."

"Better?"

"Yes."

"How?"

"Better for me, because I was always a poor hand at imitation. I imitated the minister with whom I settled from college, and nobody but myself and my wife ever guessed that my sermons were imitations of his. When I was a boy my father had me taught drawing, and my master put before me something. My copy needed to have letter press underneath to state it was an imitation of the copy. And when I set out to imitate Christ, no one could have guessed what I was trying to attain.

"But," said I, "my young friend, if my drawing-master could have infused the spirit of his skill into my brain and hand, he could have drawn through me as fair a drawing as his own; and if my great and noble friend could have only put his spirit into me, why should I not have spoken even as he? And instead of my imitating Christ far away in the glory, He will come by the Holy Spirit and dwell in me, and by His grace He shall work through my poor yielded life."

It was by the eternal Spirit that Christ offered Himself without spot to God, and it is by the eternal Spirit that the spirit of self is going to be antagonized in your life and mine. Just as in a scarlet fever case you take carbolic acid, and the carbolic acid antagonizes the germs of disease, so turning from the spirit of self I kneel before the Holy Spirit and say, "Spirit of God, fill my entire being. In the depth of my nature, when I am least thinking about it, go on day by day as the antiseptic of my flesh or self-life. Antagonize it, work against it, keep it out of sight, keep it under Christ."

The Holy Spirit will do it.

But you may say, "Mr. Meyer, I am so afraid that if I am always dealing with the self-life, it will hurt me. It will be like standing by a bier and seeing death disintegrate a corpse."

This leads me to my third point, and I reply that while the Spirit of God in the depth of our hearts is antagonizing the self-life, He does it by making Jesus Christ a living bright reality. That is the beauty of it: He fixes our thoughts upon Jesus. We do not think about the Spirit, we hardly think about self, but we think much about our dear Lord; and all the time we are thinking about Him, the process of disintegration and dissolution and death of self is going on within the heart.

A sister said to me once, "I am going to spend a whole day praying for the Holy Spirit." She went to a hut in the wood, and she came back to me at night and said, "I have had a grand day, but I am a bit disappointed. I do not feel that I have more of the Holy Spirit now than I did."

"But," I said, "is Jesus much to you?"

"Oh," she replied, "Jesus was never so sweet and precious as He is now."

"Why, my dear woman," I said, "that is the Holy Spirit, because He glorifies Christ, and when the Holy Spirit works most, you do not think about the Holy Spirit, but you think about your dear Lord."

If you want to know what you and your dear ones will someday be, study the risen Christ. This man in death and through death passed into resurrection. He spoke, and Mary recognized His voice; and our dear ones will speak to us one day, and we shall recognize their voices. Mark the risen man. I can never understand why the church has made so little of the resurrection and ascension. He was man, the glorified, risen, ascending man, the second Adam, and all Hell tried to stop him. Just as in the first man the race came out of Paradise, so in the second man, all who believe in Him will reenter Paradise.

And just as Eve was taken out of Adam as he slept, the church was taken out of Christ in His "sleep," and when He rose we streamed out a great procession from the grave. So on Easter morning I celebrate not only the resurrection of Christ but my own, for I too was raised in Him.

The church is in the world not to argue, not to defend God, not to stand forth as an advocate for God, but simply to witness to the truth of the unseen and eternal. And directly you and I step away from that position, and become advocates pleading instead of witnesses bearing testimony, we step away from the position of power. You and I and the church are called to bear witness to the death of Christ, His resurrection, His ascension, and the advent of the Holy Spirit. And while you do that the Holy Spirit says, "Amen."

Will you take this? Jesus does love you. He is always near you. I do not talk about the cross so much as about Jesus who was crucified. I do not talk about the grave, but about Jesus who rose from it. I do not talk about the ascension, but about Jesus who ascended. He is with you and me always. It is not holiness, but it is Jesus the holy one. It is not meekness, it is Jesus the meek one. It is not purity, it is Jesus the pure one. Not it, not an experience, not emotion, not faith, but Jesus!

You have been worrying about your faith. Give it up! Do not think about your faith; think about Jesus, and you will have faith without knowing it. You have been worrying about your feeling. It does not matter; it goes up and down with the barometer. Have done with it, and live in the presence of Jesus.

I had been for a long time a minister in Leicester [England], with a large church and of considerable influence in the city, but very unhappy. Conscious that I had not received the power of the Holy Spirit, I went up to the little village of Keswick. A great number of God's people gathered there to seek and to receive the power of the Holy Spirit, and they elected to have a prayer meeting from nine o'clock to eleven and onwards, to pray for the Holy Spirit.

A great many people were there agonizing. I was too tired to agonize, and somehow I felt that God did not want me to agonize hour after hour, but I had to learn to *take;* that God wanted to give, and I had only to take. So I left that prayer meeting at Keswick. It was eleven o'clock or half-past eleven, and I went out into the lane, away from the village. The lights died away in the distance, and I stood on the hill or walked to and fro, the stars shining upon me, and now and again a cloud dropping rain upon my face, as though symbolic of the refreshing my soul was to receive.

As I walked I said, "Oh, my God, if there is a man in this village who needs the power of the Holy Spirit to rest upon him it is I; but I do not know how to receive Him. I am too tired, too worn, too nervously down to agonize."

A voice said to me, "As you took forgiveness from the hand of the dying Christ, take the Holy Spirit from the hand of the living Christ."

I turned to Christ and said, "Lord, as I breathe in the whiff of warm night air, so I breathe into every part of me Your blessed Spirit."

There was no lambent flame, there was no rushing sound from Heaven, I felt no hand laid upon my head, but by faith, without emotion, without excitement, I took, and took for the first time, and have kept on taking ever since.

I turned to leave the hillside, and as I went down the Tempter said, "You have got nothing. It is moonshine."

I said, "I have."

He said, "Do you feel it?"

"I do not."

"Then if you do not feel it you have not got it."

I said, "I do not feel it, but I reckon that God is faithful. He could not have brought a hungry soul to claim by faith, and then given a stone for bread, and a scorpion for fish."[16]

Later I met a group of young clergymen who fought it out with me. They said, "No, no, we feel, we feel to have it, and we know we have got it."

But I responded, "How will you do tomorrow morning when you do not feel it?"

While we were talking, a young merchant who was listening said, "I want to say a word. In my place in Glasgow, if I miss the presence of Jesus for half an hour, I go into my counting-house and kneel down and say, 'Holy Spirit, what have I done to You that You have taken from me the sense of the presence of Christ?' " And he added, "I know I have received the Holy Spirit when I have most of Jesus."

To which I agreed, "When we know we have most of Christ, when we love Him most, live for Him most, we know that the Holy Spirit is within us in power."

Give your whole self to Jesus and He gives His whole self to you. Go to your bare garret, go to your dying child, go to scenes of trouble and sorrow and pain; He goes too. You do not need to take your pitcher to draw in some external well. You have the fountain beside you. You have Jesus in your heart, a fountain springing up to everlasting life.

The Son of Man received of the Father the promise of the Holy Spirit, not as God, because as such He was one with the Holy Spirit, but as man, as the representative man, that He might be able to communicate Him to men.

A friend of mine was in Switzerland, and two Englishmen

came into the hotel where he was staying, and engaged three guides. They were planning to attempt a precipitous ascent up the side of a mountain, by way of an icefall which was almost as steep as the side of a house: When they reached the base they roped themselves together: a guide, a traveler, a guide, a traveler, a guide. They commenced the climb, and by cutting notches in the wall of ice were able to carve steps for the toes of their feet.

So they crept up several hundred feet, and had nearly reached the summit when in some way the fifth man lost his footing and began to sway. He pulled down the climber above him and he too began to swing slowly to and fro. The two pulled down the third, and the third the fourth, and all four were dangling on the side of the precipice and in imminent danger of being dashed to pieces. The only thing that kept them from certain death was the rope around the waist of the lead man. As soon as he felt the jerk and strain, he gripped his ice axe and drove it hard into the ice just above him, and held to it for life. As he maintained his grip for an instant or two, the man next below him regained his footing, the man beneath, his, and so on to the end of the line, until the whole five stood because the first man stood.

You and I have no power; we swing to and fro; but by faith we are bound to Christ, and because He is in the glory and stands up there, we shall be pulled up at last from the difficulties of this present life, to stand with Him forever in His Father's presence.

NOTES

1. 1 Corinthians 3:2.
2. 1 Corinthians 3:4, 22.
3. Galatians 5:19-21.
4. Galatians 3:3.
5. Colossians 2:18.
6. Romans 8:3, 4.
7. Mark 8:29.
8. Matthew 16:22ff.
9. Romans 8:13.
10. Galatians 5:17.
11. Galatians 1:15, 16.
12. Colossians 1:27.
13. Exodus 34:29.
14. Galatians 1:24.
15. Galatians 2:8.
16. Luke 11:11, 12.

Peter Cartwright

Peter Cartwright (1785-1872), the person you will meet in these next pages, was for fifty years a deeply committed, circuit-riding Methodist preacher and servant of the Lord; yet he always remained his unique self—a rugged, quintessential backwoodsman.

Cartwright could do anything: plow, build, ride, plunge into politics, legislate, pray, fight, laugh, and above all, preach the gospel of Jesus Christ as could few men of any age. By mid-century he was known as the most colorful evangelist of the expanding frontier. Fearless and confident of the Lord's protection, and more than a match for any man in argument, he was really bested only once. That happened during an Illinois congressional campaign, and the man who won that election by defeating him was Abraham Lincoln. Writes Donald Dayton in his estimate of Cartwright, "Rough, uneducated and eccentric, he possessed unusual stamina, a quick wit, a clear perception of human nature, and profound devotion to the work of God."

Cartwright's lack of education, which he acknowledges in his autobiography (published in 1857), raises the perennial question as to what value an educated ministry has in reaching the common people. Cartwright himself had a low opinion of advanced training; it was the illiterate Methodist preachers, he said, who set America on fire while others were lighting their matches. "I have seen so many educated preachers," he wrote, "who forcibly reminded me of lettuce growing under the shade of a peach tree, or a gosling that had got the straddles by wading in the dew, that I turn away sick and faint."

This missionary preacher, whose father had fought in the Revolutionary War, was born in Amherst County, Virginia. In 1790 the family moved to Kentucky, where Peter grew up (as he says) with a lust for gambling, dancing and horse-racing. In 1801, during the spiritual excitement surrounding Kentucky's famous Cane Ridge revival, Cartwright heard John Page preach; what resulted is best told by himself in the following pages. Licensed as a Methodist exhorter in 1802, he was then assigned to the Livingston circuit around the mouth of the Cumberland River. In 1806 he was ordained deacon by Bishop Francis Asbury, and two years later became a presiding elder. Overall he served several circuits in Kentucky and adjoining states, preaching with tremendous power and effectiveness in churches, at camp meetings and even in dance halls.

Cartwright opposed slavery on domestic, political and moral grounds, so much so, in fact, that in 1824 he requested a transfer to the northern free state of Illinois. There he served as presiding elder of his denomination for forty-five years, and was elected twice to the state legislature. By 1856 he had preached 14,600 times, had received ten thousand persons into the church, and had baptized twelve thousand. He preached the sovereignty of God and the depravity of man, but always with the Wesleyan emphasis on free will and free grace. He died full of years at age eighty-seven in Pleasant Plains, Sangamon County, Illinois, and is honored today as one of the great figures of the Methodist Episcopal Church of America.

These following excerpts are taken from the original 1857 edition of the Autobiography of Peter Cartwright, the Backwoods Preacher, *edited by W. P. Strickland and published in New York by Hunt & Eaton.*

FIVE

From the AUTOBIOGRAPHY of Peter Cartwright

I was born September 1st, 1785, in Amherst County, on James River, in the state of Virginia. My parents were poor. My father was a soldier in the great struggle for liberty, in the Revolutionary War with Great Britain. My mother was an orphan. Shortly after the united colonies gained their independence, my parents moved to Kentucky, which was a new country.

When my father settled in Logan County, within a mile of the Tennessee border, there was not a newspaper printed south of Green River, no mill short of forty miles, and no schools worth the name. Sunday was a day set apart for hunting, fishing, horse-racing, card-playing, balls, dances, and all kinds of jollity and mirth. We killed our meat out of the woods, wild; and beat our meal and hominy with a pestle and mortar. We stretched a deer skin over a hoop, burned holes in it with the prongs of a fork, sifted our meal, and baked our bread, and it was first-rate eating.

We raised, or gathered out of the woods, our own tea. We had sage, bohea, cross-vine, spice, and sassafras tea in abundance. We made our sugar out of the water of the maple tree, and our molasses too. These were great luxuries in those days. We raised our own cotton and flax. We picked the seed out of the cotton with our fingers. Our mothers and sisters carded, spun, and wove it into cloth, and they cut and made our garments and bed-clothes. And when we got a new suit thus manufactured, and sallied out into company, we thought ourselves "so big as anybody."

I was naturally a wild, wicked boy, and delighted in horse-racing, card-playing and dancing. My father restrained me but little, though my mother talked to me, wept over me, and prayed for me, and often drew tears from my eyes. But though I often wept under preaching, and resolved to do better and seek religion, yet I broke my vows, went into young company, rode races, played cards, and danced.

At length my father gave me a young racehorse, which well-nigh proved my everlasting ruin; and he bought me a pack of cards, for I was a very successful young gambler. I was not initiated into the tricks of regular gamblers, yet I was very successful in winning money. This practice was fascinating, and became a special besetting sin to me, so that for a boy I was much captivated by it. My mother remonstrated almost daily with me, and I had to keep my cards hid from her. O, the sad delusions of gambling! Nothing but power of divine grace saved me from this wretched sin.

Somewhere between 1800 and 1801, in the upper part of Kentucky, at a memorable place called "Cane Ridge," there was appointed a sacramental meeting by some of the Presbyterian ministers, at which meeting, seemingly unexpected by ministers or people, the mighty power of God was displayed in a very extraordinary manner. Many were moved to tears, and there was bitter and loud crying for mercy. The meeting was protracted for weeks. There were at times during the meeting from twelve to twenty-five thousand people. From this camp meeting the news spread through all the churches, and all the land, and it excited great wonder and surprise. It kindled a religious flame that spread all over Kentucky and through many other states.

In 1801, when I was in my sixteenth year, my father, my eldest half-brother, and myself attended a wedding about five miles from home, where there was a great deal of drinking and dancing, which was very common at marriages. I drank little or nothing; my delight was in dancing. After a late hour in the night, we mounted our horses and started for home. I was riding my racehorse.

A few minutes after we had put up the horses, and were sitting by the fire, I began to reflect on the manner in which I had spent the day and the evening. I felt guilty and condemned. I rose and walked the floor. My mother was in bed. It seemed to me, all of a sudden, my blood rushed to my head, my heart palpitated, and in a few minutes I turned blind. An awful impression rested on my mind that death had come and I was unprepared to die. I fell on my knees and began to ask God to have mercy on me.

My mother sprang from her bed and was soon on her knees by my side, praying for me, and exhorting me to look to Christ for mercy. Then and there I promised the Lord that if He would spare me, I would seek and serve Him; and I never fully broke that promise. My mother prayed for me a long time. At length we lay down, but there was little sleep for me.

Next morning I rose, feeling wretched beyond expression. I tried to read in the Testament, and retired many times to secret prayer through the day, but found no relief. I gave up my race-horse to my father, and requested him to sell him. I went and brought my pack of cards, and gave them to Mother, who threw them into the fire, and they were consumed. I fasted, watched, and prayed, and engaged in regular reading of the Testament. I was so distressed and miserable that I was incapable of any regular business. My father was greatly distressed on my account, thinking I must die, and he would lose his only son. He bade me retire altogether from business and take care of myself.

Soon it was noised abroad that I was distracted, and many of my associates in wickedness came to see me, to try and divert my mind from those gloomy thoughts of my wretchedness; but all in vain. I exhorted them to desist from the course of wickedness which we had been guilty of together. The [Methodist] class-leader and local preacher were sent for. They tried to point me to the bleeding Lamb; they prayed for me most fervently. Still I found no comfort, and although I had never believed in the doctrine of unconditional election and reprobation, I was sorely tempted to believe I was a reprobate, and doomed, and lost eternally, without any chance of salvation.

At length one day I retired to the horse-lot, and was walking and wringing my hands in great anguish, trying to pray, on the borders of utter despair. It appeared to me that I heard a voice from Heaven, saying, "Peter, look at Me." A feeling of relief flashed over me as quick as an electric shock. It gave me hopeful feelings, and some encouragement to seek mercy, but still my load of guilt remained. I repaired to the house and told my mother what had happened to me in the horse-lot. Instantly she seemed to understand it, and told me the Lord had done this to encourage me to hope for mercy, and exhorted me to take encouragement, and seek on, and God would bless me with the pardon of my sins another time.

Some days after this, I retired to a cave on my father's farm to pray in secret. My soul was in agony. I wept, I prayed, and said, "Now, Lord, if there is mercy for me, let me find it," and it really seemed to me that I could almost lay hold of the Savior, and realize a reconciled God. All of a sudden such a fear of the Devil fell upon me that it really appeared to me that he was personally there, to seize and drag me down to Hell, soul and body, and such a horror fell on me that I sprang to my feet and ran to my mother at the house. My mother told me this was a device of Satan to prevent me from finding the blessing then.

Three months rolled away, and still I did not find the blessing of the pardon of my sins. In the spring of 1801 a Presbyterian minister, who had a congregation and meeting-house, as we called them, about three miles north of my father's house, appointed a sacramental meeting and invited the Methodist preachers to attend with them, and especially John Page, who was a powerful gospel minister, and popular among the Presbyterians. Accordingly he came and preached with great power and success.

The church would not hold the tenth part of the congregation. Accordingly the officers of the church erected a stand in a contiguous shady grove, and prepared seats for a large congregation. People came to this meeting from far and near. They came in large wagons, with victuals mostly prepared. The women slept in the wagons, and the men under them. Many stayed for a number of nights and days together. Others were provided for among the neighbors around. The power of God was wonderfully displayed; scores of sinners fell under the preaching, like men slain in mighty battle. Christians shouted aloud for joy.

To this meeting I repaired, a guilty, wretched sinner. On the Saturday evening, along with weeping multitudes, I bowed before the stand and earnestly prayed for mercy. In the midst of a solemn struggle of soul an impression was made on my mind, as though a voice said to me, "Thy sins are all forgiven thee." Divine light flashed all around me, unspeakable joy sprang up in my soul. I rose to my feet, opened my eyes, and it really seemed as if I was in Heaven. The trees, the leaves on them and everything seemed, and I really thought were, praising God.

My mother raised the shout, my Christian friends crowded around me and joined me in praising God; and though I have been since then, in many instances, unfaithful, yet I have never, for one moment, doubted that the Lord did then and there forgive my sins and give me religion.

Our meeting lasted without intermission all night, and it was believed by those who had a good right to know that over eighty souls were converted to God during its continuance. I went on my way rejoicing for several days. This meeting was in the month of May. In June our preacher, John Page, attended our little church,

Ebenezer, and there in June, 1801, I joined the Methodist Episcopal Church, which I have never for one moment regretted.

I went on enjoying great comfort and peace, and attended several camp meetings among the Methodists and Presbyterians. At all of them there were many souls converted to God. At a quarterly meeting held in the spring of 1802, Jesse Walker, our preacher in charge, came to me and handed me a small slip of paper, with these words written on it: "Peter Cartwright is hereby permitted to exercise his gifts as an exhorter in the Methodist Episcopal Church, so long as his practice is agreeable to the gospel. Signed in behalf of the society at Ebenezer, May, 1802."

I was very much surprised. I had not been talked to by the preacher, nor had I formally attempted to exhort. It is true, in class and other meetings, when my soul was filled with the love of God, I would mount a bench and exhort with all the power I had. It is also true that my mind had been deeply exercised about exhorting and preaching too. I told Brother Walker I did not want license to exhort; that if I did not feel happy I could not exhort, but if my soul got happy I felt that I had license enough. He urged me to keep the license, alleging that it was the more orderly way, and I yielded to his advice. To show how matters were done up in those early days, I will state that this permit to exhort was all the license I ever received from the church to preach until I received my parchment of ordination.[1]

The fall of this year [1802] my father moved from Logan County down toward the mouth of the Cumberland River into what was called Lewiston County. There were a good many scattering members of the Methodist Episcopal Church through that region of country. I applied to Brother Page, our presiding elder, for a letter for myself, my mother, and one sister, which he gave us.

On examination I found that mine contained a "Benjamin's mess."[2] It not only stated my membership and authority to exhort, but it gave me authority to travel through all that destitute region, hold meetings, organize classes, and, in a word, to form a circuit, and meet him the next fall with a plan of a new circuit, number of members, names of preachers, if any, class leaders, etc. I felt bad on the reception of this paper, and told Brother Page I did not want to take it, for I saw through the solemn responsibilities it rolled upon me. I told him that although I did think at times that it was my duty to preach, I had little education, and that it was my intention to go to school the next year. He told me that this was the very best school I could find between Heaven and earth, but advised me when my father got settled down there, if I could find a good moral school with a good teacher, to go to it through winter; then, in the spring and summer, form the circuit and do the best I could.

*   *   *

On our return from the General Conference in Baltimore in 1820, in the month of June, which was very warm, Brother Walker and I traveled on horseback to Knoxville. Brother Walker left me to visit friends and relatives in west Tennessee, and I journeyed on toward my home in Christian County, Kentucky. Saturday night came on, and found me in a strange region of country, and in the hills, knobs and spurs of the Cumberland Mountains.

I greatly desired to stop on the approaching Sabbath and spend it with Christian people, but I was now in a region of country where there was no gospel minister for many miles around, and where, as I learned, many of the scattered population had never heard a gospel sermon in all their lives, and where the inhabitants knew no Sabbath only to hunt and visit, drink and dance. Thus lonesome and pensive, late in the evening, I hailed at a tolerably decent house, where the landlord kept entertainment.

I rode up and asked for quarters. The gentleman said I could stay, but he was afraid I would not enjoy myself very much as a traveler, inasmuch as they had a party meeting there that night to have a little dance. I inquired how far it was to a decent house of entertainment on the road; he said seven miles. I told him if he would treat me civilly and feed my horse well, by his leave I would stay. He assured me I should be treated civilly. I dismounted and went in. The people collected, a large company. I saw there was not much drinking going on.

I quietly took my seat in one corner of the house, and the dance commenced. I sat quietly musing, a total stranger, and greatly desired to preach to this people. Finally I concluded to spend the next day (Sabbath) there, and ask the privilege to preach to them. I had hardly settled this point in my mind, when a beautiful, ruddy young lady walked very gracefully up to me, dropped a handsome curtsy, and pleasantly, with winning smiles, invited me out to take a dance with her.

I can hardly describe my thoughts or feelings on that occasion. However, in a moment I resolved on a desperate experiment. I rose as gracefully as I could; I will not say with some emotion, but with many emotions. The young lady moved to my right side; I grasped her right hand with my right hand, while she leaned her left arm on mine. In this position we walked on the floor. The whole company seemed pleased at this act of politeness in the young lady, shown to a stranger.

The colored man who was the fiddler began to put his fiddle in the best order. I then spoke to the fiddler to hold a moment, and added that for several years I had not undertaken any matter of importance without first asking the blessing of God upon it, and I now desired to ask the blessing of God upon this beautiful young lady and the whole company, that had shown such an act of politeness to a total stranger.

Here I grasped the young lady's hand tightly and said, "Let us all kneel down and pray," and then instantly dropped on my knees, and commenced praying with all the power of soul and body that I could command. The young lady tried to get loose from me, but I held her tight. Presently she fell on her knees. Some of the company kneeled, some stood, some fled, some sat still, all looked curious. The fiddler ran off into the kitchen, saying, "Lord a mercy!"

While I prayed, some wept out loud and some cried for mercy. I rose from my knees and commenced an exhortation, after which I sang a hymn. The young lady who invited me on the floor lay prostrate, earnestly crying for mercy. I exhorted again, I sang and prayed nearly all night. About fifteen of that company professed religion, and our meeting lasted next day and next night, and as many more were powerfully converted. I organized a society, took thirty-two into the church, and sent them a preacher. My landlord was appointed leader, which post he held for many years. This was the commencement of a great and glorious revival of religion in that region, and several of the young men converted at this preacher dance became useful ministers of Jesus Christ. I recall this strange scene of my life with astonishment to this day, and do not permit myself to reason on it much.

In some conditions of society I should have failed; in others I should have been mobbed; in others I should have been considered a lunatic. So far as I did permit myself to reason on it at the time, my conclusions were something like these: these are a people not gospel taught or hardened. At the early hour they have not

drunk to intoxication, and they will at least be as much alarmed at
my operations as I possibly can be at theirs. If I fail, it is no
disgrace; if I succeed, it will be a fulfillment of a duty commanded
to be "instant in season and out of season."³

I had, from some cause or other, a strong impression on my
mind that I should succeed by taking the Devil at surprise, as he
had often served me. The actions prompted by those sudden
impressions to perform religious duty often succeed beyond all
human calculation, and thereby inspire a confident belief in an
immediate superintending agency of the Divine Spirit of God. I
do firmly believe that if ministers of the present day had more of
the unction or baptismal fire of the Holy Spirit prompting their
ministerial efforts, we should succeed much better than we do, and
be more successful in winning souls to Christ than we are. If those
young men who think they are called of God to minister in the
word and doctrine of Jesus Christ were to cultivate by a holy life a
better knowledge of the supreme agency of the Divine Spirit, and
depend less on the learned theological knowledge of Biblical insti-
tutes, it is my opinion they would do vastly more good than they
are likely to do.

* * *

A Methodist preacher in those days, when he felt that God
had called him to preach, instead of hunting up a college or
Biblical institute, hunted up a hardy pony or a horse, and some
traveling apparatus, and with his library always at hand, namely,
Bible, hymnbook and Discipline, he started, and with a text that
never wore out nor grew stale, he cried, "Behold the Lamb of
God, that taketh away the sin of the world."⁴ In this way he went
through storms of wind, hail, snow and rain; climbed hills and
mountains, traversed valleys, plunged through swamps, swam
swollen streams, lay out all night, wet, weary, and hungry, held his
horse by the bridle all night, or tied him to a limb, slept with his
saddle blanket for a bed, his saddle or saddlebags for his pillow,
and his old big coat or blanket, if he had any, for a covering.

Often he slept in dirty cabins, on earthen floors, before the
fire; ate roasting ears for bread, drank buttermilk for coffee, or sage
tea for imperial; took, with a hearty zest, deer or bear meat, or wild
turkey, for breakfast, dinner and supper, if he could get it. His text
was always ready, "Behold the Lamb of God . . ." This was old-
fashioned Methodist preacher fare and fortune. Under such cir-

cumstances, who among us would now say, "Here I am, Lord, send me"?[5]

In the fall of 1827 our conference was holden in Mount Carmel and I was continued on the Illinois district. We elected our delegates that were to sit in Pittsburgh, May 1, 1828. In the month of April Brother John Dew, Brother Samuel Thompson and myself met at St. Louis to take passage on board a steamboat to the General Conference in Pittsburgh.

We had never been on board a steamboat before, at least I never had. They were then a new thing among us, so we took passage on board the *Velocipede,* Mr. Ray, captain. Before we went aboard Brothers Dew and Thompson, with the kindest feelings, thought it their duty to caution me to be very quiet, for these steamboat fellows, passengers and all, were desperadoes. They knew I was outspoken, loved everybody and feared nobody. They were afraid I would get into some difficulty with somebody. I thanked them very kindly for their special care over me. "But," said I, "brethren, take care of yourselves; I think I know how to behave myself, and make others behave themselves, if need be."

When we got aboard we had a crowded cabin, a mixed multitude; some deists, some atheists, some Universalists, a great many profane swearers, drunkards, gamblers, fiddlers, and dancers. We dropped down to the [military] barrack below St. Louis, and there came aboard eight or ten United States officers, and we had a jolly set, I assure you. They drank, fiddled, danced, swore, played cards, men and women too. I walked about, said nothing, but plainly saw we were in a bad snap, but there was no way to help ourselves. Brother Thompson came to me and said, "Lord have mercy on me, what shall we do?"

"Go to your berth," said I, "and stay there quietly."

"No," said he, "I'll reprove them."

"Now, brother," said I, "do not cast your pearls before swine."

"Well," said he, "I won't stay in the cabin. I'll go on deck."

Up he started, and when he got there, behold, they were playing cards from one end of the deck to the other. Back he came and said, "What shall I do? I cannot stand it."

"Well," said I, "Brother Thompson, be quiet and behave yourself; you have no way to remedy your condition unless you jump overboard and swim to shore."

So things went on several days and nights. At the mouth of the Ohio there came aboard a Captain Waters. He had a new fiddle and a pack of cards. He was a professed infidel. Card-playing was renewed all over the cabin. The captain of the boat was as fond of drinking and card-playing as any of them. There was a regular army lieutenant on board, and although he was very wicked, yet he had been raised by religious parents. His wife, as he told me, was a good Christian. In walking the guard this lieutenant, whose name was Barker, and myself fell into conversation, and being by ourselves, I took occasion to remonstrate with him on the subject of his profanity. He readily admitted it was wrong and said, "I have been better taught."

In this way I got to talk to many passengers on board, and they mostly ceased to swear profanely in my presence. When they commenced playing cards I walked carelessly up and looked on. Lieutenant Barker and Captain Waters looked up at me; I knew they felt reproved. Said one of them to me, "We are not blacklegs, we are not playing for money, but just to kill time." I affected to be profoundly ignorant of what they were doing, and asked them what those little spotted things were.

Mr. Barker said, "Sit down here, and I will show you what we are doing, and how we do it."

"No, no," said I, "my friends, I am afraid it is all wrong."

They insisted there was no harm in it at all.

"Well," said I, "gentlemen, if you are just playing for fun, or to kill time, would it not be much better to drop all such foolishness, and let us talk on some topic to inform each other? Then we could all be edified. As it is, a few of you enjoy all the pleasure, if indeed there is any in it; while the rest of us, who have no taste for such amusements, are not at all benefited. Come, lay aside those little spotted papers, that are only calculated to please children of a larger size, and let us talk on history, philosophy, or astronomy; then we can all enjoy it, and be greatly benefited."

Captain Waters said, "Sir, if you will debate with me on the Christian religion, we will quit all our cards, fiddles and dances."

"I will do it with pleasure, Captain," said I. "I have only one objection to debate with you. You are in the habit, I see, of swearing profanely, and using oaths, and I can't swear back at you; and I fear a debate mixed up with profane oaths would be unprofitable."

"Look, sir," said he, "if you will debate with me on that subject, I will pledge you my word and honor that I will not swear a single oath."

"Very well, sir," said I, "on that condition I will debate with you." By this time there were gathered around us a large crowd.

"Well," said Lieutenant Barker, "take notice of the terms on which this debate is to be conducted. Gentlemen, draw near, and take your seats, and listen to the arguments; and by the consent of the two belligerent gentlemen I will keep order."

We both agreed to his proposition. The captain opened the discussion by a great flourish, expressing his happiness at having one more opportunity of vindicating the religion of reason and nature, in opposition to the religion of a bastard.

I simply replied that the Christian religion was of age and could speak for itself; and that I felt proud of an opportunity to show that infidelity was born out of holy wedlock, and therefore, in the strictest sense, was a bastard. I said I thought it ill became the advocate of a notorious illegitimate to heap any reproaches on Christ.

These exordiums had one good effect: they fixed and riveted the attention of almost all the passengers, the captain of the boat, ladies and all. My opponent then proceeded to lay down his premises and draw his conclusions. When his twenty minutes expired, I replied, and in my reply quoted a passage of Scripture.

"Hold, sir," said my opponent, "I don't allow a book of fables and lies to be brought in. Nothing shall be admitted here but honorable testimony."

"Very well, sir," said I, "the Bible shall be dispensed with altogether as evidence, and then I feel confident I can overturn our system on testimony drawn from the book of nature." I then proceeded in argument.

In his second replication, Captain Waters quoted Tom Paine as evidence.

"Hold, sir," said I, "such a degraded witness as Tom Paine can't be admitted as testimony in this debate."

My opponent flew into a violent passion, and swore profanely that God Almighty never made a purer and more honorable man than Tom Paine. As he belched forth these horrid oaths, I took him by the chin with my hand, and moved his jaws together, and made his teeth rattle at a mighty rate. He rose to his feet. So did I. He drew his fist and swore he would smite me to the floor.

Lieutenant Barker sprang between us, saying, "Cartwright, stand back. You can beat him in argument, and I can whip him. If there is any fighting to be done, I am his man. He is no gentleman, for he pledged his word and honor that he would not swear; and he has broken his word and forfeited his honor."

Well, I had then to fly in between them, to prevent a bloody

fight, for they both drew deadly weapons. This ended the argument. My valorous captain made concessions, and all became
pacified. From this out, Barker was my fast friend, and would have
fought for me at any time, and my infidel, Captain Waters, became
very friendly to me. When we landed in the night at Louisville, he
insisted that I should go home with him and partake of his very
best hospitalities.

But to return, the whole company that witnessed the encounter with my infidel captain were interested in my favor. Our
boat was old and crazy, and we made but little speed; consequently,
we were detained on the river over Sunday. Early on Sabbath
morning, the passengers formed themselves into a kind of committee of the whole, and appointed a special cEmmittee to wait on
me, and invite me to preach to them that day on the boat. Lieutenant Barker was the committee; he came to me and presented the
request.

"Lieutenant," I said, "I never traveled on a steamboat before,
and it will be a very awkward affair for me to preach on the boat.
Every man on a steamboat is a free man, and will do pretty much
as he pleases, and will not be reproved. The passengers will drink
and perhaps gamble, and be disorderly. I don't know that the
captain would like such an arrangement."

Said the lieutenant, "I have consulted Captain Ray, and he is
willing, and pledges himself to keep good order. And now, sir, we
have annoyed you and your fellow clergymen all the week, and I
pledge you my word, all shall be orderly, and you shall enjoy your
religious privileges on Sunday undisturbed, and you must preach
to us. We need it, and the company will not be satisfied if you don't
comply."

I gave my consent, and we fixed on times for three sermons:
one immediately after the table was cleared after breakfast, one
after dinner, and one after supper. I led the way, taking the morning hour. The cabin was seated in good order and the deck passengers were invited down. We had a very orderly, well-behaved
congregation. Brother Dew preached in the afternoon, and Brother Thompson at night, and I rarely ever spent a more orderly
Sabbath anywhere within the walls of a church.

What good was done, if any, the Judgment Day will alone
declare. I cannot close this sketch and do justice to my feelings
without saying a few things more. After the adjournment of the
General Conference, on our return trip home, the river had fallen

very much. We could not pass over the falls, and the canal was not finished around them. Of course we had to land and reship at the foot of the falls.

The *Maryland,* a good steamboat, lay waiting there for passengers. When I entered this boat, almost the first man I met was Lieutenant Barker. He recognized me, sprang forward and seized me by the hand and said, "Is this Mr. Cartwright?" He really seemed as glad to see me as if I had been his own brother. He was returning from the east with his wife to some of the western military posts.

"Now, sir," said he, "I told you I had a good little Christian woman for my wife. She is in the ladies' cabin. I have talked to her of you a thousand times. Come, you must go right in with me, and I will introduce her to you. I know she will be glad to form an acquaintance with you." I went, and was introduced to this, as I believe, Christian lady.

We had a number of preachers on board, returning delegates from the General Conference, and we had preaching almost every day and night from that point to St. Louis, for we had almost entire command of the boat.

* * *

Before I close this feeble sketch, I wish to [pay tribute] to my fellow laborers who suffered long and endured much in spreading [the gospel] in these western wilds. The present, as well as future generations, owe, and will owe, a debt of gratitude to the indomitable courage and pious labor of early Methodist preachers for the great and good order of this vast wilderness.

When they entered it as preachers of the gospel, very few ministers would brook the hardships and undergo the privations that must necessarily be endured in preaching the gospel in these sparsely populated and frontier regions. But hardly had the early emigrant pitched his tent, and raised his temporary camp, or log cabin, when the early Methodist traveling preachers were there to preach to them the unsearchable riches of Christ.

People unacquainted with frontier life of fifty or sixty years ago can form but a very imperfect idea of the hardships the early settlers underwent at that day, when Methodist preachers went from fort to fort, from camp to camp, from tent to tent, from cabin to cabin, with or without road or path. We walked on dirt floors for carpets, sat on stools or benches for chairs, ate on puncheon tables, used forked sticks and pocket or butcher knives for knives and forks, slept on bear, deer, or buffalo skins, or sometimes on the ground in open air for downy beds, and one new suit of clothes of homespun was ample clothing for a year.

We crossed creeks and large rivers without bridges or ferry boats, often swam them on horseback, or crossed on trees that had fallen over the streams. We drove our horses over, and often waded out waist deep; and if by chance we got a dug-out, or canoe, to cross in ourselves, and swim our horses by, it was quite a treat. Thousands now in Heaven will praise God forever for [the self-sacrificing Methodist preachers who] taught them the way to life in their mud hovels and smoky cabins.

And now I must draw this imperfect history to a close. I am in the seventy-second year of my natural life. I have lived to see this vast western wilderness rise and improve, and become wealthy without a parallel in the history of the world. I have outlived every member of my father's family. I have outlived hundreds and thousands of my contemporary ministers and members. Though all these have died, they shall live again, and by the grace of God I shall live with them in Heaven forever.

Why I live, God only knows. I certainly have toiled and suffered enough to kill a thousand men, but I do not complain. Thank God for health, strength, and grace that have borne me up; thank God that during my long and exposed life as a Methodist preacher, I have never been overtaken with any scandalous sin, though my shortcomings and imperfections have been without number.

I traveled five years as a single man. I then married, and traveled forty-eight years as a married man. My wife has had nine children, seven daughters and two sons. We raised eight of those children, and have now living thirty-eight grandchildren and eight great-grandchildren. All our children are in the Methodist Episcopal Church; several of our grandchildren are also in the church.

And now I ask of all who may read this imperfect sketch of my eventful life, while I linger on these mortal shores, to pray for me, that my sun may set without a cloud, and that I may be counted worthy to obtain a part in the first resurrection, and may, O may I meet you all in Heaven! Farewell, till we meet at the Judgment.

NOTES

1. Cartwright was ordained a deacon (by Bishop Francis Asbury) in 1806 and a presiding elder in 1808.
2. Cf. Genesis 43:34, "And he [Joseph] took and sent messes unto them from before him: but Benjamin's mess was five times so much as theirs."
3. Cf. 2 Timothy 4:2.
4. John 1:29.
5. Cf. Isaiah 6:8.

Thérèse of Lisieux

When a friend suggested I look into the life of Thérèse of Lisieux (1873-1897), I manifested little interest, even though to include another woman, and particularly a French woman, into this volume seemed an excellent idea. Having taken instruction from a Roman Catholic priest in Alaska during a romantic episode in my youth, I thought I knew what to expect, and was therefore not surprised. Thérèse's writings had it all—the intense piety, the baroque imagery, the Mariolatry, the total submissiveness, the closed universe.

Yet after reading Ronald Knox's fine translation of Thérèse's autobiography, I was impressed by certain things about this young nun, despite the religious shroud in which she was wrapped. She knew how to work the Church, even to grabbing hold of the Pope and hanging on to him. That they canonized her so quickly into sainthood, in the face of all the rules; that miracles began to occur first at Lisieux and then everywhere after her death; that she was elevated to patron saint of France together with Joan of Arc—all these facts seemed rather unusual.

What truly charmed me, however, was the naturalness of the young woman, as it was portrayed in her writing. Her realistic grasp of life despite the confining regimen of the convent; her sense of humor, built upon a frank estimate of her own behavior; her courage in battling illness; and above all her total absorption in the love of God, which she saw as pervading not only her own being but all of creation—all these impressions captured my imagination, and won Thérèse a place in this volume.

Marie Françoise Thérèse Martin was the youngest of nine children born to Louis and Zelie Martin. Her father was a successful watchmaker. When she was four years of age her mother died, and her young life was deeply touched by sadness. When she was eight, the family moved from Alencon to Lisieux. A physical healing at age ten and some kind of conversion experience at age thirteen pointed her toward a life of devotion. She thought of offering herself as a missionary to some foreign field, but when two older sisters, Pauline and Marie, entered the convent of the Discalced Carmelite Nuns in Lisieux, Thérèse's one desire became to follow them.

A year later she traveled to Italy with her father and paid a visit to the Vatican in Rome. As participant in a papal audience she deliberately violated the rule of silence. When kneeling at the feet of Pope Leo XIII, she asked him if he would allow her to enter the Carmelite order when she turned fifteen. This involved another infringement of rules. As she tells the story, the Pope disappointed her by saying, "If God wants you to enter it, my dear, you will." She clung to his knees, and the Swiss guards had to carry her away by force.

In due time a bishop's letter arrived, giving Thérèse permission to enter the convent; this she did in 1888. Later, after making her formal "profession," she was appointed acting mistress of novices. During the last four years of her life she articulated what she called her "little way," based on Jesus' instructions about becoming "as little children." She saw her vocation as a call to simplicity, and quietly avoided the complex religious disciplines of would-be saints, such as mortification of the body, special methods of prayer, and pious statements intended to impress. The latter, she said, were "not like her," and she confessed to falling asleep during times of devotion.

Mystical phenomena were unknown in her life; of remarkable deeds there were none. Instead Thérèse sought to steep herself in love—a course that, as she freely admits, led her through times of anxiety, questioning, and discouragement. By order of her superior, she began to write her autobiography; but as tuberculosis overtook her, such writing became increasingly difficult. Intense suffering marked her final days.

The following excerpts are taken by permission from the Autobiography of St. Thérèse of Lisieux, *newly translated by Ronald Knox, published in New York in 1958 by P. J. Kenedy & Sons.*

LITTLE WAY
by Thérèse of Lisieux

I've always wished that I could be a saint. But whenever I compared myself to the saints there was always this unfortunate difference—they were like great mountains, hiding their heads in the clouds, and I was only an insignificant grain of sand, trodden down by all who passed by. However, I wasn't going to be discouraged. I said to myself, "God wouldn't inspire us with ambitions that can't be realized. Obviously there's nothing great to be made of me, so it must be possible for me to aspire to sanctity in spite of my insignificance. I've got to take myself just as I am, with all my imperfections; but somehow I shall have to find out a little way, all of my own, which will be a direct shortcut to Heaven."

"After all" (I said to myself), "we live in an age of inventions. Nowadays people don't even bother to climb the stairs—rich people, anyhow; they find a lift more convenient. Can't I find a lift which will take me up to Jesus, since I'm not big enough to climb the steep stairway of perfection?" So I looked in the Bible for some hint about the lift I wanted, and I came across the passage where Eternal Wisdom says, "Is anyone simple as a little child? Then let him come to Me."[1]

To that Wisdom I went. It seemed as if I was on the right track; what did God undertake to do for the childlike soul that responded to His invitation? I read on, and this is what I found: "I will console you like a mother caressing her son; you shall be like children carried at the breast, fondled on a mother's lap."[2] Never were words so touching. Never was such music to rejoice the heart. I could, after all, be lifted up to Heaven, in the arms of Jesus! And if that was to happen, there was no need for me to grow bigger; on the contrary, I must be as small as ever, smaller than ever.

* * *

During this last year God has been very gracious to me in making me understand what is meant by love. Well, of course, I did understand it before, but only in a very imperfect way. I hadn't got to the bottom of what Jesus meant when He said that the second commandment is like the first: "You shall love your neighbor as yourself."[3] I was making a special effort to love God better; and in doing that, it was borne in upon me that it was no use as long as my love simply expressed itself in words: "The Kingdom of Heaven will not give entrance to every man who calls Me Master, Master; only to the man who does the will of God, My Father."[4]

What was this will of God? Jesus kept on telling us about that; you might almost say on every page of His gospel. But at the Last Supper He makes it clearer still. He knows that the hearts of His disciples are aglow, more than ever, with love for Him. So He gives them, this dear Redeemer of ours, a new commandment. He says to them—oh, so tenderly!—"I have a new commandment to give you, that you are to love one another; that your love for one another is to be like the love I have borne you. The mark by which all men will know you for My disciples will be the love you bear one another."[5]

Well, how did Jesus love His disciples? And why did He love His disciples? You may be quite sure that their natural qualities did nothing to attract Him. After all, He stood at an infinite distance from them. He was Eternal Knowledge, Eternal Wisdom; they were only poor sinners, so ignorant, their thoughts so earthbound; and yet Jesus calls them His friends, His brothers. He wants them to reign with Him in His Father's Kingdom. He is determined to win them admission, even if it means dying on a cross for it. "This is the greatest love a man can show," as He put it Himself, "that he should lay down his life for his friends."[6]

Meditating on these words of Jesus, I began to see how imperfect my own love was. It was so obvious that I didn't love my sisters as God loves them. I realize now that perfect love means putting up with other people's shortcomings, feeling no surprise at their weaknesses, finding encouragement even in the slightest evidence of good qualities in them. But the point which came home to me most of all was that it was no good leaving love locked up in the depths of your heart. "A lamp," Jesus says, "is not lighted to be put away under a bushel measure. It is put on the lampstand to give light to all the people of the house."[7] The lamp, I suppose, stands for love; and the cheerful light it gives isn't meant simply

Thérèse of Lisieux

for the people we are fond of; it is meant for everybody in the house, without exception.

To love your neighbor as yourself—that was the rule God laid down before the Incarnation. He knew what a powerful motive self-love was, and He could find no higher standard by which to measure the love of one's neighbor. But this wasn't the "new commandment" Jesus gave to His apostles, His own commandment, as He calls it.[8] I am not just to love my neighbors as myself. I am to love them as Jesus loved them, and will love them till the end of time.

Dear Lord, You never tell us to do what is impossible, and yet You can see more clearly than I do how weak and imperfect I am. If, then, You tell me to love my sisters as You love them, that must mean that You Yourself go on loving them in and through me—You know it wouldn't be possible in any other way. There would have been no new commandment, if You hadn't meant to give me the grace to keep it. How I welcome it, then, as proof that Your will is to love, in and through me, all the people You tell me to love!

Always, when I act as love bids, I have this feeling that it is Jesus who is acting in me. The closer my union with Him, the greater my love for all the sisters without distinction. What do I do when I want this love to grow stronger in me? How do I react, when the Devil tries to fix my mind's eye on the defects of some sister who hasn't much attraction for me? I remind myself, in a great hurry, of all that sister's good qualities, all her good intentions. True enough, she's made a slip this time; but who's going to tell us how often she's fought temptation and conquered it, only she was too humble to let us notice it?

It's even possible that what I think of as a fault was in reality a praiseworthy act—it depends on the intention. I don't need to be assured on that point, because I once had experience of it myself in a small way, the moral being that you shouldn't pass judgment on other people. It was during recreation. The portress had rung twice, and that meant the big door had got to be opened to let the workmen bring in some trees for the crib. The recreation wasn't much fun, and I thought it would suit me quite well if I were sent out to lend an extra hand. Mother sub-Prioress called on me and the sister who was next to me; one of us was to go. So I started at once to fold up the piece of needlework I was doing, but rather slowly, so as to let the other sister finish first. I thought she might like the chance of lending a hand outside. The sister who was in charge of things stood there, smiling as she looked at us, and when she saw me get up last she said, "I thought as much, slowcoach! No extra jewel in your crown that time." And of course all the community must have thought I was just being selfish.

I can't tell you what a lot of good this tiny little incident did me, in making me kinder about other people's faults. Another thing—it's good for my vanity. When people speak well of me, I say to myself, "They mark it down as a fault in me, when I try to do a bit of good. What about these good qualities they find in me? Mayn't they really be faults?" And then I add, quoting from St. Paul, "I make little account of any human audit-day [judging]; I am not even at pains to scrutinize my own conduct; it is the Lord's scrutiny I must undergo."[9] And what is the best way to insure that God will judge you favorably—or rather, won't judge you at all? Why, I do my best to have none but charitable thoughts in my own mind; hasn't our Lord said, "Do not judge others, or you your-selves will be judged"?[10]

To read what I've just written, you might imagine that keep-ing the commandment of love has no difficulties for me! Well, it is true that for some months past the practice of this lovely virtue hasn't been the pitched battle it used to be; but I don't mean there haven't been any lapses. Dear me, I am much too full of imperfec-tions for that! I only mean that I don't find much difficulty, now, about picking myself up after a fall. The fact is that I had the best of it in one particular fight against temptation.

There's one sister in the community who has the knack of rubbing me up the wrong way at every turn. Her tricks of manner, her tricks of speech, her character, just strike me as unlovable. But then, she's a "holy religious"; God must love her dearly. So I wasn't going to let this natural antipathy get the better of me. I reminded myself that love isn't a matter of fine sentiments; it means doing things. So I determined to treat this sister as if she were the person I loved best in the world. Every time I met her, I used to pray for her, offering to God all her virtues and merits. I felt certain that Jesus would like me to do that, because all artists like to hear their work praised. Jesus, who fashions men's souls so skillfully, doesn't want us to stand about admiring the facade. He wants us to make our way in, till we reach the inmost sanctuary which is His chosen dwelling, and admire the beauty of that.

But I didn't confine myself to saying a lot of prayers for her, this sister who made life such a tug-of-war for me. I tried to do her every good turn I possibly could. When I felt tempted to take her down with an unkind retort, I would put on my best smile instead, and try to change the subject. Doesn't the *Imitation*[11] tell us that it's better to let other people have their way in an argument, than to go on wrangling over it? We often used to meet, outside recreation time, over our work; and when the struggle was too much for me, I used to turn tail and run.

She was quite unconscious of what I really felt about her, and never realized why I behaved as I did. To this day she is persuaded that her personality somehow attracts me. Once at recreation she actually said, beaming all over, something like this: "I wish you would tell me what it is about me that gets the right side of you? You've always got a smile for me whenever I see you." Well, of course, what really attracted me about her was Jesus hidden in the depths of her soul. Jesus makes the bitterest mouthful taste sweet. I could only say that the sight of her always made me smile with pleasure—naturally I didn't explain that the pleasure was entirely spiritual.

In the last resort, as I've told you, my recipe for victory is to run away. I must tell you about one instance of that kind, Mother, because it will amuse you. One morning, when you were having one of your attacks of bronchitis, I [being a novitiate] stole along very quietly to put some keys in your room. It was the keys to the altar-rail grille, because I was sacristan at the time. In my heart of hearts I rather welcomed this chance of getting a sight of you, but of course I took great care not to show it. And one of the sisters saw me. Actually she was very fond of me, but in the goodness of her heart she was afraid I would wake you up, so she offered to relieve me of the keys. I'm afraid I was too cantankerous to give up my rights like that, so I told her, very politely, that I was just as anxious not to wake you as she was, but giving back the keys was my job.

Of course I realize now that it would have shown a much better spirit if I had let her have her way. She was only a young nun, but she was my senior. At the time I thought otherwise; so there I was doing my best to follow her into your room, while she held the door fast to prevent me getting in, and tried to take the keys from me, till the dreadful thing happened that we were both afraid of—the noise we made woke you up.

Naturally after that I was the villain of the piece, and the poor sister I'd fallen afoul of began to indulge in a long diatribe, the burden of which was, "That was Sister Thérèse making that noise! Oh, dear, how difficult she is!"

My story was quite different, and I wanted badly to stick up for myself, but fortunately a bright idea came to me. If I started to defend myself, could I hope to preserve my peace of mind? At the same time, I didn't think I had enough patience to stand by and hold my tongue while I was being attacked like that. I had only one chance left, and that was to run away. No sooner said than done; I quitted the field without beat of drum, leaving the sister to go on with her speech, which was reminiscent of Camille's curse against Rome.[12] My heart was beating so fast that I couldn't go any distance. I just set down on the stairs to be alone with the spoils of my victory. It wasn't very heroic, was it, Mother? But I have a strong feeling that it's best not to engage in a battle when defeat is quite certain.

Oh dear, when I look back at my novitiate, I see how un-fledged I was. It makes me laugh, now, to think what heavy weather I made over nothing at all. How can I thank God enough for having made my soul grow up since then, given it the use of its wings? The arts of the fowler have no terrors for me now; "the snare is laid to no purpose, if the bird is watching."[13] Later on, no doubt, the present state of my soul will appear to me, in its turn, as full of imperfections. But at least I've learned not to be surprised at anything. It doesn't worry me to discover that I am frailty itself. On the contrary I go about boasting of it. Every day I expect to find out a fresh lot of imperfections in my character. Love, we are told, "draws the veil over a multitude of sins," and here is a rich mine Jesus has shown me.[14]

* * *

In teaching others I have learned a lot myself. One thing I've noticed is this: all souls, more or less, have to put up the same sort of fight, but on the other hand no two souls are alike. You can't treat them all in the same way. With some, I can see that I've got to fold myself up real small. I mustn't scruple to humiliate myself by telling them about my own conflicts, my own defeats. Once they've realized that I have the same weaknesses myself, these younger sisters of mine are ready to admit the faults that lie on their consciences, glad to think that I know what it's like by experience. Others, I saw from the first, needed the opposite treatment. You've got to be quite firm with them, and never go back on what you've said. In dealing with people like that, you mustn't come down to their level; it would be weaknesses, not humility. God has given me one grace—I'm not afraid of a fight. I have to do my duty, come what may.

What should I do without prayer and sacrifice? They are all the strength I've got; the irresistible weapons our Lord has granted me. I've proved it again and again—they touch souls much more surely than any words could. What an extraordinary thing it is, the efficiency of prayer! Like a queen, it has access at all times to the Royal Presence, and can get whatever it asks for. And it's a mistake to imagine that your prayer won't be answered unless you've something out of a book, some splendid formula of words, specially designed to meet this emergency. If that were true, I'm afraid I should be in a terribly bad position. I can't face the strain of hunting about in books for these splendid prayers—it makes my head spin.

I just do what children have to do before they've learned to read. I tell God what I want quite simply, without any splendid turns of phrase, and somehow He always manages to understand me. For me prayer means launching out of the heart toward God. It means lifting up one's eyes, quite simply, to Heaven, a cry of grateful love from the crest of joy or the trough of despair. It's a vast, supernatural force which opens out my heart and binds me close to Jesus.

For a long time I was in despair about this want of [more formal] devotion. I couldn't understand it. Now I don't distress myself so much. The novices themselves can't understand it; they often ask me, "How do you manage to have an answer for everything? Where do you go for these inspirations of yours?" Some of them have such nice natures that they really believe I can read their hearts, just because I sometimes know what they're going to say before they've said it. One night one of them had gone to bed in real anguish of mind, but she was determined to keep it dark from me, so she met me next morning with a smile on her face as she talked to me. And I, taking no notice of her remark, just said to her as if I knew all about it, "Something is worrying you."

She couldn't have been more surprised if I'd made the moon drop down at her feet. Indeed, her amazement was so complete that it communicated itself to me; just for a moment I felt an uncanny sense of alarm. I knew perfectly well that I hadn't the gift of reading people's hearts, and yet it had all fallen out so pat! Then of course I realized that God was there, at my elbow, and I'd simply (like a child repeating its lesson) used words that came from Him, not from me.

I sometimes get a terrible longing to hear something said about me which isn't praise! As you know, Mother, I prefer savories to sweets, and my soul is like my palate—it gets tired of food which has too much sugar in it. When that happens, our Lord arranges for somebody to give me what I call a nice little salad. Plenty of vinegar, plenty of spice about it; nothing left out except the oil, and that makes it all the more tasty. These nice little salads are served up to me by the novices at the moment when I least expect it.

The novices are quite free to tell me exactly what they think, pleasant or unpleasant, without the least restraint. That comes easy to them, because they don't feel bound to treat me with respect, as if I were a real Novice-mistress. God lifts the veil that hides my imperfections, and these dear young sisters of mine see me just as I am; they don't care for that very much. They tell me, with delightful frankness, all about the rough time I give them, and my unpleasant habits, with so little embarrassment that you would imagine they were talking about somebody else.

You see, they know they're giving me an enormous amount of pleasure by doing it; indeed, pleasure isn't a strong enough word; it's a delicious treat that simply fills my heart with joy. How a thing which runs counter to all one's natural instincts proves a source of such happiness is more than I can explain; it's a thing I couldn't believe if I hadn't experienced it.

One day when I was particularly eager to be humiliated like that, one of the novices carried out my wishes so conscientiously that I reminded me all at once of Shimei cursing King David.[15] "Yes," I said to myself, "sure enough, she must have had her orders from Heaven, to talk to me like that." No stint there of well-seasoned food in which my soul took an epicure's delight! That's the sort of way in which God, mercifully, keeps me going. He can't always be supplying me with the food that really gives me strength—I mean, public humiliation of this kind—but every now and then there are crumbs falling from the nursery table to sustain me.[16] His mercy is so wonderful that I shall have to be in Heaven before I can tell the full story of it.

*   *   *

In what follows, I mean to address our Lord Himself. I find it easier to express my thoughts that way. I'm afraid they'll be very badly expressed even so.

Jesus, my well-beloved, how considerate You are in Your treatment of my worthless soul. Storms all around me, and suddenly the sunshine of Your grace peeps out! I feel as if I were called to be a fighter, a priest, an apostle, a doctor, a martyr; as if I could never satisfy the needs of my nature without performing, for Your sake, every kind of heroic action at once. Dear Jesus, how am I to reconcile these conflicting ambitions, how am I to give substance to the dreams of one insignificant soul? Insignificant as I am, I long to enlighten men's minds as the prophets and doctors did; I feel the call of an apostle. I should want to have been a missionary ever since the creation, and go on being a missionary till the world came to an end. What are You going to say to all these fond imaginations of mine, of a soul so unimportant, so ineffective?

I was still being tormented by this question of unfulfilled longings and it was a distraction in my prayer, when I decided to consult St. Paul's epistles in the hope of getting an answer. It was the twelfth and thirteenth chapters of First Corinthians that claimed my attention. The first of these told me that we can't all of us be apostles, all of us be prophets, all of us doctors, and so on. The church is composed of members which differ in their use; the eye is one thing and the hand is another.

It was a clear enough answer, but it didn't satisfy my aspirations, didn't set my heart at rest. The Magdalen, by stooping now and again into the empty tomb, was at last rewarded for her search;[17] and I, by sinking down into the depths of my own nothingness, rose high enough to find what I wanted. Reading on to the end of the chapter, I met this comforting phrase: "Prize the best gifts of Heaven. Meanwhile I can show you a way which is better than any other."[18]

What was it? The apostle goes on to explain that all the gifts of Heaven, even the most perfect of them, without love, are absolutely nothing. Love is the best way of all, because it leads straight to God. Now I was at peace. When St. Paul was talking about the different members of the Body I couldn't recognize myself in any of them; or rather I could recognize myself in all of them. But love—that was the key to my vocation. If the church was a Body composed of different members, it couldn't lack the noblest of all. It must have a heart, and a heart burning with love. And I realized that this love was the true motive force which enabled the other members of the church to act. If it ceased to function, the apostles would forget to preach the gospel, the martyrs would refuse to shed their blood. Love, in fact, is the vocation which includes all

others. It is a universe of its own, comprising all time and space—
it's eternal.

Beside myself with joy, I cried out, "Jesus, my love! I've
found my vocation, and my vocation is love." I had discovered
where it is that I belong in the church, the niche God has appointed for me. To be nothing else than love, that's to be everything at
once.

Beside myself with joy? No, that's the wrong expression. My
feeling was rather the calm, restful feeling which comes when you
see the lighthouse which is going to guide you into harbor. The
beacon of love now shone bright before me; I could reflect its
beams. Oh, I know quite well that I am only a child, with all a
child's weaknesses, but that's precisely what emboldens me to offer
myself as a victim to Your love. Under the old law the Lord of
Hosts, the Great King, would only accept in sacrifice such beasts
as were pure and without spot; only perfect victims could satisfy
the divine justice. But now the law of fear has been replaced by the
law of love. And love has chosen me, weak and imperfect creature
that I am, for its burnt-offering. That is the gesture we might have
expected. Love cannot be content without condescending—condescending to mere nothingness, and making this nothingness the
fuel for its flame.

I know well, Jesus, that love can only be repaid by love. What
I've always looked for and found at last is some way of satisfying
my feelings by returning love for Your love. "Make use of your
base wealth to win yourselves friends who will welcome you into
eternal dwellings."[19] [NIV reads, "Use worldly wealth to gain
friends for yourselves, so that when it is gone, you will be welcomed into eternal dwellings."] That was the advice You gave to
Your disciples, after warning them that "the children of this world
are more prudent after their own fashion than the children of
light."

Well, here I was with this restless ambition to be everything
at once, to combine all the vocations which might easily prove to
be base wealth, harmful to my soul. As a child of the light, then,
I'd better use it to make myself friends in eternity. I thought of the
prayer Elisha made to our father Elijah when he asked him for a
double portion of his spirit,[20] and in that sense I prayed to all the
angels and saints in Heaven. "I'm the most insignificant of creatures," I told them, "and I couldn't be more conscious of my own
wretched failings. But I know how generous hearts like yours love
to do good to those around them, and I want you, the blessed

citizens of Heaven, to adopt me as your child. Whatever credit I win by such rash means will belong to you entirely, but don't despise the rash request I make of you when I ask you to obtain for me a double portion of your love."

Jesus, I don't know how to express it accurately, this petition of mine. If I tried to, I might find myself sinking under the weight of my own presumption. My excuse is that I'm just a child, and children don't always weigh their words. But a parent who has great resources at his disposal is ready to humor the caprices of the child he loves, even to the point of fondness, even to the point of weakness.

It's love I ask for; love is all the skill I have. But this love of mine, how to show it? Love needs to be proved by action. Well, even a little child can scatter flowers to scent the throne room with their fragrance. Even a little child can sing, in its shrill treble, the great canticle of love. That shall be my life, to scatter flowers—to miss no single opportunity of making some small sacrifice, here by a smiling look, there by a kindly word, always doing the tiniest things right, and doing it for love. I shall suffer all that I have to suffer, yes, and enjoy all my enjoyments too, in the spirit of love, so that I shall always be scattering flowers before Your throne. Nothing that comes my way but shall yield up its petals in Your honor.

And as I scatter my flowers, I shall be singing. How could one be sad when occupied so pleasantly? I shall be singing even when I have to pluck my flowers from a thorn-bush; never in better voice than when the thorns are longest and sharpest. I don't ask what use they will be to You, Jesus, these flowers, this music of mine. I know that You will take pleasure in this fragrant shower of worthless petals, in these songs of love which a worthless heart like mine sings out.

Yes, Jesus, I do love You; I do love the Church, my mother. And it sticks in my mind that "the slightest movement of disinterested love has more value than all the other acts of a human soul put together."[21] But is mine a disinterested love? Or are these wide-ranging aspirations of mine no better than a dream, a fond illusion? If so, Jesus, make it known to me; I only want to be told the truth. If my longings are presumptuous, make them fade away. Why should I suffer needless torment?

But then, how can a soul so imperfect as mine ever hope to possess love in its fullness? It is to You, Jesus, my first and only love, that I must come for the answer to such a question. Surely it would have been better to reserve these vaulting ambitions for the

really great souls, that can take their eagle-flight close to the
summits! Whereas I think of myself as a chick not yet fledged, and
no eagle in any case.

And what if God gives no sign of listening to these twitter-
ings of mine; what if the sun seems hidden away as much as ever?
Dear Jesus, how I wish I could explain to all the souls that are
conscious of their own littleness, how great Your condescension is!
I am certain that if, by some impossible chance, You could find a
soul more feeble, more insignificant than mine, You would over-
whelm it with graces still more extraordinary, provided that it
would give itself up in entire confidence to Your infinite mercy.

But why should I feel any need to tell others about the
secrets of Your love? You, nobody else, have taught them to me,
and can I doubt that You will Yourself reveal them to others as
well? I know You will, and I implore You to do it. I implore You to
look down in mercy on a whole multitude of souls that share my
littleness; to choose out for Yourself a whole legion of victims, so
little as to be worthy of Your love.

* * *

Dear Mother, you don't need to be told that God has seen fit
to subject my soul to trials of many different kinds. To judge by
outward appearance, nobody has ever had to go through so little as
I have. And yet if people could see what I've been suffering during
this last year, how it would astonish them!

There are souls which haven't got any faith, which lose,
through misuse of grace, this precious treasure, fountain of all
pure and true happiness. And in those happy days of Easter-tide,
Jesus taught me to realize that. He allowed my soul to be overrun
by an impenetrable darkness, which made the thought of Heaven,
hitherto so welcome, a subject of nothing but conflict and torment.
And this trial was not to be a matter of a few days or a few weeks; it
was to last until the moment when God should see fit to remove it.
And that moment hasn't come yet.

I wish I could put down what I feel about it, but unfortunately that isn't possible. To appreciate the darkness of the tunnel, you
have to have been through it. Now, all of a sudden, the mists
around me have become denser than ever. They sink deep into my
soul and wrap it round so that I can't recover the dear image of my
native country [Heaven] any more—everything has disappeared.

I get tired of the darkness all around me, and try to refresh my jaded spirits with the thoughts of that bright country where my hopes lie; and what happens? It is worse torment than ever. The darkness seems to borrow the gift of speech from the sinners who live in it. I hear its mocking accents: "It's all a dream, this talk of a heavenly country, bathed in light, scented with delicious perfumes, and of a God who made it all, who is to be your possession in eternity! You really believe, do you, that the mist which hangs about you will clear away later on? All right, all right, go on longing for death! But death will make nonsense of your hopes. It will only mean a night darker than ever, the night of mere non-existence."

Dear Mother, I've tried to give you some picture of the darkness in which my soul is blindfolded. If I've done Jesus an injury, may He forgive me for it; He knows well enough that I do try to live the faith, even when I get no satisfaction out of it. Sometimes, it's true, a tiny ray of light pierces through the darkness, and then, just for a moment, the ordeal is over; but immediately afterward the memory of it brings me no happiness. It seems to make the darkness thicker than ever.

Mother, I don't think I'd ever quite realized before how gracious and merciful God is to us. He has sent me this ordeal just when I was strong enough to bear it. Earlier on, I might well have given way to discouragement, whereas now it only serves to purge away all that natural satisfaction which my longing for Heaven might have brought me. Dear Mother, what's left now to hinder my soul from taking its flight? The only thing I want badly now is to go on loving till I die of love.

* * *

Acts of love aren't always such easy going. In proof of that, I'll tell you about some of my skirmishes with the enemy, which ought to amuse you. For a long time, at evening prayers, my place was just in front of a sister who had an odd nervous affection. What made me notice she was rather odd was that the moment she came in she began to make a curious little noise, rather like what one would make by rubbing two shells together. [She was grinding one of her fingernails against her teeth.] Nobody noticed it except me; but then I've got a very sensitive ear—perhaps too sensitive on some occasions.

I simply can't describe to you, Mother, how that tiny noise got me down. I longed to turn round and give the offender one look. But something told me that the right thing to do was to put up with it for the love of God, and spare the sister any embarrassment. So I stayed still, and tried to get closer to God. Perhaps I could forget it altogether, this tiny noise? . . . Absolutely useless. There I was with the sweat pouring down me, in the attempt to make my prayer into a prayer of mere suffering! Suffering—but somehow I must get rid of the nervous irritation, and suffer peaceably, joyously. So I hit on the idea of trying to *like* this exasperating noise, instead of trying vainly not to hear it. I devoted myself to listening hard, as if the sound were that of some delightful music, and all my prayer—it certainly wasn't the prayer of quiet!—consisted in offering this music to our Lord.

Another time I was helping to do the washing, and there was a sister opposite me who managed to splash my face with dirty water every time she lifted up the handkerchiefs from the ledge. [The washing was put out on a wide ledge and beaten with a wooden paddle.] My first instinct was to step back and wipe my face, by way of suggesting to this over-effusive sister that I should be obliged if she kept herself to herself. But all at once the thought occurred to me, "You're a fool not to take what's going free," so I took good care to hide my annoyance. I devoted myself, instead, to cultivating a taste for dirty water! Dear Mother, you can see for yourself that I am a very insignificant person, who can't offer to God anything but very insignificant sacrifices.

* * *

Our Lord has ascended into Heaven, so I can only follow Him by means of the traces He has left behind Him. But they're so full of light, so full of fragrance! One glance at the holy gospel, and the life of Jesus becomes a perfume that fills the very air I breathe. I know at once which way to run. Oh, I don't try to jostle into the front rank; the last is good enough for me. I won't put myself forward like the Pharisee. I'll take courage from the humble prayer of the publican.[22]

But the Magdalen [Mary Magdalene], she, most of all, is the model I like to follow. That boldness of hers, which would be so amazing if it weren't the boldness of a lover, won the heart of Jesus, and how it fascinates mine! I'm certain of this—that if my conscience were burdened with all the sins it's possible to commit, I would still go and throw myself into our Lord's arms, my heart all broken up with contrition. I know what tenderness He has for any prodigal child of His that comes back to Him. No, it's not just because God, in His undeserved mercy, has kept my soul clear of mortal sin, that I fly to Him on the wings of confidence and of love . . .

NOTES

1. NIV translates the Hebrew, "Let all who are simple come in here!" (Proverbs 9:4).
2. NIV translation reads: "You will nurse and be carried on her arm and dandled on her knees. As a mother comforts her child, so will I comfort you" (Isaiah 66:12, 13).
3. Deuteronomy 6:5; Leviticus 19:18; Matthew 22:39.
4. Matthew 7:21.
5. John 13:34, 35.
6. John 15:13.
7. Matthew 5:15.
8. John 15:12.
9. 1 Corinthians 4:3, 4.
10. Matthew 7:1.
11. *The Imitation of Christ,* by Thomas à Kempis (1380-1471).
12. In the play *Horace* by the French dramatist Pierre Corneille (1606-1684), Camille, sister of Horace, lays a savage curse upon Rome after the death of her lover in combat. She summons a hundred nations to tear the Romans to pieces to the last man, and calls down the wrath of Heaven on the ancient city with lightning, fire and total destruction.
13. Proverbs 1:17.
14. Proverbs 10:12; 1 Peter 4:8.
15. 2 Samuel 16:11.
16. Cf. Mark 7:28.
17. NIV reads, "She [Mary Magdalene] bent over to look into the tomb" (John 20:11). The text does not imply that she stooped "now and again," though, of course, she could have.
18. 1 Corinthians 12:30.
19. Luke 16:8, 9.
20. 2 Kings 2:9.
21. Quoted from the commentary on Stephen in *The Spiritual Canticle* by John of the Cross (1542-1591), chapter 29.
22. Luke 18:9-14.

Horace Bushnell

As Christian thought developed in America during the nineteenth century, the Reverend Horace Bushnell (1802-1876) became a kind of halfway house. He is included in this volume not for his mild Calvinism or for his highly volatile views of Christian nurture, but because of his pulpit mastery in expressing his love for Jesus Christ. Bushnell was a proclaimer of timeless truth. His deep insight, intense earnestness and brilliant exposition caused him to be read during his lifetime by preachers everywhere. Today's evangelical Christians would have no trouble recognizing him as a brother, though they would not perhaps adopt all of his views.

Bushnell did not attract a popular following like Spurgeon, Beecher or Talmage. His pastoral ministry was modest. All his life he served only one church, North Congregational in Hartford, Connecticut. But though he lacked the dramatic instinct necessary to oratorical popularity, his influence was as great or greater on his generation than that of any minister of his time. The reason for this will be clear to anyone who reads the sermon here selected.

When Bushnell wrote his famous sentence, "The child is to grow up a Christian and never know himself as being otherwise," he was denounced as a heretic, but quickly canonized by certain liberal religious educators. His words became their battle cry; but Bushnell himself knew better. In his most famous volume, Sermons for the New Life, he wrote, "There could be no growth if there were not something planted . . . until the new man is born, or begotten, there is not so much as a seed of true holiness . . . the soul abideth even in death, and therefore cannot grow." That volume was dedicated to "my dear flock in Hartford, who have adhered to me in days of accusation, and have upheld me for a quarter of a century in the much greater trials of a consciously insufficient and defective ministry."

Bushnell was born in Litchfield, Connecticut, and was graduated from Yale University in 1827. After serving briefly as assistant editor of the New York Journal of Commerce, he became a tutor at Yale and began studying law in 1829. During a college revival he cast aside his doubts and began studying for the Christian ministry. In 1833 he was *called and ordained to the pastorate of North Church, and served there until 1859, when ill health forced him to retire. He continued to write until his death, however. In 1856 he had assisted in organizing the College of California at Oakland, which today is the University of California.*

According to Ralph Turnbull, Bushnell "did not give up belief in conversion when he taught Christian nurture; he did not abandon faith in the atoning work of Christ when he reiterated a new facet of truth concerning the moral influence of Christ's death; and he did not surrender his faith in the sinless humanity of the Son of God." Dr. Turnbull added, "He stands as one of the superlative examples of how a sermon ought to be viewed and written."

"Every Man's Life a Plan of God" has been hailed as one of the *outstanding pulpit sermons of the century. It comes from* Sermons for the New Life, *7th edition, published in 1872 by Scribner, Armstrong & Co., New York.*

SEVEN

EVERY MAN'S LIFE A PLAN OF GOD
by Horace Bushnell

"This is what the Lord says to his anointed, to Cyrus [the Great, founder of the Persian Empire, 550-529 B.C.]. . . . I have called you by your name. I have wooed you. I have armed and equipped you, though you have not known Me." (Isaiah 45:1, 3, 4)

So beautiful is the character and history of Cyrus[1] that many have doubted whether the sketch of his life given by Xenophon[2] was not intended as an idealizing, or merely romantic picture. And yet there have been examples of as great beauty unfolded here and there in all the darkest recesses of the heathen world, and it accords entirely with the hypothesis of historic truth in the account given us of this remarkable man, that he is designated and named by our prophet even before he is born, as a chosen foster-son of God.

"I have called you by your name. I have armed and equipped you, though you have not known Me." And what should he be but a model of all princely beauty, of bravery, of justice, of impartial honor to the lowly, of greatness and true magnanimity in every form, when God has equipped him unseen, to be the minister of His own great and sovereign purposes to the nations of his time?

Something of the same kind will also be detected in the history and personal consciousness of almost every great and remarkable character. Christ Himself testifies to the girding of the Almighty when He says, "To this end was I born, and for this purpose came I into the world."[3] Abraham was prepared for a particular work and mission, in what is referred to as his call.[4] Joseph in Egypt distinguishes the provision of God's hand when he comforts his guilty brothers in the assurance, "So, it was not you who sent me here, but God."[5] Moses and Samuel were called by name and set to their great lifework in the same manner. And what is the Apostle Paul endeavoring, in all the stress and pressure of his mighty apostleship, but to perform the work for which God's Spirit equipped him at his call, and to apprehend that for which he was apprehended by Christ Jesus?

And yet these great master-spirits of the world are not so much distinguished, after all, by the acts they do, as by the sense of some mysterious engirding of the Almighty on them, whose behests they are set on to fulfill. And all men may have this: for the humblest and commonest have a place and a work assigned them, in the same manner, and have it for their privilege to be always ennobled in the same lofty consciousness. God is arming every man for a place and a calling in which, taking it from Him even though it be internally humble, he may be as consciously exalted as if he held the rule of a kingdom.

The truth I propose for your consideration, then, is this: That God has a definite life-plan for every human person, girding him visibly or invisibly, for some exact thing, which it will be the true significance and glory of his life to have accomplished.

Many persons, I am well aware, never even think of any such thing. They suppose that for most men life is a necessarily stale and common affair. What it means for them they do not know, and they scarcely conceive that it means anything. They complain, venting heavy sighs, that while some few are set forward by God to do great works and fill important places, they are not allowed to believe that there is any particular object in their existence. It is remarkable, considering how generally this kind of impression prevails, that the Holy Scriptures never give way to it, but seem in all possible ways to be holding up the dignity of common life, and giving a meaning to its appointments, which the natural dullness and lowness of mere human opinion cannot apprehend.

They not only show us explicitly that God has a definite purpose in the lives of people already great, but they show us how frequently, in the conditions of obscurity and depression, preparations of counsel are going on by which the commonest offices are to become the necessary first chapter of a great and powerful history. David among the sheep; Elisha following after the plough; Nehemiah bearing the cup; Hannah, who can say nothing more than that she is the wife of Elkanah and a woman of a sorrowful spirit: Who can be justified, after looking on these humble people at their posts of service and discovering how dear a purpose God was cherishing in them—who, I say, can be justified in thinking that God has no particular plan for him, because he is not signalized by any kind of distinction?

Besides, what do the Scriptures show us, but that God has a particular care for every person, a personal interest and a sympathy with him and his trials, watching for the use of his one talent as attentively and kindly and approving him as heartily, in the right employment of it, as if he had given him ten? And what is the giving out of the talents itself, but an exhibition of the fact that God has a definite purpose, charge and work, be it this or that, for every man?

The Scriptures also make it the privilege of every man to live in the secret guidance of God. This is plainly nugatory [worthless], unless there is some chosen work or sphere into which he may be guided. For how shall God guide him, having nothing appointed or marked out for him to be guided into, no field opened for him, no course set down which is to be his wisdom?

God also professes in His Word to have purposes prearranged for all events: to govern by a plan which is from eternity even, and which in some sense comprehends everything. And what is this, but another way of conceiving that God has a definite place and plan adjusted for every human being? Without such, He could not even govern the world intelligently, or make a proper universe of the created system; for it becomes a universe only in the grand unity of reason, which includes it. Otherwise it were only a jumble of fortuities, without counsel, end or law.

Turning now from the Scriptures to the works of God, how constantly are we met here by the fact everywhere visible that ends and uses are the regulative reasons of all existing things. This we discover often when we are least able to understand the speculative mystery of objects, for it is precisely the uses of things that are most palpable [obvious]. These uses are to God no doubt as to us, the significance of His works. Taken together, they compose a grand reciprocal system, in which part answers actively to part, constructing thus an all-comprehensive and glorious whole. The system is, in fact, so perfect that the loss or displacement of any member would fatally derange the general order.

If there were any smallest star in Heaven that had no place to fill, that oversight would beget a disturbance which no Leverrier could compute.[6] The disorder would be real and eternal, and not merely casual or apparent. So nicely balanced, and so carefully hung, are the worlds, that even the grains of their dust are count-

ed, and their places adjusted to a corresponding nicety. There is
nothing included in the gross or total sum that could be dispensed
with. One grain, more or less, of sand would disturb or even fatally
disorder the whole scheme of the heavenly motions.

The same is true in regard to forces that are apparently
irregular. Every particle of air is moved by laws of as great preci-
sion as the laws of the heavenly bodies, or, indeed, by the same
laws, keeping its appointed place and serving its appointed use.
Every odor exhales in the nicest conformity with its appointed
place and law. Even the viewless and mysterious heat, stealing
through the dark centers and impenetrable depths of the worlds,
obeys its uses with unfaltering exactness, dissolving never so much
as an atom that was not to be dissolved.

What shall we now say of man, appearing as it were in the
center of this great circle of uses? They are all adjusted for him.
Has he then no ends appointed for himself? Noblest of all creatures, and closest to God, as he certainly is, are we to say that his
Creator has no definite thoughts concerning him, no place prepared for him to fill, no use for him to serve, which is the reason
of his existence?

There is, I conclude, a definite and proper end or issue for
every person's existence: an end which, to the heart of God, is the
good intended for him or for which he was intended; that which
he is privileged to become, called to become, ought to become;
that which God will assist him to become and which he cannot
miss, save by his own fault. Every human soul has a complete and
perfect plan, cherished for it in the heart of God—a divine biography marked out, which it enters into life to live.

This life, rightly unfolded, will be a complete and beautiful
whole, an experience led on by God and unfolded by His secret
nurture, as the trees and the flowers, by the secret nurture of the
world. It is a drama cast in the mold of a perfect art, with no part
wanting; a divine study for the man himself, and for others; a study
that shall forever unfold in wondrous beauty the love and faithfulness of God, great in its conception, great in the divine skill by
which it is shaped; above all, great in the momentous and glorious
issues it prepares. What a thought is this for every soul to cherish!
What dignity does it add to life! What support does it bring to the
trials of life! What instigations does it add to send us onward in
everything that constitutes our excellence! We live in the divine
thought. We fill a place in the great everlasting plan of God's

intelligence. We never sink below His care, never drop out of His counsel.

But there is, I must add, a single but very important and even fearful qualification. Things all serve their uses and never break out of their place; they have no power to do it. Not so with us. As free beings we are able to refuse the place and the duties God appoints; but if we do, then we sink into something lower and less worthy of us. That highest and best condition for which God designed us is no more possible. We are fallen out of it, and it cannot be wholly recovered. And yet as that was the best thing possible for us in the reach of God's original counsel, so there is a place designed for us now, which is the next best possible. God calls us now to the best thing left, and will do so till all good possibility is narrowed down and spent. Then, when He cannot use us any more for our own good, He will use us for the good of others—an example of the misery and horrible desperation to which any soul must come, when all the good ends, and the holy callings of God's friendly and fatherly purpose are exhausted.

Or it may be now that, remitting all other plans and purposes in our behalf, He will henceforth use us, wholly against our will, to be the demonstration of His justice and avenging power before the eyes of mankind; saying over us as He did over Pharaoh in the day of His judgments, "Even for this same purpose have I raised you up, that I might show My power in you, and that My name might be declared throughout all the earth."[7] Doubtless God had other and more genial plans to serve in this bad man, if only he could have accepted such. But knowing his [Pharaoh's] certain rejection of these, God turned His mighty counsel in him wholly on the use to be made of him as a reprobate. How many Pharaohs in common life refuse every other use God will make of them, choosing only to figure in their small way as reprobates, and descending in that manner to a fate that painfully mimics the Pharaoh's!

God has, then, I conclude, a definite life-plan set for every man, one that being accepted and followed will conduct him to the best and noblest end possible. No qualification of this doctrine is needed save the fearful one just named: that we, by our perversity, so often refuse to take the place and do the work He gives us.

It follows in the same way that as God, in fixing on our end or use, will choose the best end or use possible, so He will appoint for us the best manner possible of attaining it. For as it is a part of

God's perfection to choose the best things and not things partially good, so it will be in all the methods He prescribes for their attainment. And so as you pass on, stage by stage, in your courses of experience, it is made clear to you that whatever you have laid on you to do or to suffer, whatever to want, whatever to surrender or to conquer, is exactly best for you. Your life is a school, exactly adapted to your lesson, and that to the best, last end of your existence.

No room for a discouraged or depressed feeling, therefore, is left you. Enough that you exist for a purpose high enough to give meaning to life and to support a genuine inspiration. If your sphere is outwardly humble, if it appears to be quite insignificant, God understands it better than you do, and it is a part of His wisdom to bring out great sentiments in humble conditions, great principles in works that are outwardly trivial, great characters under great adversities and heavy loads of encumbrance. The tallest saints of God will often be those who walk in the deepest obscurity, and are even despised and quite overlooked by man. Let it be enough that God is in your history and that the plan of your biography is His. Away, then, O man, with your feeble complaints and feverish despondencies! There is no place left for this kind of nonsense. Let it fill you with cheerfulness and exalted feeling, however deep in obscurity your lot may be, to know that God is leading you on, preparing you for a work that is worthy of His divine magnificence. If God is really preparing us all to become that which is the very highest and best thing possible, there ought never to be a discouraged or uncheerful being in the world.

Such a kind of life is to be in God and not in our own will and wisdom. This, in fact, is its dignity. It is a kind of divine order, a creation molded by the loving thoughts of God. In that view it is to the person himself a continual discovery, as it is unfolded, both of himself and God. How different, how magnificent, to live by holy consent a life all discovery: to see it unfolding moment by moment, a plan of God, our own life-plan conceived in His paternal love! Each event, incident, experience, whether bright or dark, has its mission from Him, and reveals, either now or in its future issues, the magnificence of His favoring counsel. Then we can be sure, in the dark day, of a light that will follow; that loss will terminate in gain; that trial will issue in rest, doubt in satisfaction, suffering in patience, patience in purity, and all in a consummation of greatness that even God will look on with a smile.

How strong in its repose, how full of rest, is such a life! Call it human still, decry it, let it down by whatever diminutives can be invented, still it is great. It is a charge which ought to inspire even a dull-minded person with energy and holy enthusiasm.

But this inquiry will be made, supposing all this to be true, how can we ever get hold of this life-plan God has made for us, or find our way into it? Here, to many if not all, will be the main stress of doubt. Observe, then, first of all, some negatives that are important and must be avoided. They are these:

You will never come into God's plan if you study singularity, for if God has a design or plan for every person's life, then it is exactly appropriate to his nature. And as everyone's nature is singular and peculiar to himself—as peculiar as his face or look— then it follows that God will lead every man into a singular, original and peculiar life, without any study of singularity on his part. Let him seek to be just what God will have him, and what the talents, the duties and circumstances of his life will require him to be, and then he will be just peculiar enough. He will have a life of his own; a life that is naturally and therefore healthily peculiar; a simple, unaffected life whose plan is not in himself, but in God.

As little will he seek to copy the life of another. No man is ever called to be another. God has as many plans for people as He has people; and therefore He never requires us to measure our life exactly by any other life. We are not required to have the precise feelings, or to do the works, or pass through the trials of others, for God will handle us according to what we are, and not according to what other men are. To be a copyist, working at the reproduction of a human model, is to have no faith in one's significance, and to judge that God means nothing in one's particular life, but only in the life of some other person. What can the copyist become but an affectation or a dull imposture?

In this view also we are never to complain of our birth, our training, our employments, our hardships; never to fancy that we could be something if only we had a different lot and sphere assigned us. God understands His own plan, and He knows what we want [need] a great deal better than we do. What we call hindrances, obstacles, discouragements are probably God's opportunities. It is nothing new that a patient should dislike his medicine. No! A truce to all such impatience! Choke that devilish envy which gnaws at your heart, because you are not in the same lot with others. Bring down your soul, or rather, bring it up to receive God's will and do His work in your sphere, under your cloud of obscurity, against your temptations; and then you shall find that your condition is never opposed to your good, but really consistent with it.

Another mistake to be avoided; give up the hope or expectation that God will set you in any scheme of life where the whole course of it will be known or set down beforehand. If you go to Him to be guided, He will guide you; but He will not comfort your distrust, or half-trust of Him, by showing you the chart of all His purposes concerning you. He will only show you into a way where, if you go cheerfully and trustfully forward, He will show you on still further. No contract will be made with you save that He engages, if you trust Him, to lead you into the best things all the way through. And if they are better than you can either ask or think beforehand,[8] they will be none the worse for that.

But we must not stop in negatives. How, then, can a person who really desires to do it, come into the plan God lays for him, so as to live it and rationally believe that He does? You are on the point of choosing, it may be, this or that calling, wanting to know where duty lies and what course God Himself would have you take.

1. Beginning where the generality of truth is widest, consider the character of God. All that God designs for you will be in harmony with His character. He is a Being infinitely good, just and true. Therefore you are to know that He cannot really seek anything contrary to this in you. You may make yourself contrary in every attribute of character to God; but He never made you to become anything different from, or unworthy of Himself. A great many employments or callings are, by these first principles, forever cut off. No thought is permitted you, even for a moment, of any work or calling that does not represent the industry, justice, truth, beneficence and mercy of God.

2. Consider your relation to Him as a creature. All created wills have their natural center and rest in God's will. In Him they all come into a play of harmony, and the proper harmony of being is possible only in this way. Thus you know that you are called to have a will perfectly harmonized with God's and rested in His. That gives you a large insight into what you are to be, or what is the real end of your being. Nine-tenths of your particular duties may be settled at once by a simple reference to what God wills.

3. You have a conscience, which is given to be an interpreter of God's will and thus of your duty, and of what you are to become.

4. God's law and His written Word are guides to present duty

which, if faithfully accepted, will help to set you in accordance with the mind of God and the plan He has laid for you. "I am a stranger in the earth," wrote the Psalmist, "hide not Thy commandments from me."⁹ He knew that God's commandments would give him a clue to the true meaning and business of his life.

5. Be an observer of Providence, for God is showing you by the way He leads you, whither He means to lead. Study your trials, your talents, the world's wants, and stand ready to serve God now in whatever He brings to your hand.

6. Consult your friends, and especially those who are most in the teaching of God. They know your talents and personal qualifications better, in some respects, than you do yourself. Ask their judgment of you and of the spheres and works to which you are best adapted.

7. Go to God Himself and ask for the calling of God; for as certainly as He has a plan or calling for you, He will somehow guide you into it. And this is the proper office and work of His spirit. By this private teaching He can and will show us into the very plan that is set for us. This is the significance of what is prescribed as our duty, viz., living and walking in the Spirit. For the Spirit of God is an unfailing light which, if we accept and live in, we are guided thereby into a consenting choice, so that what God wills for us we also will for ourselves—settling into it as the needle to the pole.

By this hidden union with God or intercourse with Him, we get a wisdom or insight deeper than we know ourselves—a sympathy, a oneness with the divine will and love. We go into the very plan of God for us and are led along in it by Him, consenting, cooperating, answering to Him, we know not how, and working out with nicest exactness that good end for which His unseen counsel girded us and sent us into the world. In this manner, not neglecting the other methods just named, but gathering in all their separate lights, to be interpreted in the higher light of the Spirit, we can never be greatly at a loss to find our way into God's counsel and plan. The duties of the present moment we shall meet as they rise, and these will open a gate into the next, and we shall thus pass on, trustfully and securely, almost never in doubt as to what God calls us to do.

It is not to be supposed that you have followed me in such a subject as this without encountering questions from within that are piercing. It has put you on reflection. It has set you to asking what you have been doing and becoming thus far in your course, and what you are hereafter to be. Ten, twenty, fifty, seventy years ago, you came into this living world and began to breathe this mortal air. The guardian angel that came to take charge of you said, "To this end is he born, for this cause is he come into the world." God has a definite plan for you, a good end settled and cherished for you in His heart. This it was that gave a meaning and a glory to your life. Apart from this it was not, in His view, life for you to live; it was accident, frustration, death.

What now, O soul, have you done? What progress have you made? How much of the blessed life-plan of your Father have you executed? How far on your way are you to the good, best end your God has designed for you?

Do I hear your soul confessing, with a suppressed sob within you, that up to this time you have never sought God's chosen plan at all? Have you, even to this hour, and during so many years, been following a way and a plan of your own, regardless of all God's purposes in you? Well, if it be so, what have you got? How does your plan work? Does it bring you peace, content, dignity of aim and feeling, purity, rest? Or does it plunge you into the mires of disturbance, scorch you in flames of passion, worry you with cares, burden you with bitter reflections, cross you, disappoint, sadden, sour you? And what are your prospects? What is the issue to come? After you have worked out this hard plan of your own, will it come to a good end? Have you courage now to go on and work it through?

Perhaps you may be entertaining yourself, for the moment, with a notion of your prosperity, counting yourself happy in past successes, and counting on greater successes to come. Do you call it, then, success, that you are getting on in a plan of your own? There cannot be a greater delusion. You set up a plan that is not God's, and rejoice that it seems to prosper, not observing that you are just as much farther off from God's plan for you and from all true wisdom, as you seem to prosper more. And the day is coming when just this truth will be revealed to you as the bittersweet pang of your defeat and shame.

No matter which it be, prosperity or acknowledged defeat, the case is much the same in one as in the other, if you stand apart from God and His counsel. There is nothing good preparing for any man who will not live in God's plan. If he goes a-prospecting for himself, and will not apprehend that for which he is apprehended,[10] it cannot be to any good purpose.

And really, I know not anything more sad and painful to

think of, to a soul properly enlightened by reason and God's truth, than so many years of divine good squandered and lost—whole years of that great and blessed biography which God designed for you, occupied by a frivolous and foolish invention of your own, substituted for the good counsel of God's infinite wisdom and love. O, let the past suffice!

Young man or woman, this is the day of hope to you. All your best opportunities are still before you. Now, too, you are laying your plans for the future. Why not lay them in God? Who has planned for you as wisely and faithfully as He? Let your life begin with Him. Believe that you are being equipped by your God for a holy and great calling. Go to Him and consecrate your life to Him, knowing assuredly that He will lead you into just that life which is your highest honor and blessing.

And what shall I say to the older person who is further on in his course and is still without God in the world? The beginning of wisdom, my friend, you have yet to learn. You have really done nothing, as yet, that you were sent into the world to do. All your best opportunities are gone or going by. The best end, the next best, and the next are gone, and nothing but the dregs of opportunity are left. And still Christ calls even you. There is still a place left for you: not the best and brightest, but a humble and good one. To this you are called, for this you are apprehended of Christ Jesus still. O come, repent of your dusty and dull and weary way, and take the call that is offered. How many of you are there that ought to hear this call!

The whole endeavor on your part must be Godward. You must give up every purpose, end, employment, hope that conflicts with God and takes you away from Him. It is on the ground that, in your life of sin, you are altogether in self-love, centered in yourself, living for yourself, making a god of your own objects and works. These occupy the soul, fill it, bear rule in it, and God cannot enter. You must make room for God, create a void for Him to fill, die to yourself that Christ may live within.

But this negative work of self-clearing is not enough. There must be a positive reaching after God, an offering up of the soul to Him, that He may come and dwell in it and consecrate it as His temple. For as certainly as the light will pour into an open window, just so certainly will God reveal Himself in a mind that is opened to His approach. Now this opening of the mind, this reaching after God, is faith; and hence it is that so much is made of faith. For God is revealed outwardly in the incarnate life and death of Jesus, in order that He may present Himself in a manner level to our feeling, and quickening to our love, and so encourage that faith by which He may come in to reestablish His presence in us. For God, who commanded the light to shine out of darkness, has shined in our hearts to give the light of the knowledge of the glory of God in the face of Jesus Christ.[11] O, it is there that the true God shines—let Him shine into our hearts!

All men, living without God, are adventurers out upon God's world, in neglect of Him, to choose their own course. Hence the sorrowful, sad-looking host they make. O, that I could show them whence their bitterness, their dryness, their unutterable sorrows come. O, that I could silence, for one hour, the noisy tumult of their works, and get them to look in upon that better, higher life of fruitfulness and blessing to which their God has appointed them. Will they ever see it? Alas! I fear!

Friends of God, disciples of the Son of God, how inspiring and magnificent the promise or privilege that is offered here to you. Does it still encounter only unbelief in your heart? Does it seem to you impossible that you can ever find your way into a path prepared for you by God, and be led along in it by His mighty counsel?

Let me tell you a secret. It requires a very close, well-kept life to do this; a life in which the soul can have confidence always toward God; a life which allows the Spirit always to abide and reign, driven away by no affront of selfishness. There must be a complete renunciation of self-will. God must be practically first; and the testimony that we please God must be the element of our peace. And such a disciple I have never known who did not have it for his joy that God was leading him on, shaping his life for him, bringing him along out of one moment into the next, year by year. To such a disciple there is nothing strained or difficult in saying that God's plan can be found, or that this is the true mode and privilege of life.

Nothing to him is easier or more natural. He knows God ever present, feels that God determines all things for him, rejoices in the confidence that the everlasting counsel of his Friend is shaping every turn of his experience. He does not go hunting after this confidence; it comes to him, abides in him, fortifies his breast, and makes his existence itself an element of peace. And this, my brethren, is your privilege, if only you can live close enough to have the secret of the Lord with you.

Every man's life, practically speaking, is shaped by his love. If it is a downward, earthly love, then his actions will be tinged by it, all his life will be as his reigning love. This love, you perceive, is not a mere sentiment, or casual emotion, but is the man's settled affinity. It is that which is, to his character, what the magnetic force is to the needle, the power that adjusts all his aims and works, and practically determines the man, It only must be a downward love, or an upward love, for being the last love and deepest of the person, there cannot be two last and deepest, it must be one or the other. And then, as this love changes, it works a general revolution of the person.

Hence it is that so much is said of the heart in the gospel, and of a change of the heart; for it is what proceeds out of the heart that defiles the man. The meaning is, not that Christianity proposed to give us a new organ of soul, or to extract one member of the soul and insert another, but that it will change the love of the heart. In his prior, unregenerate state as a sinner, man was separated from God and centered in himself, living in himself and to himself. And he was not made to live in this manner. He was made to live in God, to be conscious of God, to know Him by an immediate knowledge, to act by His divine impulse; in a word, to be inspired by Him.

If a man love Me, says the Savior, he will keep My words, and My Father will love him, and We will come unto him and make Our abode with him.[12] That abode in the soul is a new condition of divine movement, for it is the movement of God. All things, of course, are new. Life proceeds from a new center, of which God is the rest and prop. The Bible is a new book, because there is a light in the soul by which to read it. Duties are new, because the divine love the soul is in has changed all the relations of time and the aims of life. The saints of God on earth are no longer shunned, but greeted in new terms of celestial brotherhood. The very world itself is revealed in new beauty and joy to the mind, because it is looked upon with another and different love, and beheld as the symbol of God.

How sacred, how strong in its repose, how majestic, how nearly divine is a life thus ordered! The simple thought of a life which is to be the unfolding, in this manner, of a divine plan is too beautiful, too captivating to suffer one indifferent or heedless moment. Living in this manner, every turn of your experience will be a discovery to you of God, every change a token of His Fatherly counsel. Whatever obscurity, darkness, trial, suffering falls upon you; your defeats, losses, injuries; your outward state, employment, relations; what seems hard, unaccountable, severe, or, as nature might say, vexations—all these you will see are parts or constitutive elements in God's beautiful and good plan for you, and as such are to be accepted with a smile.

Trust God! Have an implicit trust in God! And those very things will impart the highest zest to life. If you were in your own will, you could not bear them; and if you fall, at any time, into your own will, they will break you down. But the glory of your condition as a Christian is that you are in the mighty and good will of God.

Hence it was that John Bunyan called his hero "Greatheart,"[13] for no heart can be weak that is in the confidence of God. See how it was with the Apostle Paul: counting all things but loss for the excellency of the knowledge;[14] enduring, with Godlike patience, unspeakable sufferings; casting everything behind him, and following on to apprehend that for which he was apprehended. He had a great and mighty will, but no self-will; therefore he was strong, a true lion of the faith.

Away, then, with all feeble complaints, all meager and mean anxieties. Take your duty, and be strong in it, as God will make you strong. The harder it is, in fact, the stronger you will be. Understand, also, that the great question here is, not what you will get, but what you will become. The greatest wealth you can ever get will be in yourself. Take your burdens, and troubles, and losses, and wrongs, if come they must and will, as your opportunities, knowing that God has girded you for greater things than these. O, to live out such a life as God appoints, how great a thing it is! To do the duties, make the sacrifices, bear the adversities, finish the plan, and then to say with Christ (who of us will be able?) "It is finished!"[15]

NOTES

1. The Persian emperor Cyrus II, whose rule began in 550 B.C., is honored in Jewish literature as few other Gentiles. He repatriated the exiled Jews living in Babylonia, and ordered the restoration of the Temple in Jerusalem. The book of Isaiah mentions him several times with distinction. Says the *International Standard Bible Encyclopedia,* "He was not only one of the greatest conquerors of history, but by the tradition of his clemency to those he had defeated, and his policy of religious toleration, he . . . left an example to mankind that, had it been followed, would have saved the world immeasurable suffering" (Vol. 1, art. "Cyrus").
2. Xenophon (430-355? B.C.), Greek philosopher, wrote the *Cyropaedia,* a fanciful description of the boyhood and training of Cyrus, well over a century after the emperor's death.
3. John 18:37.

4. Cf. Hebrews 11:8.
5. Genesis 45:8.
6. Urbain Jean Joseph Leverrier (1811-1877), French astronomer, investigated a disturbance in the motion of Uranus and deduced the presence of an unknown planet which was later discovered and named Neptune.
7. Exodus 9:16.
8. Cf. Ephesians 3:20.
9. Psalm 119:19.
10. Cf. Philippians 3:12.
11. 2 Corinthians 4:6.
12. John 14:23.
13. In *Pilgrim's Progress*, Part II.
14. Cf. Philippians 3:8.
15. John 19:30.

Joseph Parker

Sunday mornings in London in the late nineteenth century, as Warren Wiersbe has pointed out, must have been wonderful times for Christians just to be alive. They could choose to hear Charles Spurgeon at the Metropolitan Tabernacle, or F. B. Meyer at Regent's Park Chapel, or Canon Henry Liddon at St. Paul's Cathedral, or Joseph Parker at the City Temple. What a feast for mind and soul! The anguish would be having to make a selection between such alternatives.

Among this galaxy of great English pulpit masters, Joseph Parker (1839-1902) seems to have had the most forceful personality. To some observers his rugged physique and his commanding appearance lent a semblance of colossal egotism, and he certainly was not lacking in self-esteem. On one occasion, when a congregation smaller than his present one invited him to become its pastor, he replied, "An eagle does not roost in a sparrow's nest." Someone who knew Parker well said of him, "He was boisterous, sometimes bombastic, but he had drama, he had passion, he had genius, he had great flashes of inspiration which made other preachers seem dull by comparison. When Parker died our greatest preacher passed. We shall not see his like again."

By his admission, the man lived for his work. He married twice, but had no children. He owed little to his origins; his father was a stonemason in Northumberland. The autobiographical account of his early schooling reads like something out of Nicholas Nickleby. Later study was largely self-administered. He preached his first sermon at age eighteen, and it convinced him that he wanted to be a minister. At twenty-two he was invited to London by an editor he had come to know, and preached in Whitefield's tabernacle. He later wrote that the ministers who heard him "unanimously agreed that there was absolutely no need for me to go through any preparatory course." Instead he studied Greek and moral philosophy at University College, London.

The following year, at age twenty-three, he was ordained a Congregational minister and called to Banbury Church in Oxfordshire. During his five-year pastorate there his popularity grew to such an extent that Parker received seven invitations to other pulpits. He finally accepted a call to the wealthy Cavendish Street Chapel in Manchester, *where he remained for eleven years. The congregation grew to two thousand, and he had no expectations of moving. In 1869, however, a call came from what was then known as the Poultry Church in London; and despite his initial refusal, the appeal persisted. Finally Parker agreed to go if the congregation would relocate and rebuild in London.*

Thus the City Temple was erected near Holborn Viaduct, and for the next thirty-three years Joseph Parker was its pastor and leader. The church became a prominent tourist attraction of London. Three thousand regularly attended Sunday services, and another thousand came to hear him at weekday noontime services.

No one questioned who was in charge. After the stewards took the offering they handed it to him. He managed all the monies of the church and gave an accounting to none. Alexander Gammie wrote, "His massive figure, his leonine head with its shaggy locks, would have attracted attention anywhere. The gleaming eyes, the sweeping gestures, the constantly changing inflection of his wonderful voice, held any audience spellbound; and there was always the element of the unexpected."

Central to Parker's outstanding ministry were his solid evangelical views on the inspiration and authority of Scripture, doctrines which he loved to expound. The following pages show how fearlessly he grappled with the rising tide of Biblical criticism. Seven years before his death Parker wrote, "In my judgment the only preaching that can do profound and lasting good must be Biblical." His successors at City Temple did not choose to emulate Parker's obvious masculinity. Unfortunately they also veered away from what Parker called "the pure Gospel of Christ," and chose other paths. This excerpt is taken from his book about the Bible, None Like It: A Plea for the Old Sword, *published in 1893 by Fleming H. Revell, New York.*

EIGHT

NONE LIKE IT: A PLEA FOR THE OLD SWORD
by Joseph Parker

Some writers, of the highest Christian standing, have brought themselves to look upon the Bible as a book obviously marked by incongruity, self-contradiction, historical impossibility, and occasional moral outrage. Nevertheless [they say] many a direct and genuine message from God may be found if sought for with a reverent, humble and obedient spirit.

Such writers decline to speak of the Bible as "the Word of God," yet happily they are equally emphatic in declaring that in ancient times the Word of God came to individual prophets and suppliants, and that a record of the communication is to be found in the Bible. The writers go much farther than this. Their urgent contention [is] that the Word of God not only came, but it comes, is coming, has always been coming, and will always come to living and holy souls.

We are dealing with friends and allies who are spending their lives in the exposition and propagation of their own view of "the truth as it is in Jesus."[1] We are dealing with brethren, not with enemies; with believers, not with infidels. On all sides of these great inquiries we are in quest of truth. We want to get down to the rock of reality. It is a worthless orthodoxy that cannot stand the test of all fair criticism.

The brethren whose theory I am about to consider, and in parts strongly to oppose, are of opinion that no little harm has been done to the Bible itself by claiming that as a book it is "the Word of God." They wish the Bible to be properly defined. They regard it not as *being* but as *containing* the Word of God. They are not afraid to say that the Bible as a book abounds in errors, that some of the authorships are nominally fictitious, that many of its dates are incorrect, that some of its books are of composite and not of individual authorship, that Moses may have written little or none of the books which bear his name, and that David may never have heard of the Psalms which are ascribed to his harp and pen. Yet they claim that humble and obedient souls may find "the Word of God" in the Bible, but not in the Bible alone, for that Word, they say, comes to men every day as a distinct and direct message from God. Every day brings its own message.

It has been said that the Bible itself nowhere claims to be "the Word of God." There are some rights which do not require to be formally "claimed." They wait for recognition; they are self-revealing. The Bible cannot live upon testimonials, or "claims" or official sanctions. It can only live by such a supremacy of influence as entitles it to the faith, the love, and the veneration of the world. If it has exercised that influence, that influence is the Bible's best claim.

It is said that Jesus Christ is the Word of God. That he was, some persons who deny His Deity might have no difficulty in admitting. To myself Jesus Christ is not only the Word of God, He is God the Word. I do not ask what "claim" Jesus Christ made for Himself. I do not set store upon mere "claim." History has given us too much reason to suspect it. I study Christ Himself, His words, His ways, His thoughts, His deeds, and thus I am led to exclaim, "My Lord and my God."[2]

When we speak of the Bible as "the Word of God," we may be using a symbolic idiom—an idiom which represents the supreme purpose of the Book, its vital content and soul—in a sense and measure which no merely literary definition can fully express. To describe the Bible as "the Word of God" is, in my view, to describe the Book by its supreme purpose, which purpose is the revelation of God in such degree and proportion as the human mind is able to receive it. I cannot escape mystery in receiving the Bible, but I escape the greater mystery by receiving it as a message from God.

It must be remembered that we are dealing with no less a theme than the revelation of God. How to bring it into words! Eternity is incommoded when endeavoring to typify itself upon the dial-space of time. It is the culmination of irony. The Bible is the revelation of God—ineffable—in the only setting or framework possible in the present conditions of life. To bring God into language is to bring Him within limitation. So when I am challenged to define the phrase "the Word of God" I am not ashamed to own that to my mind the phrase typifies a reality which it is impossible fully to express in terms which would not themselves require to be defined.

A special danger [in interpreting the Bible] arises in the form of a temptation to judge the part out of its relation to the whole. I have been enabled to regard the Bible as a unit. I know it is a collection of what may be called tracts or pamphlets, and that probably no one writer knew, or in many instances could possibly know, what the others had written. Yet to my view the Bible is a unit. One part belongs to another. One part explains another. This is indeed very marvelous, considering the different authorships, the different dates, the different environments. It is not difficult to believe that the authors must have been moved by a common impulse, and must have been building a common temple without knowing it. The parts of the temple come together most wonderfully, as if proportioned and fitted by the same Architect.

So wondrous is the effect upon my own mind that if any teacher should explain the marvel by saying, "Holy men of old wrote as they were moved by the Holy Spirit,"[3] I could accept the solution. My reason, my imagination, and my heart could unite in exclaiming, "God is here, and I knew it not; this is none other than the Word of God, and this is the light of Heaven!"[4]

Nor am I to be troubled by having my attention called to the real or supposed defects of certain portions of the Bible. Can Ecclesiastes, say some, be looked upon as the Word of God? Look at its materialism, its sensuousness, its pessimism. The Book of Ecclesiastes is part of a larger book. Its pessimism is a shadow upon a landscape. There is undoubtedly a pessimistic side of life, and I am glad to have it expressed exactly as it is found in the Book of Ecclesiastes. The Bible would have been incomplete without it. If it [Ecclesiastes] were the whole Bible, it would cover the soul with deep darkness; but as part of the Bible it is true to human experience, and the very recognition of it is itself an encouragement to faith and hope.

Others say, can the Book of Esther be part of the Word of God when the name of God is not so much as mentioned in it? For my own part I can see little but God in the main action of that tragedy. God does sometimes govern anonymously. To me it is not an unacceptable conception that sometimes the light is reflex rather than direct. The Bible, having been made into a unit, is to be judged in its unity even in the act of considering its parts. Books which may be difficulties when torn out of their setting may assume new color and meaning when regarded in their relation to an organic whole.

So also with texts, separate verses, and special commandments which are supposed to present such stumbling-blocks to that sensitive creature, that highly-wrought and delicately-constructed machine, the infidel. Some teachers are painfully careful of his feelings. He is most sensitive. When he hears that God visits the iniquities of the fathers upon the children to the third and fourth generation, he faints. When he is told that the Canaanites and other persons in whose feelings and sufferings he is deeply interested were driven out of the land with great slaughter and loss, he is overpowered. When he comes to passages which seem to direct that the heads of little ones are to be dashed against the stones, he simply lays down the Bible in horror and becomes a larger infidel than ever.

Yet after all (and speaking with trembling deference), even an infidel may be wrong. Yet in what white-faced awe we stand before him! How anxious the commentators are to explain verse 36 to him in a way that will soothe his exasperated feelings! How deeply anxious the preachers are so to explain the Almighty that the dear and sensitive infidel may take a more lenient and hopeful view of the general way in which the universe is managed as a whole.

For my part I will not make an idol of an infidel. Again and again I would say, notwithstanding the apparent impious audacity of the assertion, that even an infidel may sometimes be wrong. I can at least imagine it possible that in the final audit the Bible writers may have seen farther than some who are shocked by their statements. Evils do run out their consequences to the third and fourth generation. Nations are as a matter of fact displaced and replaced in a mysterious way. Even little children are dashed against the stones. If these facts be degraded into mere anecdotes, they are made horrible by first being made contemptible; but set in their right atmosphere, thrown into their true perspective amid the ever-coming and ever-vanishing centuries, read in the larger light—even in God's high noon—who knows but that it may yet be proved that it was the infidel who was wrong?

Some teachers suppose that they have met the case by describing the Bible as "a record." But a "record" of what? Surely more than a record of names, births, ages, wars, migrations, and anecdotes. These may properly come under such a designation as "record." But is there nothing more in the Bible? Is there not something more in Moses than Moses ever dreamed? Why have a Bible at all? What is it that gives the Bible its uniqueness? That is the quality which I wish to get at and appreciate. When I have discovered that quality, I can have no difficulty in making a definite claim for the Bible.

Is there anything in the Bible of the nature of prophecy, communion, fellowship with God, insight, motive—anything about or bearing upon prayer, eternity, sanctification, election, trust, destiny—anything that goes beyond records, schedules, registers, and genealogies—anything that takes in all the centuries and gathers up human history into a unit? What is the supreme purpose of the Book? Does the Book anywhere claim to have a supreme purpose? If it has not a supreme purpose, why was it collated and published? If its supreme purpose, claimed or unclaimed, is the revelation of God to the world, I have no difficulty in regarding it as the inclusive and authoritative Word of God.

What then is the permanent qualtity that is in the Bible, the qualtity without which there could be no Bible in the sense in which we understand that term? It is, compendiously, the revelation of God. It is in detail every law that can beneficially affect the condition and the perfecting of human life—"profitable for teaching, for reproof, for correction, for instruction which is in righteousness, that the man of God may be complete, furnished completely with every good work."[5] It is evident that the man who wrote the Second Epistle to Timothy believed that some Scripture, somewhere, written by some pens, was inspired; that there was some writing somewhere which he regarded as "Holy Scripture," and that such Holy Scripture undertook the whole spiritual culture and perfecting of man.

According to the Apostle Paul any Scripture which is not profitable, vitally and permanently useful, which does not complete the man of God and furnish him unto every good work, cannot be regarded as inspired, and every Scripture covering and fulfilling this ministry may be accepted as inspired by the Holy Spirit. Now on the ground of history and on the ground of personal experience it is claimed that the Bible, as we have it, brings men to God, makes them men of God, fills them with thoughts of God, and creates in them a desire to be holy after the manner of God, and because it does this, does it openly and subtly, does it constantly and unexceptionally, it is no exaggeration of claim to represent it as "the Word of God." Nor can we so re-edit the Bible as to say with definiteness that the exclusion of what may be called local and limited history would not affect the parts which are avowedly moral, spiritual, universal and permanent. The Bible is impregnated through and through with one infinite and glorious purpose.

My submission, then, is that the Bible is more than a book. It is marked by a peculiar quality, a separating and differentiating quality. Call it supremely spiritual, or call it distinctively supernatural; that quality can only be penetrated by a spirit kindred to its own. It is admitted by all who regard the Bible as something more than an interesting collation of very ancient literature, that there is some kind of inspiration in it; that God is revealed in it, and that God's will in some sense or degree is made known in it. The Apostle Paul puts the matter in the most lucid and acceptable manner when he says, "The natural man receiveth not the things of the Spirit of God, and he cannot know them because they are spiritually discerned, judged, or examined."[6] I claim, then, that in the degree in which the Bible is inspired, it can be truly read only by the ministry of the inspiring Spirit, and that he only who receives the Holy Spirit can feel the power of the Holy Scripture.

In nothing whatsoever that is wise, good, true, can present-day inspiration make any advance upon the Bible. That is a clear issue. Happily it is an issue that can be submitted to practical tests. Take the supreme question of character. The quality of manhood that is produced or contemplated by any book is a good test of the quality of the book itself, provided that the character is not merely pictorial, but vital and beneficent. What, then, can transcend the Biblical conception of character? It is character founded upon a New Birth.

At this moment we are dealing with the conception and not with the inner mystery. Has modern inspiration made any advance upon that conception? The New Birth means new creatureship, completeness of the divine image in the soul, and eternal life. Can present-day inspiration indicate any omissions of excellence [in the Bible] and supply them?

Take the question of social beneficence. Socialism is the rage of the hour. Have we moved one step beyond the Bible line? Has any man added one tint of beauty to the parable of the Good Samaritan? Has the modern prophet ever sent a tenderer message to wandering souls than the parable of the Prodigal Son? Is social service poorly represented in the 25th chapter of the Gospel of Matthew? The Bible is saturated with the spirit of sympathy, and alive with the doctrine of social responsibility.

What, then, can present-day inspiration do? It will find its function in obedience. New forms and new applications are possible and may be desirable, but the root ideas are in the Bible. The Bible is more than a record. Records refer to the past, the Bible claims and rules the whole future. The Bible is a record, but it is also a revelation. It is not only a tree on whose fruit the ancients fed, it is a Tree of Life, and its leaves are for the healing of nations yet unborn.[7]

If the Bible had not survived so many examinations, assaults, and afflictions, one might despair of its happy issue out of present-day inquiry and so-called dissection. What we want, however, and what we must have at all costs, is the truth. If the [present] discussion turned upon some particular doctrine contained in the Bible, a doctrine known to be open to various interpretations, the ground would be significantly limited. But in this case the question turns upon the genuineness and credibility of the Bible itself.

Our scholars and experts offer us "a series of tentative suggestions"; they refer us to "a true historical instinct." They are not able to say this or that "at present"; they give "legitimate weight" to the results or possibilities of "future excavations." Adam, as he has been popularly apprehended, was removed from the Bible long ago by the naturalists. There is no Adam; there never was any Adam; there never could have been any Adam. The account of the Creation is a poem, but who wrote it no man knows. Adam could not have written it, for there never was an Adam. It would be a "childish misinterpretation" to treat the first known story in Genesis "as literal fact." The serpent never talked, the flood never came. Abraham was ideal and cumulative, a noun of multitude rather than a real, historical personality.

We are getting accustomed to hear without special emotion that [the books of] Ruth, Daniel and Esther "rest upon a very slender historical basis." Moses did not write the Pentateuch, David did not write the Psalms, Solomon had little or nothing to do with the Proverbs, and "the authors of the books which compose the Bible did not dream of making the claim that what they were writing was written by God or spoken by God." Yet in spite of all this we are assured that on all spiritual matters the Bible may be trusted.

Surely this is imposing a severe strain upon the mind of anyone but an expert! But we must not consider that. What we want to get at is fact, rise or fall what may. The front gates are fired down, the castle guns have been silenced, the moat has been crossed, the roof has been battered in, but the household hearth still remains. Does it? How long will it remain? What I fear is that where criticism has so completely beaten back orthodoxy it may one day drive in the battle on Calvary itself and seize the cross as a trophy of war. It is easy to deprecate this view, [but] if ninety-nine of a hundred points have been carried, I cannot feel quite secure about the hundredth.

I feel that if such men are right, I must be wrong. I was preaching in some blundering way before they were born, but they come up with all the new learning, and they take away, or permit to be taken away, Adam and Abraham, and David and Isaiah and Daniel, in the sense in which I have always cherished these illustrious names. They drive Christ out of the Messianic Psalms and prophecies. They tell me that the Bible is wrong in history, wrong in chronology, wrong in dates, wrong in sequence. But they assure me that the whole purpose of the book is to bring men to Christ. Whose Christ? Presently they may take away my Lord Himself without telling me where they have lain Him.

My mother knew nothing about God but what she had read in the Bible. Of course this cuts a mean figure in the eyes of formal logic and in the view of the new learning. Yet I am going to cling to it. My reason for referring to it is to remind the critics that there is a Bible dear to the common people. They were made by it, converted by it, comforted by it, and they live upon it; and I do not want the critics to take it away until they have something better to give than "a series of tentative suggestions" and the hope of finding some help in "future excavations."

I would only take away an idolater's idol because I think I have something better to put in its place. Neither would I take away Adam and Moses and Abraham and Isaac and Isaiah and Daniel, and fill the ghastly vacancy with nothing more than "a series of tentative suggestions."

But what would the infidel say? I never consult the infidel upon anything. I go to the infidel for infidelity; I never go to him for faith. What then is to be done? Do not let the soul shiver in nakedness while the new tailors are wrangling over the texture and pattern of the new clothes. What, then, is my personal standpoint, my individual and peace-bringing faith? I will try to make it clear.

At the outset I feel sure that the Bible was written, edited, put together, and otherwise made into a book by somebody. It is something to know beyond doubt that the Bible had a personal origin. But it might have a personal origin and be a bad book.

Exactly. But we know that it is not a bad book. Even some schools of rationalism admit that the book has moral merits.

Certainly it is a most religious book. Its key word is GOD. That must be most clearly recognized. When creation is accounted for, where is God put? In the very first sentence. When man is accounted for, where is God put? In the very first sentence. When the law is given, where is God put? In the first sentence. When the prophets were called, where is God put? In the first sentence. When Jesus began to preach, where was God put? In the very first sentence. When Jesus Christ rose from the dead, to whom was He about to ascend? To "My God and My Father."[8] When Jesus shall end His mediation, who shall reign? "God shall be all in all."[9] When Jesus shall come again, how will He come? "With the trumpet of God."[10]

From whom is the new Jerusalem to descend? "I, John, saw the new Jerusalem coming down from God."[11] Before whom did the twenty-four elders fall down in Heaven? They fell down and worshiped God that sat on the throne.[12] Who promised the seed of the woman? God. Who so loved the world that He gave His only begotten Son? God. Who shall destroy the last trace of sorrow? "God shall wipe away all tears."[13] So rolls the thunder-music. God! God! God! I simply note the fact, and I especially note it because it is one of those facts which do not terminate in themselves. Whenever God comes, He comes with thousands of angels and chariots innumerable. When God comes, Creation came, and Providence, and Redemption.

Finding as I do so much implied by the introduction of the divine Name, I at once, and necessarily, think of the Book in vital connection with that all-including Name. In a very clear and intelligible sense, the Name is to me the Book, and the Book is the Name. I hardly so much as see the human names; they are the names of clerks, scribes, secretaries or amanuenses. I am interested in them only in a very secondary and remote way. Why? Because the other Name fills all the space and becomes the focal point of all attention.

It would not surprise me if the writers themselves were to tell me that they were very slow and laborious penmen, and that often they did not know what they were writing. The prophecy may have been greater than the prophet. Jeremiah may have shrunk into a child when the heavenly charge sought to enter into his soul, and Moses never really knew how much he hesitated and stammered until God called him to service.[14] Then the hesitancy was felt. We chaffer on equal terms with Eliphaz, Bildad, and Zophar, but when the Voice out of the whirlwind thrills us, we abhor ourselves in dust and ashes.[15]

It is that Voice which I hear most distinctly in the Bible. That Voice is indeed the Bible. Without that Voice there would be no Bible. I therefore call the Bible the Word of God, and if I called it by any other name I should be as one who was busy here and there and who let the King pass by. It is more than possible to think too much about the scribes and amanuenses, and to think too little about what is actually written. Sometimes we should pity them. Surely it was not easy to bear "the burden" of the Lord. I thank the men through whom the message came, but I must not forget that my business is with the message itself.

If, when I read the wonderful words of Peter, I were to fall down at his feet and worship him, he would take me up and say, "Stand up; I myself also am a man."[16] If I were to think only or largely of Moses and Ezra and Isaiah, this same Peter would rebuke me, saying, "The prophecy came not in old time by the will of man, but holy men of God spoke as they were moved by the Holy Spirit."[17] And the prophets themselves would rebuke our criticism and our admiration, saying, "Why marvel at this? Or why look so earnestly on us, as though by our own power or holiness we had brought you this message?"[18]

They would refer us to the true Source: "Not that we are sufficient of ourselves to think anything as of ourselves; but our sufficiency is of God."[19] In the New Testament as well as the Old the reference is always to God. Thus not in a "few scattered texts" but uniformly and passionately we are referred to God. Prophets and apostles ask no recognition; they constantly point us to God. The dominant and unchanging tone of the Bible is God. That is my reason for thinking and speaking of the Bible as the Word of God.

This gives me the right point of approach to the Bible and all its contents. All the detail I can now survey from a true elevation. So long as I mistook the telegraph messenger for the telegram itself, I was in great confusion. Who was he? Who were his parents? What was his age? How did he come to be connected with a great electrical system? I made a puzzle of him. Was he old enough to have written a telegram? Had he and another boy concocted the telegram? After all, was the missive a telegram? If it was a telegram, why was it not sent immediately to me without the intervention of a messenger? And if a messenger had to come, why almost insult me by sending a boy? I asked the boy if he had written the telegram and he said No. I demanded to see the clerk who had penciled down the message, and he turned out to be little more than a boy himself, but he had sufficient sense to suggest that I had better open the envelope and read the message. When I read it, the boy and the clerk became of small consequence to me.

The message was full of love. It was the message for which I had been waiting many a weary day. I could have loved even the boy who brought it to me. I had at length looked at the whole action from the right point of view, and now the shadows were dispersed by the full shining of the light. The right point of view is exactly what we want in everything.

We are told by surveyors that the setting up of the theodolite was one of the most difficult operations in carrying out the trigonometrical survey of the country. The theodolite itself may be in perfect condition, yet the triangulation will be bungled if it is not set up on the right spot and at the right height. Sometimes a scaffold had to be built up to a great height. The surveyors say that they had sometimes to build a solid foundation for it in the middle of a bog, and sometimes it had to be carried to the very summit of a rocky mountain.

So in our looking out upon wider spaces, we must not only have a well-adjusted theodolite, we must find the elevation on which the instrument must stand, even if that elevation has to be built or attained at the greatest cost. Then must follow the three specific adjustments of the instrument, any one of which being wanting or incorrect, triangulation is impossible.

It seems to me that the higher critics have not always placed themselves at the right point of view in attempting to survey the almost boundless field of inspiration. In some conspicuous instances they are mere word-grubbers who cannot find through grammars and lexicons what can only be found by incessant and sympathetic communion with God. If I start my survey of the Bible from any other point than God, I am lost in details. The Author, not the book in its mechanical form, is the point at which to begin.

We must first know the dominating Personality of the book. That Personality is Jesus Christ. The Worker, not the works, must first be studied. It is beautiful that the New Testament begins with the genealogy of the Man. God has no genealogy, so He plunges at once into the act of revelation by creation. Jesus comes to us by every human genealogy, as they trace the incarnation of the Son of

Man. Jesus is every man's ancestor and every man's descendant.
The root is in every twig, and every twig is in the root. Buddha is
in the genealogy, and the woman who was a sinner, and the man
who murdered his brother, and the saint almost wholly white, and
Judas Iscariot who betrayed Innocence with a kiss, since this
Coming One was the Son of Man. "The Son of Man!" That is His
genealogy in three syllables. It reaches beyond the timeline, for He
who is thus the Son of Man is of necessity the Son of God, and He
who is thus the Son of God is to me, and to unnumbered millions,
God the Son!

Thus, in surveying the New Testament, I think I place the
theodolite on the true base. And thus the miracles fall into their
right position and yield their mystery in response to faith. It was
only when I approached the miracles from the wrong point that
they staggered my inexperience. I talked of nature, and laws of
nature, and the order of the universe, and continuity, until I settled
into that kind of wonder the lower side of which looks toward
unbelief.

But all was changed when I approached the miracles from
the point of long and deep communion with Christ. The miracles
were but the dust of His feet. They ceased to be miracles. They
were syllables in one great speech of love. In the first instance I
struggled up to them through the weakness and gloom of fear. In
the second I descended upon them in the strength and glory of
faith. Then I understood how He came to make so little of miracles and so much of holiness. Then there shone upon me the
meaning of His promise that the glory of His miracles should be
eclipsed by the "greater works" which He would do through His
disciples when He worked from the height of the heavens.[20]

It is important to remember that inspiration and revelation
are not one and the same thing. Probably there cannot be revelation without inspiration, but there may be inspiration without
revelation. It may be proper to define revelation as including such
truths and facts as are not discoverable by human reason: for
example, the personality and attributes of the Godhead. But inspiration may guide the mind into all truth: into a right construction
of history, into a right grouping and coloring of the facts of life,
into the right use of the moral sense; in short, into a true knowledge of all things pertaining to the whole culture of the soul. A
man may be inspired to carve a statue, or paint a picture, or
compose a poem, yet have no revelation of the living and gracious
God.

As to some of the Biblical books being supposedly less inspired than others, such as Esther, Daniel, Ecclesiastes, and Jonah, the case is not proved; but if proved, the issue would be of limited importance. In the matter of gradation, or degree, or other obscure variety, the construction of the Bible is most remarkable. In some cases the personality of the prophet goes for much, as Jeremiah, Isaiah, and Ezekiel. In others the prophet is lost in the prophecy. Who knows anything of Obadiah? Or Joel? Who knows precisely when Amos took up his work, except that it was two years before the earthquake? Of Amos and Hosea we know some interesting particulars, but who knows anything of Micah, whose father's name is unknown, and whose birthplace owes its fame to his own prophecy? Yet Micah spoke of justice and mercy and the humble walk with God.[21]

The minor prophets had their share of inspiration. Inspiration is not a mechanical term. The great and the small are the Lord's. Inspiration touches the highest and lowest grades of faculty. There is a common inspiration, as well as an inspiration that is unique. "There is a spirit in man, and the inspiration of the Almighty gives him understanding."[22]

The church is entitled to claim this inspiration in reading the Bible. Some parts of the Bible are personal and local, and in that degree they may have been allowed to fall into desuetude. "The valley of craftsmen" is of no importance to us.[23] Many of us are compelled to do with the Bible as we do with a country: some valleys are fruitful, some rocks are barren. My pastoral advice to inquirers is founded upon the example of Christ. When He was asked great questions He referred the inquirers to the law, the commandments and the prophets. That is what His ministers must do. He never referred to the difficulties of the Old Testament, but to its gospels. The valley of Megiddo may be blotted out; the garden of Gethsemane is the road to forgiveness.

Am I expected, then, to receive from so small a people as the Jews so great a gift as a Book which is regarded by Christendom as the vehicle of a divine revelation? Am I in any prescriptive degree whatever to be bound by that Book? Why not go to the Greek, the Roman, or the Indian mind for my revelation? Why not collate all revelations, dreams, visions, and aspirations, and get out of them a common revelation?

Why God should have chosen the Jew and not the Greek we cannot explain. Why Sinai was chosen, and prouder heights passed by, no man can tell. There is only One who can carry

forward the mystery into light. That One is our Father. I therefore
take my stand upon that Father's sovereignty. I know that the end
will be right. Theories and criticisms will come and go. Confidence and panic will alternate in the experience of the church, but
the truth advances by night and by day. We should determine to
see the good that is in each other. We do not want uniformity of
creed; we want individual conviction sanctified by universal love.
Men can surely meet on the ground of common service for Christ's
sake, and find in love the end of the commandment.

One might naturally resent being driven to Palestine to learn
who God is, and what He is, and what He wants. [One seems to]
enter into the sanctuary of revelation by some ill-kept postern gate,
rather than through the portals of a federal and representative
humanity. [But] I have no difficulty as to my reply. From beginning to end there is not in the Bible a shadow of suggestion that
the revelation was a message to the Jew alone. Infinitely beyond
all other sacred books I might argue that the Bible is pervaded and
penetrated by what I may call the spirit of universality. When it
begins there are no Jews; when it ends there are no Gentiles, for at
the end the whole earth is as a rose in the garden of God.

But I have a larger answer. I am already committed to the
Jews by an infinite obligation. From the Jews I have accepted the
Christ. "Salvation is of the Jews."[24] This acceptance determines
everything. I am not ashamed to receive the Writing where I
received the Life.

Such is my personal testimony. If one ungracious word has
escaped me I have done myself grievous injustice, for I love and
honor the brethren whose views I am least able to adopt. They
have taken their course and I have taken mine, and in all instances
the action has been taken under a solemn sense of responsibility to
the adorable Head of the church. He will judge us all, and in His
mercy He will save the weakest, and spare even the bruised reed
that He may breathe more music through it. Christ's men should
be stronger in love than in any other quality.

I am not able so to divide the Bible into human and divine,
natural and supernatural, as to impair in any degree its absolute
authority in doctrine and morals. To me it was not so much the
writer who was inspired as the *man*—Moses or Ezra, Isaiah or
Paul. The man's personality was a greater miracle than his inspiration. Consider when he wrote, what he wrote, and consider the
influence which still flows from his writings, and then—account
for him! Do not be so modern as to be a critic; be so ancient as to

be a contemporary, then—account for him! Do not get at this man through a grammar and a concordance, but through sympathy, assimilation, and spiritual kinship.

To understand the building you should commune with the architect. A word from him might fill his cathedral with light. In the Bible we have to deal with inspired manhood as certainly as with inspired literature, with character more than with ability, with holiness rather than with office. The grammarian, as such, will never understand the prophet. The lexicon will never explain the Bible. That Book of books—that poem which absorbs all poetry— can only be understood in one way, and that is by our daily walking and conscious fellowship with God the Holy Spirit.

NOTES

1. Cf. Ephesians 4:21.
2. John 20:28.
3. 2 Peter 1:21.
4. Cf. Genesis 28:17.
5. 2 Timothy 3:17.
6. 1 Corinthians 2:14.
7. Cf. Revelation 22:2.
8. Cf. John 20:17.
9. 1 Corinthians 15:28.
10. 1 Thessalonians 4:16.
11. Revelation 21:2.
12. Revelation 4:10.
13. Revelation 21:4.
14. Jeremiah 1:6, 7; Exodus 4:10.
15. Cf. Job, *passim.*
16. Acts 10:26.
17. 2 Peter 1:21.
18. Cf. Acts 3:12.
19. 2 Corinthians 3:5.
20. John 14:12.
21. Micah 6:8.
22. Job 32:8.
23. Nehemiah 11:35.
24. John 4:22.

Charles Grandison Finney

It takes an exceptional lawyer to make a good preacher of the gospel, and Charles Grandison Finney (1792-1875) was such a man. A master at the skills of his profession, he built a case for his Lord that seemed almost airtight. Further, he demanded a verdict from his hearers and often got it. The very brilliance of his arguments caused controversy to swirl about his head. Today the issues are largely forgotten, but the memory of the man's greatness remains.

Finney was a theological innovator. He declared that people had the means to bring about revival whenever they determined to pray, repent, and confess their sins. He invented the "anxious seat" for struggling seekers. A firm Bible believer, he did not hesitate to hide fleeing Negro slaves in the presidential attic at Oberlin College. He conducted revival services for his own theological students whose homiletics he considered faulty. And he split the Presbyterian Church by denouncing the Westminster Confession.

In 1835 Finney traveled by Erie Canal barge to Rochester, New York, and when he had concluded his meetings there, it was said that every lawyer in town had been converted to Christ. As a New School Calvinist, he opened fire on the question of predestination, contending that Christ died for everyone, and that the "elect" were actually free agents with the power to choose life or death. Yet the "elect" at the same time were destined to eternal life because God foreknew that in the perfect exercise of their freedom, they could be induced to repent and embrace the gospel.

For all his gifts, this unique man never attended college or seminary, and when an offer was made to send him to Princeton, he declined. Instead he taught himself Latin, Greek and Hebrew. He was admitted to the bar after some training in a law office. Following his conversion he was told by a client on one occasion that he was due in court to try the man's case. "I have a retainer from the Lord Jesus Christ to plead His cause," replied Finney, "and I cannot plead yours." When asked at a prayer meeting if he wanted prayer, he responded, "No, because I do not see that God answers your prayers. You have prayed enough to have prayed the Devil out of town, but here you are, praying on and complaining still."

Finney was born in Warren, Connecticut, to non-Christian parents, and was reared in Oneida County, New York. As a young man he attended Presbyterian services in the town of Adams, conducted by George W. Gale. He began to study the Bible, and in 1821 experienced a remarkable work of the Holy Spirit. After Presbyterian ordination in 1824, he began conducting revivals that led him through New York, Pennsylvania, Ohio, Massachusetts, Rhode Island and other states. Hundreds of thousands were brought to faith in Christ; similar results occurred later in England and Scotland. His autobiographical account of these meetings makes fascinating reading.

In 1835 Finney became professor of theology at Oberlin, a new college in Ohio, and from 1851 to 1866 served as president. Two years later, having completed his autobiography, he continued pastoring the local Congregational Church and lecturing at the seminary. It was said that "the quiet power of his life was felt as a benediction upon the community which, during forty years, he had done so much to guide and mold and bless." He completed his last course of lectures only a few days before his death in 1875.

This sermon, originally titled, "The Excuses of Sinners Condemn God," was preached at Oberlin sometime between 1845 and 1861, and was recorded in shorthand by Henry Cowles. It was published in a volume by Finney entitled Sermons on Gospel Themes *in 1876 by Fleming H. Revell Co., New York.*

NINE

THE WAY OF THE TRANSGRESSOR IS— AN EXCUSE
by *Charles Grandison Finney*

Every excuse for sin condemns God. This will be apparent if we consider that nothing can be sin for which there is a justifiable excuse. This is entirely self-evident. It needs neither elucidation nor proof. If [then] God condemns that for which there is a good excuse, He must be wrong. This also is self-evident. If God condemns what we have good reason for doing, no intelligence in the universe can justify Him.

But God does condemn all sin. He condemns it utterly, and will not allow the least apology or excuse for it. [So] either there is no apology for it, or God is wrong. Consequently every excuse for sin charges blame upon God, and virtually accuses Him of tyranny. Whoever pleads an excuse for sin, therefore, charges God with blame.

We will consider some of these excuses, and see whether the principles I have laid down are not just and true.

1. "Men cannot do what God requires." No excuse is more common. It is echoed and re-echoed over every Christian land with unblushing face. God, it is said, requires what men cannot do. And does He know that men are unable? Most certainly. Then the requisition is most unreasonable. Human reason can never justify it.

Upon what penalty does God require what man cannot do? The threatened penalty is eternal death! God requires of men, on pain of eternal death, to do that which He knows I cannot do. Truly this condemns God in the worst sense. You might as well charge God outright with being an infinite tyrant.

Perhaps, sinner, you little think when you urge the excuse of inability, that you are really arraigning God on the charge of infinite tyranny. And you, Christian, who make this dogma of inability a part of your "orthodox" creed, may have little noticed its blasphemous bearings against the character of God; but your failure to notice it alters not the fact.

I have intimated that this charge is blasphemous against God—and most truly. Far be it from God to do any such thing! Shall God require natural impossibilities, and denounce eternal death upon men for not doing what they have no natural power to do? Never! Yet good men and bad men agree together to charge God with doing this very thing, not once or twice only, but uniformly, through all ages, with all the race, from the beginning to the end of time! Horrible! Nothing in all the government of God ever so insulted and abused Jehovah! Nothing was ever more blasphemous and false!

You declare that His commands are not only grievous, but are even naturally impossible. Hark! What does the Lord Jesus say? "My yoke is easy and My burden is light."[1] And do you deny this? Do you say, "Lord, Your yoke is so hard that no man can possibly endure it"?

2. A second excuse is *want of time.*

Suppose I tell one of my sons, "Go, do this or that duty, on pain of being whipped to death."

He replies, "Father, I can't possibly do it, for I have not time. I must be doing that other business which you told me to do; and besides, if I had nothing else to do, I could not possibly do this new business in the time you allow." Now if this statement be true, and I knew it when I gave him the command, then I am a tyrant.

So if God really requires of you what you have not time to do, He is infinitely to blame. For He surely knows how little time you have. What? Is God so reckless of justice, so regardless of the well-being of His creatures, that He can sport with red-hot thunder-bolts? *Never!* NEVER! This is not true; it is only the false assumption the sinner makes when he pleads as his excuse that he has not time to do what God demands of him.

Let me ask you, sinner, how much time will it take you to do the first great duty which God requires—namely, *give Him your heart?* How long will this take? How long need you be in making up your mind to serve and love God? Do you not know that this, when done, will be done in one moment of time? And how long need you be in persuading yourself to do it?

Your meaning may be this: "Lord, it takes me so long to

make up my mind to serve You, it seems as if I never should get time enough for this." Is this your meaning? Let us look on all sides of the subject. Suppose I said to my son, "Do this now, my son," and he replied, "I can't, father, for I must do that other thing you told me to do."

Does God do so? No. God only requires the duty of each moment in its time. That is all. He only asks us to use faithfully all the power He has given us—nothing more. He only requires that we do the best we can. When He prescribes the amount of love which will please Him, He does not say, "Thou shalt love the Lord thy God with the powers of an angel." No, but only "with all thy heart."[2] This is all. Thou shalt do the best that thou art able to do, says God to the sinner. Ah, says the sinner, I am not able to do that. Oh, what stupid nonsense!

God asks only that we should use each moment for Him, in labor or in rest, whichever is most for His glory. Oh, but you say, I cannot be religious, for I must be up in the morning and get my breakfast. And how much longer will it take you to get your breakfast ready to please God, than to do the same to please yourself? The farmer pleads, "I can't be religious; I can't serve God—I must sow my wheat." Well, sow your wheat, but do it *for the Lord.* Oh, but you have so much to do! Then do it all for the Lord. Get your lesson, but get it for the Lord.

3. Men plead *a sinful nature* for their excuse. What is this sinful nature? Do you mean by it that every faculty and even the very essence of your constitution were poisoned and made sinful in Adam, and came down in this polluted state by inheritance to you? Do you mean that you were so born in sin that the substance of your being is all saturated with it, and so that all the faculties of your constitution are themselves sin? Do you believe this?

I admit if this were true, it would make out a hard case. Until the laws of my reason are changed, it would compel me to speak out openly and say, "Lord, this is a hard case, that You should make my nature itself a sinner, and then charge the guilt of its sin upon me!" But the dogma is an utter absurdity. For, pray, what is sin? God answers, "transgression of law."[3] And now you hold that your nature is itself a breach of the law of God; that it has always been, from Adam to the day of your birth. Was man his own creator? Do you believe any such thing? No; you ascribe your nature and its original faculties to God, and upon Him, therefore, you charge the guilty authorship of your "sinful nature."

But how strange a thing is this! The fact is, sin can never

consist in having a nature, nor in what nature is; but only and alone in the bad use which we make of our nature. That is all. Our Maker will never find fault with us for what He has Himself done or made. He will not condemn us, if we will only make a right use of our powers—of our intellect, our sensibility, and our will. Think what mischief [this monstrous dogma] has wrought. Think how it has scandalized the law, the government, and the character of God. Think how it has filled the mouths of sinners with excuses from the day of its birth to this hour!

4. Sinners in self-excuse say they are *willing to be Christians*. They are willing, they say, to be sanctified. Oh yes, they are very willing; but there is some great difficulty lying further back— perhaps they do not know just where—but it is somewhere, and it will not let them become Christians.

Now the fact is, if we are really willing, there is nothing more we can do. Willing is all we have to do morally. But the plea as in the sinner's mouth maintains that God requires of us what is naturally impossible. It assumes that God requires of us something more than right willing; and this is of course to us an impossibility. If I will to move my muscles, and no motion follows, I have done all I can do. There is a difficulty beyond my reach, and I am in no blame. Just so, if I were to will to serve God, and absolutely no effect should follow, I have done my utmost, and God never can demand anything more.

Do tell me, parent, if you had told your child to do anything, and you saw him exerting himself to the utmost, would you ask anything more? This plea is utterly false, for no sinner is willing to be any better than he actually is. If the will is right, all is right; and universally the state of the will is the measure of one's moral character. To will is the very thing which God does require. Those men, therefore, who plead that they are willing to be Christians while yet they remain in their sins, talk mere nonsense.

5. Sinners say *they are waiting God's time*. A lady in Philadelphia had been in great distress of mind for many years. On calling to see her, I asked, "What does God require of you?"

"Oh," she said, "God waited on me a long time before I began to seek Him at all, and now I must wait for Him as long as He did for me. So my minister tells me."

Now what is the real meaning of this? God urges me to duty, but is not ready for me to do it. He tells me to come to the gospel feast, and I am ready; but He is not ready to let me in. Does not this throw all the blame upon God? The sinner says, "I am ready, and willing, and waiting; but God is not yet ready for me to stop sinning."

When I first began to preach I found this notion almost universal. Often after pressing men to duty I have been accosted: "What, you throw all the blame upon the sinner!"

"Yes, indeed I do," would be my reply.

An old lady once met me after preaching and broke out, "What! You set men to getting religion themselves! You tell them to repent themselves! You don't mean so, do you?"

"Indeed I do," said I. She had been teaching for many years that the sinner's chief duty is to await God's time.

6. Sinners plead in excuse that *their circumstances are very peculiar.* And does not God understand your circumstances? Has not His Providence been concerned in making them what they are? If so, then you are throwing blame upon God. You say, "O Lord, You are a hard Master, for You have never made any allowance for my circumstances."

But do you mean that your circumstances are so peculiar that God ought to excuse you, at least for the present? If you do not mean this, why do you make your circumstances your excuse at all? If you do mean this, then you are mistaken. For God requires you, despite your circumstances, to abandon your sin. If, now, your circumstances are so peculiar that you cannot serve God in them, you must abandon them or lose your soul. If they are such as admit of your serving God in them, then do so at once.

But you say, "I can't get out of my circumstances."

I reply, "You can. You can get out of the wickedness of them. For if it is necessary in order to serve God, you can change them; and if not, you can repent and serve God in them."

7. The sinner's next excuse is that *his temperament is peculiar.* "I am very nervous," he says, or, "My temperament is very sluggish." Now, what does God require? Does He require of you another or a different sensibility from your own? Or does He require only that you should use what you have according to the law of love?

A woman came to me and pleaded that she was naturally too excitable, and dared not trust herself, and therefore she could not repent. Another person had the opposite trouble—too sluggish, scarce ever sheds a tear. But does God require you to shed more tears than you are naturally able to shed? Or does He only require that you should serve Him? Certainly this is all. Serve Him with the very powers He has given you. Let your nerves be ever so excitable, come and lay those quivering sensibilities in the hands of God. I know how to sympathize with that woman, for I know much about a burning sensibility; but does God require feeling and excitement? Or à consecration of all our powers to Himself?

8. But, says another, *"my health is so poor* that I can't go to meeting." Again, what does God require? That you should go to all the meetings, by evening or by day, whether you have the requisite health for it or not?

Infinitely far from it. If you are not able to go to meeting, yet you can give God your heart. If you cannot go in bad weather, be assured that God is infinitely the most reasonable being that ever existed. He makes all due allowance for every circumstance. Does He not know all your weakness? Indeed He does. And do you suppose that He comes into your sickroom and denounces you for not being able to go to meeting? No, not He; but He comes into your sickroom as a Father.

He comes to pour out the deepest compassions of His heart in pity and in love. He comes to you and says, "Give Me your heart, My child."

And now you reply, "I have no heart." Then He has nothing to ask of you; He thought you had. He thought, too, that He had done enough to draw your heart in love and gratitude to Himself.

9. Another excuse is in this form: *"My heart is so hard that I cannot feel."* In reality it is only another form of the plea of inability. In fact, all the sinner's excuses amount only to this: "I am unable. I can't do what God requires." If the plea of a hard heart is any excuse at all, it must be on the ground of real inability.

But what *is* hardness of heart? Do you mean that you have so great apathy that you cannot get up any emotion? Or do you mean that you have no power to will or to act right? On this point it should be considered that the emotions are involuntary; they go and come according to circumstances. They are not, properly speaking, either religion itself or any part of it. God asks you to yield your will and consecrate your affections to Himself, and He asks this whether you have any feeling or not.

Real hardness of heart, in the Bible use of the phrase, means stubbornness of will. The sinner cleaves to his self-indulgence, and will not relinquish it, and then complains of hardness of heart. This complaint is extremely common: "My will is so set to have my own way that I cannot possibly yield." Many a sinner makes it who has been often warned, often prayed with and wept over, and has been the subject of many convictions. And does he really mean by this plea that he finds his will so obstinate that he cannot make up his mind to yield to God's claims? Does he mean this, and does he really intend to publish his own shame?

Suppose you go to the devils in Hell and press on them the claims of God, and they should reply, "O, my heart is so hard, I can't." What would be their meaning? Only this: I am so obstinate. My will is so set in sin that I cannot for a moment indulge the thought of repentance. This would be their meaning, and if the sinner tells the truth of himself, and uses language correctly, he must mean the same.

Suppose a murderer arraigned before the court, and permitted before his sentence to speak, should rise and say, "May it please the court, my heart for a long time has been as hard as a millstone. I can kill a man without the least compunction of conscience. Indeed, I have such an insatiable thirst for blood that I cannot help murdering whenever I have a good opportunity. My heart is so hard that I find I like this employment as well as any other."

How long will the court listen to such a plea? "Hold there! Hold," the judge would cry, "you infamous villain, we can hear no more such pleas. Sheriff, bring in a gallows, and hang the man within these very walls of justice, for I will not leave the bench until I see him dead! He will murder us all here in this house if he can!"

Now, what shall we think of the sinner who says the same thing? "Oh, God," he says, "my heart is so hard I can never love You. I hate You so sincerely I can never make up my mind to yield this heart to You in love and willing submission." How many of you in this house have made this plea: "My heart is so hard, I can't repent; I can't love and serve God"?

Go, write it down; publish it to the universe. Make your boast of being so hardhearted that no claims of God can ever move you. You would not be half through before the whole universe would hiss you from their presence and chase you from the face of these heavens. The voice of indignation would rise up and ring along the arch of Heaven like the roar of ten thousand tornadoes, and whelm you with unutterable confusion and shame! When the sympathy of your Christian friends has pressed you with entreaties to repent, and they have made you a special subject of their prayers; when angels have wept over you, you turn up your face of brass toward Jehovah and tell Him your heart is so hard you can't repent, and don't care whether you ever do or not! You seize a spear and plunge it into the heart of the crucified One, and then cry out, "I can't be sorry, not I; my heart is hard as a stone!"

10. Another form of the same plea is, *"My heart is so wicked I can't."* Since you bring this forward as your excuse, your object must be to charge this wickedness of heart upon God. Covertly, perhaps, but really, you imply that God is concerned in creating that wicked heart. You would feel no interest in your excuse, and it would never escape your lips but for this tacit implication that God is in fault for your wicked heart.

11. Another kindred plea is, *"My heart is so deceitful."* Suppose a man should make this excuse for deceiving his neighbor: "I can't help cheating you. I can't help lying to you and abusing you; my heart is so deceitful!" Would any man in his senses ever suppose that this could be an apology or excuse for doing wrong? Never. Of course, unless the sinner means in this plea to set forth his own guilt and condemn himself, he must intend it as some sort of justification; and if so, he must cast the blame upon God. And this is usually his intention. He does not mean sincerely to confess his own guilt. No, he charges the guilt of his deceitful heart upon God.

12. Another person excuses himself by the plea, *"I have tried to become a Christian."* I have done all I can do; I have tried often, earnestly, and long.

You have tried, then, you say, to be a Christian. What is being a Christian? Giving your heart to God. And what is giving your heart to God? Devoting your voluntary powers to Him; ceasing to live for yourself and living for God. This is being a Christian—the state you profess to have been trying to attain.

No excuse is more common than this. And what is legitimately implied in this trying to be a Christian? A willingness to do your duty is always implied: that the heart (that is, the will) is right already; and the trying refers only to the outward efforts—the executive acts. For there is no sense whatever in a man's saying that he is trying to do what he has no intention or will to do. The very statement implies that his will is not only in favor, but is thoroughly committed and really in earnest to attain the end chosen.

Consequently, if a man tries to be a Christian his heart is obedient to God, and his trying must respect his outward action. These are so connected with the will that they follow by a law of necessity unless the connection is broken. Thus the sinner ought to mean by this plea, "I have obeyed God a long time, I have had a right heart." That is, he has tried sincerely to secure such external action as comports with Christian character. Now, if this be true, you have done your duty. But do you mean to affirm all this? No, you say.

Then what do you mean?

Suppose I should say to my son, "Do this, my son. Why have you not done it?"

"Oh," he says, "Father, I have tried." But he does not mean that he ever intended to do it. He only means, "I have been willing to try. I made up my mind to try to be willing"—that is all.

So you say, "I have tried to get religion." And what *is* religion that you could not get it? How did you fail? Probably you have been trying in this way. God has said, "Give Me your heart," and you turned round and asked God to do it Himself; or perhaps you simply waited for Him to do it. He commanded you to repent, and you have tried to get Him to repent for you. He said, "Believe the gospel," and you have only been thinking of getting Him to believe for you. No wonder you have tried for a long time in vain. How could it be otherwise? You have not been trying to do what God commanded you to do, but to induce God to change His system of moral government and put Himself in your place to do Himself the duty He enjoins upon you. What a miserable perversion is this.

As to this whole plea of having tried to be a Christian, what is the use of it? You will easily see its use when you realize that it is utterly false when understood as you intend it, [and] that it is a foul implication of the character of God. You say, "Lord, I know I can't. I have tried all I can, and I know I cannot become a Christian. I am willing, but I cannot make it out."

Who, then, is to blame? Not yourself, according to your statement of your case. Where, then, is the blame? Let me ask: what would be said in the distant regions of the universe if you were believed there, when you say, "I have tried with all my heart to love and serve God, but I can't"? They never can believe such a libel on their own infinite Father!

13. Another excuses himself by the plea, *"it will do no good to try."* And what do you mean by this? Do you mean that God will not pay well for services done Him? Or do you mean that He will not forgive you if you do repent? Do you think, as some do, that you have sinned away your day of grace?

[A man] dreamed that he was just going to Hell, and as he

was parting with his brother, [who was] going, as his dream had it, to Heaven, he said, "I am going down to Hell, but I want you to tell God for me that I am greatly obliged to Him for ten thousand mercies which I never deserved. He has never done me the least injustice. Give Him my thanks for all the unmerited good He has done me." At this point he awoke and found himself bathed in tears of repentance and gratitude to his Father in Heaven.

Oh, if men would only act as reasonably as that man dreamed, it would be noble—it would be *right*. If when they suppose themselves to have sinned away the day of grace, they would say, "I know God is good. He has done me no injustice. I will at least send Him my thanks." Sinner, will you do this?

14. Another, closely pressed, says, *"I have offered to give my heart to Christ, but He won't receive me. I have no evidence that He receives me or ever will."* In the last inquiry meeting[4] a young woman told me she had offered to give her heart to the Lord, but He would not receive her. This was charging the lie directly upon Christ, for He has said, "Him that cometh to Me I will in no wise cast out."[5] You say, "I came and offered myself and He would not receive me." Jesus Christ says, "Behold, I stand at the door and knock, if *any* man"—not "if some particular, some favored one"—but "if *any* man hear My voice and open the door, I will come in to him."[6]

And yet when you offered Him your heart, did He spurn you away? Did He say, "Away, sinner, BEGONE?" No, He never did, never. He has said He would never do it. "He that seeketh, findeth; to him that knocketh it shall be opened."[7] But you say, "I have sought and did not find." Do you mean to make out that Jesus Christ is a liar? Do you make your solemn affirmation, "Lord, I laid myself at Your gate and knocked, but all in vain"? And do you mean to bring this excuse of yours as a solemn charge of falsehood against Jesus Christ and against God?

15. But another says, *"There is no salvation for me."* Do you mean that Christ has made no atonement for you? But [the New Testament] says He tasted death for every man. It is declared that God so loved the world that He gave His only begotten Son, that whosoever believeth in Him shall have eternal life.[8] And now do you affirm that there is no salvation provided and possible for you? Are you mourning all your way down to Hell because you cannot possibly have salvation? When the cup of salvation is placed to your lips, do you dash it away, saying, "That cannot be done for

me"? And do you *know* this? Can you prove it even against the word of God Himself?

Stand forth, if there be such a sinner on this footstool of God.[9] Speak it out, if you have such a charge against God, and if you can prove it true. Ah, is there no hope? None at all? The difficulty is not that there is no salvation provided for and offered to you, but that there is no heart for it.

16. But perhaps you say in excuse, *"I cannot change my own heart."* Suppose Adam had made this excuse when God called him to repent after his first sin. "Indeed," responds his Maker, "how long is it since you changed your heart yourself?" You changed it a few hours ago from holiness to sin, and will you tell your Creator that you can't change it from sin to holiness?

The change of heart is a voluntary thing. You must do it for yourself or it is never done. True, there is a sense in which God changes the heart, but it is only this: God influences the sinner to change, and then the sinner does it. The change is the sinner's own voluntary act.

17. You say again, *you can't change your heart without more conviction.* Do you mean by this that you have not enough knowledge of your duty and your sin? You cannot say this. You do know your sin and your duty. You know you ought to consecrate yourself to God. Well, then, what do you mean? Can't you do that which you know you ought to do? Ah, there is the old lie—that shameless refuge of lies—that same foul dogma of *inability.* What is implied in this new form of it? That God is not willing to convict you enough to make it possible for you to repent. He will not do His work, and you, alas, have no alternative but to go down to Hell. All because God will not do His part toward your salvation. Do you really believe that?

18. Again, you say in excuse, that *you must first have more of the Spirit.* And yet you resist the Spirit every day. God offers you His Spirit; [more than that,] He bestows His Spirit, but you resist it. What, then, do you mean when you pretend to want more of the Spirit's influence? The truth is, you do not want it. You only want to make it appear that God does not do His part to help you repent, and that as you can't repent without His help, therefore the blame of your impenitence rests on God. It is only another form of the old slander: He has made me unable and won't help me out of my inability.

19. The sinner also excuses himself by saying, *"God must*

change my heart." But in the sense that God requires you to do it, He cannot do it Himself. God is said to change the heart only in the sense of persuading you to do it.

This excuse implies that there is something more for God to do before the sinner can become [devout]. I have heard many professors of religion take this ground. Yes, thousands of Christian ministers have said to the sinner, "Wait for God. He will change your heart in His own good time. You can't do it yourself, and all that you can do is put yourself in the way for the Lord to change your heart. When this time comes, He will give you a new heart— perhaps while you are asleep. God acts in this matter as a sovereign, and does His own work in His own way."

So they teach, filling the mouth of the sinner with excuses and making his heart like an adamant against the real claims of God upon his conscience.

20. The sinner pleads, again, *"I can't live a Christian life if I were to become a Christian. It is unreasonable for me to expect where I see so many fail."* I recollect the case of a man who said, "It is of no use for me to repent and be a Christian, for it is altogether irrational for me to expect to do better than others have done before me." Sinners who make this excuse come forward very modestly and tell God, "I am very humble. You see, Lord, that I have a very low opinion of myself. I am so zealous of Your honor, and so afraid that I shall bring disgrace upon Your cause! It does not seem at all best for me to think of becoming a Christian, I have such a horror of dishonoring Your Name."

Yes, and what then? "Therefore I will sin on and trample the blessed gospel under my feet. I will persecute You, O my God, and make war on Your cause, for it is better by far not to profess than to profess and then disgrace my profession." What logic! A fair specimen of the absurdity of the sinner's excuses. This excuse assumes that there is not enough grace provided and offered to sustain the soul in a Christian life. Away with such teaching to the nether pit whence it came!

Is God so weak that He can't hold up the soul that casts itself on Him? Or is He so parsimonious in bestowing His gracious aid that it must be expected always to fall short of meeting the wants of His dependent and depending child? So you seem to suppose. So hard to persuade the Lord to give you a particle of grace? Can't get grace enough to live a Christian life with honor? What is this but charging God with withholding sufficient grace?

But what say the Word and the oath of Jehovah? "Because

God wanted to make the unchanging nature of His purpose very clear to the heirs of what was promised, He confirmed it with an oath. God did this so that, by two unchangeable things in which it is impossible for God to lie, we who have fled to take hold of the hope offered to us may be greatly encouraged."[10] You say, however, "If I should flee and lay hold of this hope, I should fail for want of grace. The oath of the unchanging God can never suffice for me." So you belie the Word of God, and make up a miserably slim and guilty apology for your impenitence.

21. Another excuse claims that *"this is a very dark, mysterious subject. This matter of faith and regeneration—I can't understand it."* Did you ever meet the Lord with this objection, and say, "Lord, You have required me to do things which I can't understand"? You know that you can understand well enough that you are a sinner—that Christ died for you—that you must believe on Him and break off your sins by repentance. All this is so plain that "the wayfaring man though a fool, need not err therein."[11] Your plea therefore is as false as it is foul. It is nothing better than a base libel on God.

22. But you say, *"I can't believe."* You mean, do you, that you can't believe a God of infinite veracity as you can believe a fellow-man? Would you imply that God asks you to believe things that are really incredible? But you urge again that you *can't realize these things.* You can't realize that the Bible is true; that God does offer to forgive; that salvation is actually provided and placed within your reach. What help can there be for such a case? What can make these truths more certain? But on your own showing, you do not want more evidence. Why not, then, act upon the known truth?

But you also plead that *you can't repent.* You can't be sorry you have abused God. You can't make up your mind now to break off from all sin. If this be really so, then you cannot make up your mind to obey God, and you might as well make up your mind to go to Hell. But at any rate *you can't become a Christian now.* You mean to be converted sometime, but you can't make up your mind to do so now. Well, God requires it now, and of course you must yield or abide the consequences. But you say that you can't now. Then God is very much to blame in asking for it! If however the truth be that you *can,* then the lie is on your side.

No sinner under the light of the gospel lives a single hour in sin without some excuse, either tacit or avowed, by which he justifies himself. It seems to be a law of man's intelligent nature that when accused of wrong, either by his conscience or any other agent, he must either confess or justify. The latter is the course taken. It is so hard to abandon all excuses and admit the humbling truth that [sinners] themselves are all wrong and God all right. Thus it becomes the great business of a gospel minister to search out and expose the sinner's excuses; to demolish if possible his refuge of lies, and lay open his heart to the shafts of truth.

I can recollect very well the year I lived on excuses, and how long it was before I gave them up. I had never heard a minister preach on the subject. I found however by my experience that my excuses and lies were the obstacles in the way of my conversion. As soon as I let these go utterly, I found the gate of mercy wide open. And so would you.

Now, what use do you calculate to make of this sermon? Are you ready to say, "I will henceforth desist from all my excuses, now and forever, and God shall have my whole heart"? What do you say? Will you set about to hunt up some new excuse? Do you say, "Let me go home first. Don't press me to yield to God here on the spot. Let me go home and then I will"—do you say this? And are you aware how tender is this moment, how critical this passing hour?

Remember, it is not I who press this claim upon you, it is God. God Himself commands you to repent today, *this hour.* You know your duty. You know what it is to give God your heart. And now I come to the final question: *Will you do it?* Will you abandon all your excuses and fall, a self-condemned sinner, before a God of love, and yield to Him yourself, your heart and your whole being, henceforth and forever? Will you come?

NOTES

1. Matthew 11:30.
2. Deuteronomy 6:5.
3. Cf. 1 John 3:4.
4. What evangelical churches today call "counseling rooms" or "prayer rooms" were sometimes called "inquiry rooms" by nineteenth-century evangelists. People were invited into such a room at the close of an evangelistic service.
5. John 6:37.
6. Revelation 3:20.
7. Matthew 7:7.
8. John 3:16.
9. Isaiah 66:1; Acts 7:49.
10. Hebrews 6:18.
11. Isaiah 35:8.

Dora Greenwell

There must have been thousands like her in Victorian England: quiet, devout, frail maiden ladies living out their seemingly uneventful lives in big houses and then fading into obscurity. They were remembered by the next generation as Aunt Lettie or Aunt Sophy, if they were remembered at all. But Dora Greenwell (1821-1882), much as she may have seemed like other spinsters, was different. She could think deeply and write beautifully. In fact, bishops of the Church of England read her essays for their own spiritual growth. Her volume of poems, Carmina Crucis, *which she labeled "roadside songs," proved highly popular. Her best-known lines are found even today in hymnbooks. One stanza reads:*

> *And was there then no other way*
> *For God to take?—I cannot say;*
> *I only bless Him, day by day,*
> *Who saved me through my Savior.*

The account of Dora Greenwell in the British Dictionary of National Biography *betrays the gentle restraint of someone who had "personal knowledge" of her. Dora was born at Greenwell Ford in the English county of Durham. Her father was an "active country gentleman" who "became embarrassed" (that is, he lost his fortune through some mishap) and in 1847 sold his home to pay his debts. We hear no more of him, but concerning Dora we learn that for the next eighteen years she lived with her mother somewhere in Durham, and that her "very poor health served to deepen her religious views."*

We are told nothing of her education, but she was obviously quite literate, as the following pages indicate. Her books are filled with erudite footnotes that discuss even the profoundest theological issues with an ease born of a thoroughgoing knowledge of the subjects. Her impeccable orthodoxy reflects Anglicanism at its finest.

She wrote admiringly about the reform-minded French Catholic priest Jean Baptiste Lacordaire, whose sermons at Paris' Notre Dame Cathedral were, according to the Britannica, *"the delight of the city." She also wrote a memoir of the American Quaker John Woolman, who sailed to England to urge the abolition of that country's lucrative African slave trade. He contracted smallpox and died during his tour (see the second volume of the Christian Heritage Classics,* Spiritual Awakening, *Crossway, 1986.)*

While she continued to publish poetry (Songs of Salvation, Stories That Might Be True, The Soul's Legend *and* Camera Obscura), *Dora also began during her thirties to write prose. A* Present Heaven *was issued in 1855 and was followed by* The Patience of Hope *and* Two Friends. *In 1866 her volume of* Essays *appeared, a compilation of pieces that had appeared in British periodicals. One of the essays, "Our Single Women," was a pioneering effort to emancipate women from the thraldom of limited educational opportunities. While its tone was neither strident nor radical, it constituted an earnest plea for a change in the British education system. To keep Aunt Sophy and Aunt Lettie (the names are mine, not hers) housebound and ignorant was, to Dora Greenwell, to waste a valuable national resource of talent.*

The poet John Greenleaf Whittier wrote of Miss Greenwell's work, "It assumes the life and power of the gospel as a matter of actual experience. Christianity is not simply historical and traditional, but present and permanent, the eternal spring and growth of divine love." An accident in 1881 impaired Miss Greenwell's delicate constitution, and she died a year later.

The following excerpt, originally titled "Prayer Considered in Its Relation to the Will of Man, and in Its Dependence on the Sacrifice of Christ's Death," is taken from her Essays, *published in 1866 by Alexander Strahan, London and New York.*

THE KEY TO PRAYER
by Dora Greenwell

Christianity is a living whole. It is a system transcending the world system with which it is now connected. It is a supernatural system based upon a series of supernatural transactions. It is a solemn, world-appealing, world-accusing fact—a fact existing with many other facts, with which it seems in apparent disagreement. It is a Kingdom, as was emphatically declared by its Great Founder, "not of this world."

It is simply idle, therefore, in considering any of the great laws of this Kingdom, to speak of the doctrines of expiation, sacrifice, and the like as "mystical enthusiasm, a dithyrambic mode of expression"—as idle as it would be in a person wholly ignorant of the great laws of the natural kingdom in discussing light or heat to set down electricity as "a mystical theory." Let us at least learn something about this great Kingdom. Let us make ourselves familiar with its genius, its laws, its administration, and then to talk nonsense about it will at least be a conscious and responsible act.

An unbeliever is, in a simple and literal sense, a man of this world. He lives and is guided by the natural order, by what he sees, as well as for what he sees. The believer, or Christian, moves also among facts, but facts of a supernatural order. He also lives by what he sees, but faith has enlarged his range of vision, and brought within its ken a world of spiritual realities, with laws by which his actual life is explained and guided.

All things in Christianity hold by its great central truth, redemption. Each doctrine, each rite of the Christian church, each instinct of the Christian heart leads, if tracked home, to that meritorious sacrifice which burst the gates of death for our ran-somed race, and made a highway of peace and reconciliation between the redeemed spirit and its God.

We know not the nature and degree of intercourse that Adam

originally enjoyed with his Maker. It was probably close and intimate to a degree which we cannot now realize even in thought. It
might be natural to him to talk to God simply, confidingly, as a
child talks to its parent; but since the entrance of sin into humanity
there has been a wall of separation between man and God. They
have stood farther off each other, and it seems evident that since
the Fall there has been no true approach to God, no living communion with Him, in fact, no prayer without sacrifice. Sacrifice
makes prayer possible; it opens the way to God.

Even the altar of incense, that great type of the prayers of the
Christian church, on which no bleeding sacrifice was offered, but
only incense, representing the prayers of the congregation, was
itself sprinkled by the priest with the blood of atonement.

Then came Christianity, a better covenant, established on
better promises and on better sacrifices.[1] The way into its holiest
places, its deepest spiritual communions, was obtained through
the might of that one perfect, all-sufficient sacrifice through
which it still lives, and moves, and breathes, and prays.

Even the most false religions, so long as they retain the idea
of sacrifice, always retain along with that idea the instinct of
prayer. In this respect paganism is a deeper thing than so-called
natural religion, and contains within it seeds of which pure Deism
knows nothing, doubtless derived from primeval knowledge of the
true God. Mohammedanism is, on the other hand, a creed without
sacrifice, without mystery, and (so far as I am informed on this
point) without prayer. Its deep-rooted fatalism leaves no room for
the pleading human voice of supplication; its only language is that
of acquiescence in that "inexorable will which it calls god."[2] Deism also adores and acquiesces, it does not pray. "I accustom my
mind," says Rousseau,[3] "to sublime contemplations. I meditate
upon the order of the universe, not for the sake of reducing it to
vain systems, but to admire it unceasingly, to adore the wise Creator who makes Himself felt within it. I converse with the Author
of the universe; I imbue all my faculties with His divine essence.
My heart melts over His benefits. I bless Him for all His gifts, but
I do not pray to Him. What have I to ask Him for?"

We might say, what is there so simple as prayer? What so
natural as to seek the help and favor of One who is confessed to be
the cause and ruler of all things? Yet it may be doubted whether
the natural man ever prays. It may be doubted whether any heart
save that which is renewed by the Holy Spirit ever lifts up to God
that fervent, inwrought prayer which avails much. The sense of

fixity and order is so deep within the human spirit that a secret distrust of prayer seems native to it, and it appears idle to expect that God, whose goings are from everlasting, will break His appointed order at a request from mortal lips.

So strong is the sense of this fixity, that there seems but one other thing strong enough to break it—the voice of a risen Savior, which, when the spiritually dead hear, they come alive and pray. The realm of nature, however fair and fruitful, is but the house of bondage; and until man's spirit hears the voice that calls him out of it, baptizing him in the cloud and in the sea, he is unable to break through the network of the subtle spells and sorceries she weaves around him.

He is a captive to the strength of her continued miracle, her procession of days and nights, of summer and winter, of youth and age. The exhibition of God's power lays such hold upon him, that the sense of the Divine as *power* only grows upon the mind (as it does in every form of paganism) till it leaves no room for any action of the human will. [It does, that is,] until it is met by the other great, ever-enduring miracle of God's love, as it is manifested in Him who lived and died and rose again for man; in Him who for man and as man ever lives, the everlasting Witness, who bears record in Heaven, as he bore it on earth, to God's sympathy with His creature. Nature is God's going forth, terrible in splendor and majesty; grace is His coming forth in pity and in love—the Father coming forth to meet His erring son.

Nature shows us no Father. "Nature," says George Jacob Holyoake [English social reformer] who acknowledges no other God, "acts with fearful uniformity. Stern as fate, absolute as tyranny, merciless as death, too vast to praise, too inexorable to propitiate, it has no ear for prayer, no heart for sympathy, no arm to save." [But] he who has seen Christ has seen a greater sight than that of "suns on suns that rise and set/from creation to decay." He has seen God sympathizing with and aiding man. He has come to a break in nature's adamantine chain. He has passed from a world of fixity into a world of life. "If you believe in the Son, the Son shall make you free."[4] The sight of the cross, God's mighty interference for man, is the death-blow to fatalism, which but for it reigns over all the sons of Adam.

It is the sight of the cross, and of all the tremendous associations that are bound up with it—the sense of guilt, of condemnation, of deliverance, of infinite loss, and everlasting gain—that brings, that binds the soul to prayer. It is this sight that makes of every awakened soul a priest, an intercessor, no longer trusting in his own repentance, his own faith, his own prayer, but joining his every petition to the might of that prevailing blood which is "itself the most powerful of all intercessions."[5]

To talk to nominal believers on the subject of prayer is generally to find that they have little confidence in prayer as a power. Do they believe that prayer effects, alters anything? No, for nominal Christianity is but a refined naturalism. It wears the cross as an ornament, but never presses it to its heart. It [the cross] is to it a thing extrinsic, adventitious, out of harmony with all that it really believes. Nominal Christianity contains within it no deep-seated sense of sin, of need, or of dependence. How then can it lay its grasp upon the great truths of sacrifice, expiation, and mediation?

The Christian's prayer is a supernatural intercourse founded upon a supernatural work. It is built upon Christ's express command, and linked forever with His explicit promise, "Ask in My Name and you will receive." It is based upon faith in his meritorious work, and it is vain to come before God without the sacrifice of a free heart, the offering up of the human will, prized by Him long after He has ceased to delight in burnt-offerings and material sacrifices for sin.

So close and evident is the union between prayer accepted and answered by God, and the sacrifice of the human will, that it has led me to meditate upon the meaning of those lives on which God has laid so heavy a burden of pain and repression, lives so filled up by endurance, that there is little room left in them for self-denial or sacrifice. A life filled with pain is perhaps meant by God to be a life filled with prayer. However blank and unintelligible it may be to men, its Godward aspect may be full of meaning. Stripped of leaf and blossom, it may stand bare like a cross, appealing and interceding. Pain is as deep a mystery as sin, and like that mystery, grows more obscure and perplexing for being closely tracked. When we have allowed that pain is remedial and purifying, we feel we have not exhausted its meaning. Even in that which is simply physical and inarticulate, [there is] a power which in the extent of its working can be but dimly guessed at.

Prayer is the voice of one who was created free, although he was born in chains. It is at once self-assertion and self-surrender. It claims a will even in surrendering it when it says, "Not my will, but Thine, be done."[6] Nothing so dignifies human nature as does prayer. When God gave man reason, says Milton [in the *Areopagitica*], He gave him freedom to choose, for freedom is but choosing.

Prayer is God's acknowledgment, His endorsement of His own gift of freedom to man. It is His royal invitation to man to exert this privilege, to use this power. Prayer is spirit acting upon Spirit. It is the will of man brought to bear upon the will of God, but it must be believing to be effectual.

Now, in any natural action, say that of sowing a seed, the mental attitude of the sower signifies nothing. The seed will come up whether he expects it to or not. But in any act between two conscious intelligent beings, the mental attitude is obviously everything. Thus the measure of faith is the measure of prayer. In a literal sense, faith gives the soul a claim and hold upon God.

It is in life acting upon life that renewal unto God consists. The Spirit of God, in acting upon the human spirit, acts upon that which can attract, which can invite, which can *resist* Him. He acts upon a living agent which, having once received an impulse, needs not to be dragged or propelled. It [the soul] can say, "Draw me, and I will run after Thee."[7] "I will run in the way of Thy commandments, when Thou shalt enlarge my heart."[8] Work, says the apostle, because God is working in you to will and to do.[9] Pray, says the believer, because the Holy Spirit Himself is praying in your prayers.

We know that God's nature is unchangeable; are we sure that His will is equally so? Is the wish, the submitted wish of a human heart, able to alter the counsel of the Almighty? Can the humble request of believing lips restrain, accelerate, change the settled order of events? Can prayer make things that are not to be as though they were? Are events, in short, brought about through prayer that would not otherwise take place? *Yes, a thousand times yes!*

To believe anything short of this is to take the soul out of every [Bible] text that refers to prayer. It is to do away [with] the force of every Scriptural illustration that bears upon it. To believe anything short of this is to believe that God has placed a mighty engine in the hands of His creature, but one that will not work; useful only as a scientific toy might be, that helps to bring out a child's faculties, and valuable only as a means of training the soul to commune with God.

Yet what is so easy for the unbeliever as to cavil at prayer? What is so easy even for the Christian as to fail and falter in this region, and to stop short of the fullness of God's own Land of Promise through unbelief? The commonplace objection to prayer, founded upon the supposed immutability of the laws by which

God governs the world, is easily met and answered by the fact that *prayer is itself one of these laws,* upon whose working God has determined that a certain result shall follow:

> An element
> That comes and goes unseen, yet doth effect
> Rare issues by its operance.

But not so easily answered are other and deeper objections, to which this great question lies open. If prayer is indeed so effective, it may be asked, why not so universally, and why not so immediately? Sincere experience will testify, how long have we prayed in faith for certain objects, how long and how vainly! To a thousand such thoughts and surmises we may be unable to give a single satisfactory answer. We shall only do well to remember that there is not one of them which does not tell equally against any other part of the system included in the work of Christ for man.

All that we as yet see of the Christian dispensation would lead a thoughtful person to expect in prayer an apparent check and inadequacy. For all that we see as yet of Christ's work presupposes a deficiency. All connected with Christ's office is remedial and partial in its efficacy, as the remedial must ever be.

Why, it may be asked, has Christ's great sacrifice of Himself for the world, His abiding gift of the Holy Spirit to His church, told so partially on the mass of mankind, so feebly even in the hearts that have received them? Why, to go back a step further, was man created a being needing to be redeemed? To all such questions, not only any one part, but the whole plan to salvation lies open, and if we could answer any one of them, sin, pain, death, redemption, earth's darkest shadows, Heaven's most dazzling light, would probably be no longer mysterious to us, and the veil would be lifted from all hearts and all nations.

Meanwhile all that we see around and within us testifies to the presence of a mighty opposing agency, and bears witness also to a reserve or economy of grace, a hiding of God's power, in which we can discern, as through a glass darkly, a merciful purpose. All that we now see of Christ's Kingdom bears upon it the marks of cost and labor, of infinite gain secured by finite loss. The song of the church carries on from age to age to age the burden of the old Greek chorus: "Sing sorrow, strife and sorrow, but let Victory remain."

The work of our salvation, it is evident, is a *work*. Nature brings forth with ease and rejoicing. The earth [yields] its grass, its herb, its fruit-bearing tree; the waters bring forth abundantly; but every birth of the redeemed is single, and bears upon it the marks of the Lord Jesus, the birthmark of a mighty soul that has travailed for it betwixt life and death. Why should we expect that the work of prayer would be easy, swift, and triumphant, while the work of grace in general is so slow and difficult, while the march of the church is so uneven and hesitating, and the miracle of conversion so tardy and interrupted?

All that we see in Christ's Kingdom bears witness to powerful outward resistance on the part of an enemy, and also testifies to a secret restraint on the part of a friend. We find in it reserve, economy, something kept in store, not yet wholly given. This reserve enters largely into prayer. It is not every faithful Christian who can say to his Lord, "You have given me my heart's desire, You have not denied me the request of my lips."[10] Neither can all of God's children join in that fervent ascription of the Psalmist: "I love the Lord because He has heard the voice of my supplications."[11] We hear another, a deeper voice exclaim, "O my God, I cry in the daytime and You hear not, and in the night season also I take no rest."[12]

Yet God, the Eternal, lives, and while He lives, no prayer that has been truly lifted up to Him can die. The Christian rejoices in an answered prayer; he waits for the accomplishment of a yet unfulfilled one. He is inured to delay and resigned to denial. Through Christ who strengthens him, he can do all things except cease to pray. A Christian's daily common life is full of unseen, unrecognized miracles, and among the greatest of all miracles worked by prayer is faith in prayer itself. The Christian believes in Christ, though he sees not yet all things put under Him. He believes in prayer, though he sees not yet floods descend in answer to it. Prayer is the instinct of the redeemed soul.

Praise is often spoken of as something higher and more complete than prayer. It may be so insofar as it is more suited to the glorified state, the state which has all and abounds, and has nothing to desire or to ask for. But in our present order there is no voice so sweet, so powerful, so essentially human, as that of prayer—none so natural to a being like man, at once rational, fallen, and redeemed.

It is possible, without any great strain upon imagination, to conceive of inanimate creation as filled with praise. It is easy to think of the winds and waves in their restless movement, the birds in their song, the stars in their silence, the very grass and flowers, as worshiping God in their beauty and gladness. Often the air around us seems full of thanksgiving, breathless with adoration. But who, even in poetry, ever dreamt that nature *prayed?* Prayer is the voice of one who errs and loves; of one who sins, and suffers, and aspires. It is the voice of a child to its father, the voice of man to his God.

And in entering even a very little way into the perplexed question of denials and delays in prayer, it seems well to touch upon a point too little taken into account in the general Christian mind: that question of the times and seasons which the Father has left in His own hand, and which we cannot take into ours. All things, said a pagan philosopher, are not possible to all men at all times; and for want of duly acknowledging this statute of limitation, many devotional books, and a great deal of religious teaching, tend only to bring strain and anguish upon the sincere mind, which feels it cannot rise to the prescribed level until it is lifted there by God Himself.

Alike to individuals and churches there come days of refreshing from the Lord, times of visitation which the strongest urgency of the human spirit cannot antedate, but which it is its highest wisdom to meet, so as to be found willing in the day of God's power. If the whole year were one long harvest, where then were the sowing, the patient expectation, the ploughing in the cold? A vintage comes once in a year, a triumph perhaps once in a lifetime. So has the Christian life its seasons, its epochs, its days of benediction. There are times, probably, in the life of every faithful believer when things long desired and sought after are dropped like golden gifts within his bosom.

Few tried Christians have not known times when God, suddenly or gradually, has lifted a weight from their lives, has brought a power within their souls, has so mitigated some affliction, as to make that endurable which was previously intolerable, or has rendered some long-desired and apparently unattainable temporal or spiritual aim possible, practicable, and easy. How many blessings at such a season will God, by one sweep of His mighty arm, bring within the soul's grasp! He will at once enlarge the soul's border, and visibly defend the land He has made so broad and fruitful, giving it rest from all its enemies round about. Often in times of great tribulation the prophecy of such a season will be borne like a breath from Heaven across the wasted and desolate spirit.

In prayer there are many voices, none of them, however faint and formal, altogether without significance; but there is among these one, the instant prayer, which the soul even while offering it feels that God *must* answer. We know not why it is that in prayer, man's direst necessity should be God's chosen opportunity, [but it happens:] the fierce onset of temptation, the pang of sharp tribulation, the pressure of some irresistible weight impending over the whole being, and threatening to crush out life itself, [enables] the soul to lift itself straight up to God as it cannot do under ordinary circumstances, [giving] it power to plead with God and to prevail, to take hold of His great strength against His great strength, to contend with Him in His own might—the might of love.

Why it should be so it seems impossible to explain; but it seems certain that times of danger, distress, and keen anguish are often times of chosen access to God. When the heart is driven into its deepest recess, it finds itself nearest to its God. But let its distress stop short of despair, which makes prayer impossible. Despair is the last, worst device of the enemy which would rob the soul of its God.

There are times in the life of every Christian when some great truth is clearly revealed to him, some long-locked door of promise left with the key hanging in the wards, only waiting to be turned by a prayer. At these times God is waiting to be gracious, and what He appears to wait for is the full consent and submission of the human will. Often at such times the Holy Spirit will allure the soul into the direction where God intends to meet and bless it. The life will be drawn toward the attainment of some specific object. The heart will be enticed to covet earnestly some peculiar grace. God will appear to invite the soul to pray for the special gift He intends to bestow.[13] "Yet for this thing," He says, speaking of some boon which He kept in store for His ancient church, "will I be inquired of by them."[14] God sometimes seems to wait in His dealings with the world until He has secured the cooperation of man's wish and will.

"Pray," says our Lord Himself, "to the Lord of the harvest, that He may send forth laborers into His harvest."[15] The harvest is God's, and He must send the laborers; still man must pray. His great Father does not work alone. He has need of man's voice, man's heart, man's energy, man's prayer.

As great as is the admitted mystery of prayer, there can be little doubt that much of its secret lies wrapped in the cooperation of the divine and human will. In prayer man is a laborer together

with his God. We have had enough in our day of the shallow
evangel of labor, man's gospel preached to man. We have been told
till we are weary of hearing it that "he who works prays." Let us
lift up our hearts high enough to meet a fuller, deeper, richer
truth. Let us learn that "he who prays works," works even with his
God. Such a person is humble enough, is bold enough to help
Him who upholds all things with the word of His power.

Let us look through the history of the whole church, beginning with that elder one, whose story is but the initial of our own
writ large and plain. What is the Old Testament but the record of
the universal Christian heart and life rudely dramatized? It is flung
forth as a deep spiritual truth might be shadowed and outlined in
some medieval mystery play, and left in that picture-writing forever.

And what do we find in its every record but this: God
instructing, pardoning, blessing man through man. "He makes
His angels spirits, and His ministers a flaming fire."[16] They are, as
their names import, God's messengers, His flaming pursuivants,
His heralds of peace and goodwill. But who, through the whole
spiritual history of our fallen yet mighty race, have been chosen by
God as teachers, as enlighteners, as intercessors for man but [such]
men—"prophets from among our brethren"?[17]

When it is an angel who is the medium of communication
between God and man, the work is an outward one; it is something to be done or told. When *man* bears the Lord's message and
burden, the work is intimate, searching, spiritual. The word sent,
be it of reproof or of consolation, is a true gospel, bringing man
nearer to his God, placing him in a new and spiritual relation with
his Creator. It is not angels, but men, who are the princes of both
the new and old covenant, "having power with God." "Surely the
Lord will do nothing without revealing His plan to His servants
the prophets."[18] The time would fail me to tell of Abraham, of
Jacob (the type of so many feeble yet faithful believers), of Moses,
of Hezekiah, of Job, of Elijah, of Daniel, men whose attitude with
God is that of priests, whose outstretched hands at once deprecate
wrath and draw down blessing.

The New Testament is but one long acknowledgment to
man's power with God, in form less striking, perhaps, than in the
Old, because less concentrated, but in fact more wonderful, because it is referred to as such a simple thing. Paul, throughout his
epistles, not only confidently intends and expects to bless his
converts through his prayers for them; but continually claims their

prayers for him as something which he absolutely needs. It is through their prayers that he must be "enlarged," "helped," "furthered."

But what need to multiply examples? Why seek further illustrations of the truth that God, through him whom He has chosen, has made of man "a priest forever"?[19] When God would bless man, He chooses ofttimes to bless him through man. Yes, when God would save man, it was His will (to borrow the sublime expression of Jeremy Taylor) to save him by way of a Man.

Therefore let men pray always. Our present day seems full of question, of urgency on all points connected with prayer. It seems disposed to put it to the proof, to ask what it can effect or alter. It appears inclined to ask for a sign from Heaven; but what sign can be given it but the sign of the Son of Man in Heaven? The warfare of prayer, the accomplishment of the cross, is a conquest through apparent defeat. Its work is one with that great effectual Work [i.e., our salvation] in which its strength lies wrapped and hidden. Like [our salvation], it is a real and effective work, though one of which the believer, with his Lord, must sometimes be content to say, "I have labored in vain, I have spent my strength in vain, yet surely my judgment is with the Lord, and my work with my God."[20]

* * *

"My soul thirsts for God," says the Psalmist, "for the living God." There is a point beyond which neither the experience of others, or the utterances of the inspired Word can instruct or comfort the heart. It must have rejoicing in itself, and not in any other. It must learn of its Lord as none except Himself can teach. Its prayer is, "Make me to hear Your voice." It knows much about Jesus, but it desires to know *Him*. It can no longer rest on opinions, on ordinances, on Christianity received as a system, in anything save in Christ, and in actual communion with Him.

But whence comes this sigh, the broken language of every Christian heart, "More of Christ!" How is it that our Lord has been so long a time with us, and yet we have not known Him?

Who among us has not experienced moments, and these perhaps often recurring, in which the heart has communed with itself and been sad, desiring that Jesus would Himself draw near? Yet the heart is ready, in its discouragement, to ask whether, in the very urgency of its desire and endeavor, it may not be expecting too much of itself, may not be expecting too much of God.

In this urgency, have we considered that saying of our Savior's, "I have yet many things to say to you, but you cannot bear
them now"?[21] The natural man dies hard within us, and the man
from Heaven is not born without a pang. First the anguish, then
the joy. Are our souls willing, are they able to endure that anguish,
ardently as we may desire the joy which makes it to be remembered no more? When the fullness of time is come, the fullness of
strength will be given to meet it, and not before. Meanwhile, the
way of life continues to have its own ache, a sadness peculiar to
itself.

Here we are reminded of what the prophet tells us, that
God's thoughts are not our thoughts, neither His ways our ways.[22]
God has time for everything, but it is far otherwise with his
creature [man]. The tendency of all human effort is to go straight
to a desired aim, putting on all possible strain and pressure. If we
could see clearly into the depths of the divine counsels, it is
probable, indeed certain, that we should find nothing arbitrary or
left to chance in any of the works or decrees of the Almighty;
nothing, I mean, which could have been otherwise than that
which it is. Choice is the glory of humanity, its distinctive attribute. It raises a human being as high above the inferior creatures
as it sinks him below Deity. For to choose is obviously as human as
to err, but infinite Wisdom can see and take but one way.

God, as His apostle tells us, cannot deny or contradict Himself;[23] and upon this, His moral obligation, the moral freedom of
man is founded—a freedom which the gospel of life and immor-
tality has brought to light, and which it alone reveals. All systems
founded upon nature tend to bondage.

When we turn to God's inner Kingdom [i.e., the church], we
must confess that God wraps up His great designs in a husk or
envelope, which will not fall off until the appointed time. What is
the sacred history, but that of a labor working to a mighty, far-seen
and remote end? What is Christianity but "an infant of days"? We
naturally think that God might make all things as He wishes them
to be at once; but we find it is not His way to do so. God does not
heal us with a touch. He uses means and processes, tedious often
and peculiarly afflicting. When God would tune a soul, says John
Bunyan, He most commonly begins at the lowest note. So it has
been in the tuning of the world's wide discord. In the depths of the
great atonement God has sounded the lowest note. We know little
of either sin or love until we learn of them at the cross.

When we feel—as what Christian at times does not?—an impatience with the slowness of our own growth, let us look from ourselves into the universal church of Christ, and ask this: How shall the growth of the part be rapid, when that of the whole has been so slow?

Yet the Christian would prefer to see otherwise. He sees Satan exalting himself against Christ, and the gates of Hell advancing upon that against which they shall never prevail. Therefore he is often perplexed and baffled, as one that knows not what his Lord is doing. It is this which gives such terrible, blighting power to the words and writings of unbelievers. What they urge against Christianity is true. The believer already knows all that the infidel can tell him. The eye of love can see as clearly as that of hate, and has already mourned over all that the other exults in.

The Christian desperately wants to explain and account for these long delays, this partial efficacy, this intermittent working [of God's goodness and power]. He feels that he is in possession of the key which is to open all these intricacies, but at present, like that of the Pilgrims, "it grinds hard in the lock." He sees Jesus, but he sees not yet all things put under Him. The world around him is the same world which crucified his beloved Lord.

Often must the believer, like Antaeus,[24] grow stronger for having touched the ground. Often must he experience the sentence of death in himself. He must feel himself a being without heart or hope, incapable and even insensible, so that he may learn to trust not in himself or in any other, but in Him who raises the spiritually dead. The Christian must hold on to God through conflicts and agonies. He must fight while his blood runs down and glues his hand to the sword. He must hold on when that hand is benumbed and stiff with cold; when strength and consciousness seem gone together, and only an instinct remains through which the soul is able to fling itself like a dead weight upon Christ. Yet even here is

> an overthrow
> worth many victories.

Through being chilled and mortified in the smallest, most inwardly humiliating things; through being beaten away from the broken cisterns of self and of all creatures, we learn to look to Christ as our well of life, and so to find all our fresh springs in

Him, that we are able to say with a simple and sincere heart, "Lord, evermore give me of this water, so that I thirst not, neither come hither to draw."[25]

I know not how to speak of that great era in the Christian's soul when, whether through the strength of a patient following, or through the sweetness of a loving recognition, it finds Him whom it has long loved, and passes in that finding from the straitened life within itself into the free outlooking from self into Christ. When it ceases to confer with flesh and blood, to watch over its own changes and fluctuations, for the sake of attaching itself implicitly to Him who is the whole of what we have in part; when it lives no longer by faith but by Christ, holding Him too surely to think of what it holds by; it has done with self-questioning, with self-analysis. It believes in the love by which it lives, and can appeal for all answers to the fact of its own life.

How quiet such a life is! How fruitful! Fruitful because it is so quiet. It works not, but lives and grows. The uneasy effort has passed out of it. Unresting, because it rests always, it has done with task-work and anxiety. It serves, yet is not cumbered with much serving. It has ceased from that sad complaint, "Thou hast left me to serve alone."[26] Such a life will seem less spiritual only because it has grown more natural. The soul moves in an atmosphere which of itself brings it into contact with all great and enduring things, and it has only to draw in its breath to be filled and satisfied.

As the Christian advances upon his way, a sweet and solemn sense of the unity of life grows upon his spirit. "We are complete in Him."[27] Gradually, almost imperceptibly, the believer will find the current of his existence sweeping into a broader channel. He will find doors opening upon him, doors of happiness, doors of usefulness, which will be to him a gate of Heaven. Windows will open, letting in the breath of summer upon his soul, filling it with sunshine and sweet air. Suddenly some new interest, some friend, will appear in the thick of the battle, vanishing perhaps when the fight is over, yet blessing him even in vanishing from his sight.

That terrible saying of Anne of Austria to Richelieu holds true for mercy as well as for judgment: "My Lord Cardinal, God does not pay at the end of every week, but at the last *He pays*." God may put His faithful ones upon a long and painful apprenticeship, during which they learn much and receive little. Yet at the last He pays; pays them into their hearts, pays them into their hands also.

We may remember long seasons of faint yet honest endeavor,

the prayers of a soul yet without strength, the sacrifices of an imperfectly subdued will. We may remember such times, or we may forget them. Some of the good seed sown in tears is now shedding a heavenly fragrance within our lives, and some of it will blossom and perhaps bear fruit over our graves.

Light is good, and it is a pleasant thing to behold the sun. Yet far dearer than outward peace, far sweeter than inward consolation, is the solace of the Christian's heart, the imperishing root, the dry tree[28] that shall flourish when every green tree of delight and of desire fails. It is to the cross that the heart must turn for that which will reconcile it to all conflicts, all privations. When Christ is lifted up within the believing soul, nothing is too hard for it to venture upon or endure. It rests upon a power beyond itself, and can bring its whole strength to bear upon generous, exalted enterprise. Show your servant Your work, and his own will be indeed easy!

"Midnight is past," sings the sailor on the southern ocean. "Midnight is past; the Cross begins to bend."[29] Outward duties weary, inward consolations fail. Love never fails. Let us now turn aside and look upon this great sight[30] of love that burns with fire yet is not consumed; of love that, having poured out its soul unto death, yet lives to see of that soul's long travail and to be satisfied with it.[31] "Behold the Lamb of God, that takes away the sins of the world."[32]

When were love's arms stretched so wide as upon the cross? When did they embrace so much as when You, O Christ, gathered within Your bosom the spears and arrows of the mighty to open to us a Lane for Freedom?

NOTES

1. Cf. Hebrews 9:23.
2. From *Arabia,* by William Gifford Palgrave, English Jesuit missionary.
3. In his *Émile, ou Traité de L'Éducation.*
4. Cf. John 8:36.
5. From the writings of Frederick W. Faber.
6. Luke 22:42.
7. Cf. Song of Solomon 1:4.
8. Psalm 119:32.
9. Cf. Philippians 2:13.
10. Cf. Psalm 21:2.
11. Psalm 116:1.
12. Psalm 22:2.
13. Cf. Ezekiel 36:36, 37.
14. *Ibid.*

15. Matthew 9:38.
16. Cf. Hebrews 1:7.
17. Cf. Deuteronomy 18:18.
18. Amos 3:7.
19. Psalm 110:4; Hebrews 5:6.
20. Isaiah 49:4.
21. John 16:12.
22. Cf. Isaiah 55:8.
23. Cf. 2 Timothy 2:13.
24. In Greek mythology, Antaeus was a Libyan giant wrestler who, when thrown, became stronger by contact with his mother, the Earth.
25. John 4:15.
26. Cf. Luke 10:40.
27. Cf. Colossians 2:10.
28. Ezekiel 17:24.
29. The reference is to the Southern Cross constellation, by which sailing ships chartered their courses in the southern hemisphere.
30. Cf. Exodus 3:3.
31. Cf. Isaiah 53:11.
32. John 1:29.

T. De Witt Talmage

"Florid, sensational, eccentric, inaccurate"—these were among the epithets leveled at the Reverend Thomas De Witt Talmage (1832-1902) during the closing decades of the past century. Whether they were appropriate, the reader can perhaps judge from the pages that follow. On balance, the man was immensely popular; the secular press hailed him as "the greatest one-man attraction in America." Six hundred newspapers throughout the English-speaking world printed his sermons each Monday morning. In Britain his words appeared regularly alongside those of Charles Spurgeon.

At Brooklyn Tabernacle in New York, which had twenty members when he took over in 1869, he was soon preaching to three thousand to five thousand every Sunday, and continued to do so for thirty years. When he lectured at Chautauqua assemblies, special trains were run in from every direction. If it were known he would be delayed at a railroad junction, his friends would wire ahead and set up impromptu stopover meetings for the crowds they knew would gather at the depot.

Talmage makes easy reading, even today. His was the consummate art of the storyteller. Each week, both in the pulpit and in the various publications he edited, he poured out an astonishing fund of information about the world of his day and did so in colorful and dramatic ways. Twenty years after his death Talmage's daughter, May, published The Wisdom and Wit of T. De Witt Talmage *(Doran, 1922). She wrote, "His was an everyday religion, full of sunshine, flowers, music, health, hope and encouragement. His principal theme was Heaven, and his messages have not grown stale with the passing years."*

While critics dismissed Talmage as extravagant and flamboyant, others characterized his garnished language as that of a prose poet. His voice, it was said, was rather high and melodious, but his crisp enunciation and earnest manner lent what was called "indescribable" power to his words. He was not above visiting the New York underworld in company with local police, to see for himself the conditions of vice and crime in the metropolis. His sermons reporting on such visits made Talmage a target for harsh attacks by other clergy, but the public's interest, whether prurient or not, brought considerable increase in church attendance.

Talmage was born into a godly Dutch Reformed family in Bound Brook, New Jersey. He professed faith in Christ at age eighteen, and after a rather frustrating attempt to study law at the University of the City of New York, he entered New Brunswick Theological Seminary to prepare for the ministry. He graduated in 1856, and then pastored Dutch Reformed churches in Belleville, New Jersey; Syracuse, New York; and Philadelphia.

In 1869 he was called to Central Presbyterian Church, Brooklyn, which became known as Brooklyn Tabernacle. As the young pastor developed the pulpit oratory for which he became famous, the congregation grew by leaps and bounds. Despite his success as preacher, lecturer, writer and editor, however, his life was not easy. Three times his Tabernacle burned to the ground during his tenure. Finally in 1894 it was abandoned, Talmage resigned, and the church with its membership of two thousand was dissolved. Talmage moved to Washington, D.C., and became co-pastor of a Presbyterian Church together with an aged minister. He remained there until his death.

Any final judgment on De Witt Talmage must take cognizance of the fact that he was a person of sincerity and integrity. His was an evangelical, Biblical message, with stronger ties to D. L. Moody than to Henry Ward Beecher. The sermon that follows was one that he preached in Washington. It is taken by permission from 500 Selected Sermons of T. De Witt Talmage, Volume 19, published in 1957 by Baker Book House, Grand Rapids, Michigan.

ELEVEN

THE BUSYBODY
by T. De Witt Talmage

"A busybody in other men's matters." (1 Peter 4:15)

Human nature is the same in all ages. In the second century of the world's existence people had the same characteristics as people in the nineteenth century [of our era], the only difference being that they had the characteristics for a longer time. It was five hundred years of goodness or five hundred years of meanness, instead of goodness or meanness for forty or fifty years.[1] Well, Simon Peter, who was a keen observer of what was going on around him, one day caught sight of a man whose characteristics were severe inspection and blatant criticism of the affairs belonging to people for whom he had no responsibility, and with the hand once browned and hardened by fishing-tackle he drew this portrait for all subsequent ages: "A busybody in other men's matters."[2]

That kind of person has been a troublemaker in every country since the world stood. Appointing himself to the work of exploration and detection, he goes forth mischief-making. He generally begins by reporting the infelicity discovered. He is the advertising agent of infirmities and domestic inharmony and occurrences that but for him would never have come to the public eye or ear. He feels that the secret ought to be hauled out into light and heralded.

If he can get one line of it into the newspapers, that he feels to be a noble achievement to start with. But he must not let it stop. He whispers it to his neighbors, and they in turn whisper it to their neighbors, until the whole town is a-buzz and agog. You can no more catch it or put it down than you can a malaria. It is in the air and on the wing and afloat. Taken by itself, it seems of little importance, but after a hundred people have handled it, and each has given it an additional twist, it becomes a story, in size and shape marvelous. If it can be kept going, after a while it will be large enough to call the attention of the courts or the presbyteries or conferences or associations. Most of the scandals abroad are the work of the one whom Peter in the text styles, "A busybody in other men's matters."

First, notice that such a mission is most undesirable, because we all require all the time we can get to take care of our own affairs. To carry ourselves through the treacherous straits of this life demands that we all the time keep our hand on the wheel of our own craft. While, as I shall show you before I get through, we all have a mission of kindness to others, we have no time to waste in doing that which is damaging to others.

There is our worldly calling, which must be looked after or it will become a failure. Who succeeds in anything without concentrating all his energies upon that one thing? All those who try to do many things go to pieces, either as to their health or their fortune. They go on until they pay ten cents on the dollar, or pay their body into the grave. We cannot manage the affairs of others and keep our own affairs prosperous. While we are inquiring how precarious is the business of another merchant, and finding out how many notes he has unpaid and how soon he will probably be wound up or make an assignment or hear the sheriff's hammer smite his counter, our own affairs are getting mixed up and endangered.

While we are criticizing our neighbor for his poor crops we are neglecting the fertilization of our own fields or allowing the weeds to choke our own corn. While we are trying to extract the mote from our neighbor's eye, we fall under the weight of the beam in our own eye. Those men disturbed by the faults of others are themselves the depot at which whole trains of faults arrive, and from which whole trains of faults start. The men who have succeeded in secular things or religious things will tell you that they have no time for hunting out the deficits of others. On the way to their counting-room they may have heard that a firm in the same line of business was in trouble, and they said, "Sorry, very sorry," but they went in and sat down at their table and opened the book containing a full statement of their affairs to see if they were in peril of being caught in a similar cyclone.

Gadders about town, with hands in pockets and hats set far back on their heads, waiting to hear baleful news, are failures now or will be failures. Christian men and women who go around with mouth and looks full of interrogation points to find how some other church member is given to exaggeration or drinks or neglects his home for greater outside attractions, have themselves so little grace in their hearts that no one suspects they have any. In proportion as people are consecrated and holy and useful, they are lenient with others and disposed to say, "Wait until we hear the other side of that matter. I cannot believe that charge made against that man or woman until we have some better testimony than that given by these scandal-mongers. I guess it is a lie."

If God had given us whole weeks and months and days with nothing to do but gauge and measure and scrutinize the affairs of others, there might be some excuse for such employment, but I do not know anyone who has such a surplus of time and energy and qualification that he can afford much of the time to sit as a coroner upon the dead failures of others. I can imagine that an astronomical crank could get so absorbed in examining the spots on the sun as to neglect clearing the spots off his own character. A successful man was asked how he had accumulated such a fortune. He replied, "I have accumulated about one-half of my property by attending strictly to my business, and the other half by letting other people's alone."

Furthermore, we are incapacitated for the supervising of others because we cannot see all sides of the affair reprehended. People are generally not so much to blame as we suppose. It is never right to do wrong, but there may be alleviations. There may have arisen a conjunction of circumstances which would have flung any one of us. The world gives only one side of the transaction, and that is always the worst side. The defaulter at the bank who loaned money he ought not to have loaned did it for the advantage of another, not for his own. That young man who purloined from his employer did so because his mother was dying for the lack of medicine. The young woman who went wrong did not get enough wages to keep her from starving to death. Most people who make moral shipwreck would do right in some exigency, but they have not the courage to say No.

Better die than do the least wrong, but moderate your anathema against the wrongdoer by the circumstances which may yet develop. Be economical of your curses when all the community is hounding some man or woman. Wait, consider, pause and hope that which is charged is a base fabrication. Do not be like a jury who should render verdict against the defendant without allowing him to present his side of the case.

I know not what your observation has been, but I have never known a case of default in character but there were some circumstances which ought to weigh on the side of the recreant. The most repugnant character on earth to me is the man who believes everything he hears against others and hurls all the slandered down the same embànkment of denunciation. I dislike such a one more than I dislike the offender for whom he has no mercy.

Furthermore, we make ourselves a disgusting spectacle when we become busybodies. What a diabolical enterprise those undertake who are ever looking for the moral lapse or downfall of others! As the human race is a most imperfect race, all such hunters find plenty of game. There have been sewing societies in churches which tore to pieces more reputations than they made garments for the poor. With their sarcasms and sly hints and depreciation of motives, they punctured more good names than they had needles. With their scissors they cut character bias, and backstitched every evil report they got hold of.

Meetings of boards of directors have sometimes ruined good businessmen by insinuations against them. The bad work may not have been done so much by words, for they would be libelous, but by a twinkle of the eye or a shrug of the shoulder or a sarcastic attenuation of a word. "Yes, he is all right when he is sober." "Have you inquired into that man's history?" "Do you know what business he was in before he entered this?" "I move that the application be laid on the table until some investigations now going on are consummated." It is easy enough to start a suspicion that will never down, but what a despicable man is the one who started it!

There is not an honest man in Washington or New York or any other city who cannot be damaged by such infernalism. In a village where I once lived a steamboat every day came to the wharf. An enemy of the steamboat company asked one day, "I wonder if that steamboat is safe?" The man who heard the question soon said to his neighbor, "There is some suspicion about the safety of that steamboat." And the next one who got hold of it said, "There is an impression abroad that there will be an accident on that steamer." Soon all that community began to say, "That steamer is very unsafe," and as a consequence we all took the stage rather than risk our lives on the river.

The steamer was entirely sound and safe, but one interrogation in regard to her started a suspicion that went on until the steamboat company was ruined. Precisely so noble reputations and good enterprises and useful styles of business are slain by interrogation points. Can you imagine any creature so loathsome as the one who feels himself or herself called to question all integrity, all ability, all honesty, all character? Buzzards looking for carrion.

While I believe enough in human depravity to be orthodox, I tell you that most of the people whom I know are doing the best they can. Faults? Oh, yes; all people except you and I have faults. But they are sorry about it, repentant on account of it, and are trying to do better. About all the married people I know are married to the one person best suited. Nearly all the parents with whom I am acquainted are doing the best they can for their children. All the clerks in stores, so far as I know, are honest; and all persons in official position, city, state, or nation, are fulfilling their mission as well as they can. Most of those who have failed in business, so far as I know, have failed honestly.

The singers are singing their best songs, the sculptors chiseling their best statues, the painters penciling their best pictures, the ministers preaching their best sermons. Take any audience that assembles in any church, and if there are five hundred people assembled, I think at least four hundred fifty are doing the best they can, and if there be five thousand assembled, at least forty-five hundred are doing the best they can.

While I was thinking upon this subject, I made a visit to one of the national bureaus in this capital,[3] and found that out of $1,100,000,000 in money that had passed through the hands of more than four hundred employees, only three cents were unaccounted for, and the three cents were afterwards found. What a compliment to common honesty!

All people make mistakes—say things that afterward they are sorry for, and miss opportunity of uttering the right word and doing the right thing. But when they say their prayers at night these defects are sure to be mentioned somewhere between the name of the Lord, for whose mercy they plead, and the amen that closes the supplication.

"That has not been my observation," says someone. Well, I am sorry for you, my brother, my sister. What an awful crowd you must have got into! Or, as is more probable, you are one of the characters that my text sketches. You have not been hunting for partridges and quail, but for vultures. You have been microscoping the world's faults. You have been down in the marshes when you ought to have been on the uplands. I have caught you at last! You are a "busybody in other men's matters."

How is it that you can always find two opinions about anyone, and those two opinions exactly opposite? I will tell you the reason. It is because there are two sides to every character—the best side and the worst side. A well-disposed man chiefly seeks the best side. The badly-disposed seeks chiefly the worst side. Be ours the desire to see the best side, for it is healthier for us to do so and it stirs admiration, which is an elevated state; while the desire to find the worst side keeps on in a spirit of disquietude and disgust and mean suspicion, and that is a pulling down of our own nature, a disfigurement of our own character. I am afraid the imperfections of others will kill us yet.

The habit I deplore is apt to show itself in the visage. A kindly man who wishes everybody well soon demonstrates his disposition in his looks. His features may fracture all the laws of handsome physiognomy, but God puts into that man's eyes and in the curve of his nostril and in the upper and lower lip the signature of divine approval. And you see it at a glance, as plainly as though it had been written all over his face in rose color: "This is one of My princes. He is on the way to coronation. I bless him now with all the benediction that infinity can afford. Look at him. Admire him. Congratulate him."

On the other hand, if one be cynical about the character of others, and chiefly observant of defects and glad to find something wrong in character, the fact is apt to be demonstrated in his looks. However regular his features, and though constructed according to the laws of Kaspar Lavater,[4] his visage is sour. He may smile, but it is a sour smile. There is a sneer in the inflation of the nostril. There is a bad look in the eye. The devil of sarcasm and malevolence and suspicion has taken possession of him, and you see it as plainly as though from the hairline of the forehead to the lowest point in the round of his chin it were written: "Mine! Mine! I, the demon of the pit, have soured his visage with my curse. Look at him! He chose a diet of carrion. He gloated over the misdeeds of others. It took all my infernal engineering to make him what he is—'a busybody in other men's matters.' "

The slanderer almost always attempts to escape the scandal he is responsible for. When in 1741 John Wesley was preaching at Bristol and showing what reason he had to trust in the Captain of his salvation, a hearer cried out, "Who was your captain when you hanged yourself? I know the man who saw you when you were cut down!" Wesley asked the audience to make room and let the slanderer come to the front, but when the way was open, the slanderer instead of coming forward fled the room. The author or distributor of slanders never wants to face his work.

On the Day of Pentecost there were people endowed with what was called the "gift of tongues," and they spake for God in many languages. In our time there are people who seem to have the gift of evil tongues, and there is no end to their iniquitous gabble. Every city, village and neighborhood of the earth has had driven through it these scavenger carts. When anything is said to you defamatory of the character of others, imitate Joseph John Gurney of England who, when a bad report was brought to him concerning anybody, asked, "Do you know any good thing to tell us concerning her? Since there is no good to relate, would it not be kinder to be silent on the evil? Love rejoices not in iniquity."[5]

But there is a worthy and Christian way of looking abroad upon others, not for the purpose of bringing them to disadvantage or advertising their weaknesses or putting in "great primer" or "paragon" type[6] their frailties, but to offer help, sympathy, and rescue. That is Christlike, and he who does so wins the applause of the high heavens. Just look abroad for the people who have made great mistakes, and put a big plaster of condolence on their lacerations. Such people are never sympathized with, although they need an infinity of solace. Domestic mistakes. Social mistakes. Ecclesiastical mistakes. Political mistakes. The world has for such only jocosity and gesture of deploration. There is an unoccupied field for you, my brother. No one has ever been there. Take your case of medicines and go there and ask them where they are hurt and apply divine medicament.

There is a public man who has made a political mistake from which he will never recover. At the next elections he will be put back and put down into a place of disapproval from which he will never rise. Just go to that man and unroll the scroll of one hundred splendid Americans who, after occupying high places of promotion, were relegated to private life and public scorn. Show him in what glorious company he has been placed by the anathema of the ballot-box.

There is a man or woman who has made a conjugal mistake, and a vulture has been put into the same cage with a dove, or a lion and a lamb in the same jungle. The world laughs at the misfortune, but it is your business to weep with their woe. There is a merchant who bought at the wrong time or a manufacturer whose machinery has been superseded by a new invention or who under change of tariff on certain styles of fabric has been dropped from affluence into bankruptcy. Go to him and recall the names of fifty businessmen who lost all but their honesty and God and Heaven. Let him know there are hundreds of good men who have gone under that are thought of in heavenly spheres more than many who are high up and going higher. All will acknowledge that good and lovely Arthur Tappan,[7] who failed in business, was more to be admired than William Tweed in possession of his stolen millions.[8]

Go to that literary man who is starving with a brilliant pen in his right hand, his literary position lost, his books unsalable, and tell him of the mightiest of the past and the present who suffered from nonappreciation. Show the discouraged author, whose manuscript the publishing house will not take, that among the rejected manuscripts of the publishing houses for a while were *Paradise Lost* and *Jane Eyre* and Thackeray's *Vanity Fair* and *Vestiges of Creation* and *Uncle Tom's Cabin*, and that Shakespeare was comparatively unknown in England until Germany acclaimed its appreciation of the greatest of dramatists.[9] Unroll before that discouraged public man the cartoons in the time of Andrew Jackson and Abraham Lincoln and James G. Blaine, and show all the misinterpreted and pursue the fact that they have it no worse than many who have preceded them, and that in most cases it is jealousy at success that has caused the assault.

In literature it has always been hard for one man to speak well of another. Voltaire hated Rousseau. Charles Lamb could not endure Coleridge. Coleridge derides DeQuincy because, while they both used opium, Coleridge says DeQuincy used it for pleasure, while he, Coleridge, took it to relieve pain. Waller wars against Cowley. The hatred of Plato and Xenophon is as immortal as their works. Corneille had utter contempt for Racine. At Westminster Abbey, in the "Poets' Corner," sleeps Drayton, the poet, and Goldie, who said Drayton was not a poet. There rests Dryden, and not far off poor Shadwell, who had pursued him with a fiend's fury; Alexander Pope and John Dennis, his implacable enemy.[10] Show those wronged of criticism that they are not exceptional cases, and so comfort them to bear the outrage.

Hear it! The more you go to busying yourselves in other men's matters the better, if you have design of offering relief. Search out the quarrels, that you may settle them; the fallen, that you may lift them; the pangs, that you may assuage them. Arm yourselves with two bottles of divine medicine, the one a tonic and the other an anaesthetic; the latter to soothe and quiet, the former to stimulate, to inspire to sublime action. A man's matters need looking after in this respect. There are ten thousand men and women who need your help, and need it right away. They do not sit down and cry. They make no appeal for help, but within ten yards of where you sit in church, and within ten minutes' walk of your home there are people in enough trouble to make them shriek out with agony if they had not resolved upon suppression.

If you are rightly interested in other men's matters, go to those who are just starting in their occupations or professions and give them a boost. Those old physicians do not want your help, for they are surrounded with more patients than they can attend to, but cheer those young doctors who are counting out their first drops to patients who cannot afford to pay.

Those old attorneys at the law want no help from you, for they take retainers only from the more prosperous clients, but cheer those young attorneys who have not had a brief at all lucrative. Those old merchants have their business so well established that they feel independent of banks, of all changes in tariffs, of all panics; but cheer those young merchants who are making their first mistake in bargain and sale. That old farmer who has two hundred acres in best tillage, and his barns full of harvested crops, and the grain merchant having bought his wheat at high prices before it was reaped, needs no sympathy from you; but cheer up that young farmer whose acres are covered with a big mortgage and the drought strikes them the first year. That builder, with contracts made for the construction of half a dozen houses and the owners impatient for occupancy, is not to be pitied, but give your sympathy to that mechanic in early acquaintance with hammer and saw and bit, and amid all the limitations of a journeyman.

We pity people who have met with bereavements or accidents or great losses, but there are "other men's matters" that are never reported, though they are crushing to the last degree. Search them out. Alleviate them. Give them practical help. Have a word of appropriate sympathy. Do not go in at some case of bereavement and quote conventionally from the Bible, as I have heard it quoted amid such circumstances: "We all do fade as a leaf," "Man that is born of woman is of few days, and full of trouble,"[11] and so on. The Bible, like an apothecary store, has many medicines, and they are all good, but are not alike suited to all cases. I have heard

verses of the Bible quoted when they were no more appropriate to
the particular case than would be a chapter of Homer's *Iliad* or
Virgil's *Georgics*.

Go forth to be a busybody in other men's matters, so far as
you can helping them out and helping them on. The world is full
of instances of those who spend their life in such alleviations. But
there is one instance that overtops and eclipses all others. He had
lived in a palace. Radiant ones waited upon Him. He was chariot-
ed along streets yellow with gold and stopped at gates glistening
with pearl hosannaed by immortals coroneted and in snowy white.
Centuries gave Him not a pain. The sun that rose on Him never
set. His dominions could not be enlarged, for they had no bound-
aries, and uncontested was His reign. Upon all that lustre and
renown and environment of splendors He turned his back and put
down His crown at the foot of His throne, and on a bleak December night trod His way down to a house in Bethlehem of our
world. Wrapped in what plain shawl and pursued by what enemies
on swift camels and howled at by what brigands and thrust with
what sharp lances and hidden in what sepulchral crypt, until the
subsequent centuries have tried in vain to tell the story by sculp-
tured cross and painted canvas and resounding doxologies and
domed cathedrals and redeemed nations.

He could not see a woman doubled up with rheumatism, but
He touched her, and inflamed muscles relaxed and she stood
straight. He could not meet the funeral of a young man, but He
broke up the procession and gave him back to his widowed mother. With spittle on the tip of His finger He turned the midnight of
total blindness into the midnoon of perfect sight. He could not see
a man down on his mattress helpless with [paralysis] without
calling him up to health, and telling him to shoulder the mattress
and walk off. He could not find a man tongue-tied, but He gave
him immediate articulation. He could not see a man with the
puzzled and inquiring look of the deaf without giving him capacity
to hear the march of life beating on the drum of the ear. He could
not see a crowd of hungry people but He made enough good bread
and a surplus that required all the baskets.

He scolded only twice that I remember, once at the hypocrites with elongated visage[12] and the other time when a dinful
crowd had arraigned an unfortunate woman, and the Lord with
the most superb sarcasm that was ever uttered gave permission to
anyone who felt himself entirely commendable to hurl the first
missile.[13] All for the others. His birth for others. His ministry for

others. His death for others. His ascension for others. His enthronement for others.

That spirit which leads one to be busy for the betterment of others induced John Pounds to establish "ragged schools" and Father Matthew to become a temperance reformer and Peter Cooper to establish his Institute and Slater to contribute his fund for schools and Baroness Hirsch to leave more than $100,000,000 for the improvement of her race, and Cornelius Vanderbilt to flood churches and charitable institutions with his beneficence.[14] "Other men's matters!" Be busybodies in improving them. With kind words, with earnest prayers, with self-sacrificing deeds, with enlarging charities, let us go forth on a new mission.

I stand here and tell you, my hearers, of a great salvation. Do you understand what it is to have a Savior? He took your place. He bore your sins. He wept your sorrows. He is here now to save your soul.

A soldier, worn out in his country's service, took to the violin as a mode of earning his living. He was found in the streets of Vienna, playing his violin; but after a while his hand became feeble and tremulous, and he could no more make music. One day, while he sat there weeping, a man passed along and said, "My friend, you are too old and feeble; give me your violin." He took the man's violin and began to discourse most exquisite music, and the people gathered around in larger and larger numbers, and the aged man held his hat, and the coins poured in until the hat was full.

"Now," said the man who was playing the violin, "put those coins in your pockets." The coins were put in the old man's pockets. Then he held his hat again, and the violinist played more sweetly than ever, and played until some of the people wept and some shouted. And again the hat was filled with coins. Then the violinist dropped the instrument and passed on, and the whisper went, "Who is it? Who is it?"

Someone just entering the crowd said, "Why, that is Bucher,[15] the great violinist, known all through the realm!" The fact was, he had just taken that man's place and assumed his poverty and borne his burden and played his music and earned his livelihood and made sacrifice for the poor old man.

So the Lord Jesus Christ comes down, and He finds us in our spiritual penury, and across the broken strings of His own heart He strikes a strain of infinite music which wins the attention of earth and Heaven. He takes our poverty; He plays our music;

He weeps our sorrow; He dies our death. A sacrifice for you; a sacrifice for me.

And now my words are to the invisible multitudes I reach week by week, but yet will never see in this world, but whom I expect to meet at the bar of God, and hope to see in the blessed Heaven.[16] The fact is, a great many of the churches in this day are being doctrined to death. They have been trying for twenty-five years to find out all about God's decrees, and they want to know who are elected to be saved and who are reprobated to be damned, and they are keeping on discussing that subject when there are millions of souls who need to have the truth put straight at them.

They sit counting the number of teeth in the jawbone with which they are to slay the Philistines,[17] when they ought to be wielding skillfully the weapon. They sit on the beach and see a vessel going to pieces in the offing, and instead of getting into a boat and pulling away for the wreck, they sit discussing the different styles of oarlocks. God intended us to know some things, and intended us not to know others. I have heard scores of sermons explanatory of God's decrees, but came away more perplexed than when I went. The only result of such discussion is a great fog. Here are two truths which are to conquer the world: man, a sinner; Christ, a Savior.

[But] where there is one man in the church of God shouldering his whole duty, there are a great many who never lift an axe or swing a blow. It is as if there were ten drones in every hive to one busy bee, as though there were twenty sailors sound asleep in their ship's hammock to four men on the stormy deck, or fifty thousand men belonging to the reserve corps, and only one thousand active combatants. Oh, we all want our boat to get over to the golden sands, but most of us are seated either in the prow or in the stern, wrapped in our striped shawl, holding a big-handled sunshade, while others are blistered in the heat, and pull until the oarlocks groan, and the blades bend until they snap.

A young man has got into bad company. He has offended the law and he is arraigned. All blushing and confused, he is in the presence of judge and jury and lawyers. He can be sent straight in the wrong direction. He is feeling disgraced and desperate. Let the district attorney overhaul him as though he were an old offender. Let the ablest attorneys at the bar refuse to say a word for him, because he cannot afford a considerable fee. Let the judge give no opportunity for presenting the mitigating circumstances. Let him hurry up the case, and hustle the young man up to Auburn or Sing Sing.

If he lives seventy years, for seventy years he will be a criminal. Each decade of his life will be blacker than its predecessor. In the interregnums of prison life he can get no work, and he is glad to break a window-glass, or blow up a safe, or play the highwayman, so as to get back again within the walls where he can get something to eat, and hide himself from the gaze of the world. Why does not his father come and help him? His father is dead. Why not his mother? She is dead. Where are all the ameliorating and salutary influences of society? They do not touch him.

Why did not someone long ago, knowing the case, understand that there was an opportunity for the exploit which would be famous in Heaven a quadrillion of years after the earth has become scattered ashes in the last whirlwind? Why did not the district attorney take that young man into his private office and say, "My son, I see that you are the victim of circumstances. This is your first crime. You are sorry. I will bring the person you wronged into your presence, and you will apologize and make all the reparation you can, and I will give you another chance."

Or that young man is presented in the courtroom, and he has no friends present. The judge says, "Who is your counsel?" And he answers, "I have none." And the judge says, "Who will take this young man's case?" And there is a dead halt, and no one offers, and after a while the judge turns to some attorney who never had a good case in all his life, and never will, and whose advocacy would be enough to secure the condemnation of innocence itself. And the professional incompetent crawls up beside the prisoner—when there ought to be a struggle among all the best men of the profession as to who should have the honor of trying to help that unfortunate.

How much would such an attorney have received as his fee for such an advocacy? Nothing in dollars, but much every way in a happy consciousness that would make his own life brighter, and his own dying pillow softer, and his own Heaven happier—the consciousness that he had saved a man!

Oh, you religious sleepyheads, wake up! While we have in our church a great many who are toiling for God, there are some too lazy to brush the flies off their heavy eyelids. You have been so long in one place that the ants and caterpillars have begun to crawl over you! What do you know, my brother, about a living gospel made to storm the world? My idea of a Christian is a man on fire with zeal for God.

The last word that Dwight L. Moody, the great evangelist, said to me at Plainfield, New Jersey, was, "Never be tempted under any circumstances to give up your weekly publication of sermons throughout the world." That solemn charge I will heed as long as I have strength to give them and the newspapers desire to take them.

Oh, you people back there in the Sheffield mines of England, and you in the sheep pastures of Australia, and you amid the pictured terraces of New Zealand, and you among the cinnamon and color-enflamed groves of Ceylon, and you Armenians weeping over the graves of murdered households in Asia Minor, and you amid the idolatries of Benares on the Ganges, and you dwellers on the banks of the Androscoggin and the Alabama and the Mississippi and the Oregon and the Shannon and the Rhine and the Tiber and the Danube and the Nile and the Euphrates and the Caspian and Yellow Seas; you of the four corners of the earth who have greeted me again and again—accept this point-blank offer of everything for nothing! Of everything of pardon and comfort and illumination and safety and Heaven "without money and without price."[18]

What a gospel for all lands, all zones, all ages! Gospel of sympathy, gospel of hope, gospel of emancipation, gospel of eternal victory! Take it, all you people, until your sins are all pardoned and your sorrows all solaced and your wrongs all righted. Let your dying pillow be spread at the foot of a ladder which, though like the one that was let down at Bethel,[19] may be thronged with descending and ascending immortals, [still] shall have room enough for you. May you climb foot over foot on rungs of light, till you go clear up out of sight of all earthly perturbation, into the realm where "the wicked cease from troubling and the weary are at rest."[20]

NOTES

1. The author is referring to the ancient Hebrew patriarchs in the Book of Genesis.
2. 1 Peter 4:15.
3. This sermon was delivered in Washington, D.C.
4. Johann Kaspar Lavater (1741-1801) was a Swiss writer who developed a so-called science of physiognomy.
5. Joseph John Gurney (1788-1847) was an English Quaker philanthropist and social reformer.
6. The author is using printers' terms for large typefaces.

7. Arthur Tappan (1786-1865), American philanthropist.
8. William M. ("Boss") Tweed (1823-1878), corrupt New York politician.
9. *Vestiges of Creation* I have been unable to locate.
10. Lesser-known writers in this list include Edmund Waller (1606-1687) and Abraham Cowley (1618-1667), both royalist English poets; Michael Drayton (1563-1631), and Thomas Shadwell (1642-1692), also poets; and John Dennis (1657-1734), critic and dramatist.
11. Isaiah 64:6; Job 14:1.
12. Cf. Matthew 6:16.
13. Cf. John 8:1-8.
14. John Pounds (1766-1839), English shoemaker, is considered the originator of the idea of "ragged schools." Peter Cooper (1791-1883), American locomotive builder and philanthropist, founded New York's "Cooper Union." Baroness Clara Hirsch (1833-1899) joined her wealthy German husband in improving conditions of Jews, notably in Russia. Cornelius Vanderbilt (1794-1877), better known as a railroad magnate than a philanthropist, endowed Vanderbilt University and other charities, many of them Christian.
15. Famous as Bucher may have been, I have been unable to identify him.
16. Talmage's sermons were (according to some accounts) printed weekly in over 3,500 newspapers around the world, over a period of several years.
17. Cf. Judges 15.
18. Isaiah 55:1.
19. Cf. Genesis 28:12.
20. Job 3:17.

Hans Nielsen Hauge

If it be true, as Oswald Chambers says, that life is tragic, then one aspect of that tragedy is unrecognized greatness. Were the Christian church to establish an "unsung hall of fame," Hans Nielsen Hauge (1771-1824) would be an honored member. The self-taught son of a poor Norwegian peasant, he became the inspiration of a Christian laymen's movement that not only pumped new life into the official Lutheran Church, but also established Norway as a true democracy in the family of nations.

During his fifty-three years, eleven of them spent in prison, Hauge suffered repeated persecution by both church and state. His followers were marked for ridicule and vilification, for no other reason than their public witness for Christ. Listen to this description by the (Lutheran) bishop of Bergen: "Their books are very badly written and incoherent. They interpret the Bible incorrectly here and there. . . . They are miserable speakers and win only the most simple people. . . . Their speakers [meaning Hauge] assume a kind of melancholy attitude, hanging their heads and talking in plaintive voices. . . . All kinds of hypochondriacs and neurotics resort to them and become worse rather than better. . . . Nearly all of Hauge's followers are miserable weaklings, the least influential part of the commonwealth."[1]

Yet Norwegian history has proved that it was from these "Least in the Kingdom" (to use a Biblical phrase) that the spirit of the modern free nation emerged.

Hauge was born in the parish of Thuno and grew up on his father's farm. Following his conversion at age twenty-five he sensed God's call, summoning him to exhort the people of Norway to repentance and godly living. For the next eight years, from 1796 to 1804, he traveled widely throughout the land by ski and on foot, finding a warm response in both cities and hamlets. State law forbade itinerant evangelism by laypersons, and conflict with religious and government authorities eventually landed Hauge in prison after prison.

Despite his limited education, Hauge early sensed the value of literature in furthering his mission. Fellow Norwegians began to recognize him as a born leader, and avidly read his writings. Like the

Anglican John Wesley, he never formally broke with the state church, but remained a faithful Lutheran; and to the ordinary citizen of Norway he became the symbol of true New Testament Christianity.

At last the Danish court in Copenhagen (the seat of authority) pronounced the final verdict in Hauge's long-drawn-out case, and he was freed. In January 1815 he married Andrea Nyhus, who kept house for him after his release. She died, leaving him an infant son, and in 1817 he married again, this time to Ingeborg Oldsdatter, by whom he had three sons. His farm at Breddwill, near Christiania (Oslo), became the center of the Haugean movement in Norway.

In his final years Hauge achieved a certain amount of acceptance throughout Scandinavia and Germany. Bishops, pastors and theological professors who had formerly berated him now made their way to Breddwill to pay their respects. But his health had been broken by the many years in damp prisons, and he died on Sunday, March 28, 1824, with the words, "Follow Jesus!" on his lips.

These excerpts from his books Religious Experiences *and* My Travels, *written during his retirement, are taken by permission from the* Autobiographical Writings of Hans Nielsen Hauge, *translated by Joel M. Njus and published in 1954 by Augsburg Publishing House, Minneapolis.*

TWELVE

MY LIFE AND TRAVELS
by Hans Nielsen Hauge

I still remember my confirmation day. It was the custom on the occasion to dress with particular care, but I had not intended to be any different than I usually was. Then one of my sisters took it upon herself to fix me up a little. On the way to church one of the other confirmands said to the rest of the group, "Today even Hans Nielsen has combed his hair!"

From early youth I was of an outwardly quiet temperament. When somebody talked about religious or spiritual things, I was deeply interested; but later on I became more conformed to the world. Although memory of the reaffirmation of my baptismal promise, and the reading of godly books, kept me from open vices, still a love of the world and other sins were not overcome. My carelessness, instability and disobedience to my parents disturbed my conscience. Often after remorse over sin and a renewal of good intentions to walk the way of the blessed, I was well satisfied, found my pleasure in God, and sang spiritual songs.

When working or traveling I found that singing these hymns cheered one greatly. But although they edified me, and although I was of a quiet disposition, my liking for fun carried me into various worldly enjoyments. I found pleasure in hunting and card-playing, not for money but to the extent of a sinful waste of time. The older I grew, the more I lost my capacity for noble feeling. Various anxieties began to weigh heavily upon me as on different occasions I met with adversity and knew fear. Terror overwhelmed me when I was in the dark, as if evil spirits were after me. Such things troubled me until I was twenty-five years old.

At this time I wanted to try to improve my personal fortunes, so I went to a suburb of Fredrikstad. Here I was exposed to many temptations by evil-minded companions. I took an early liking to liquor, so much so that I think I could soon have fallen into the vice of drunkenness. As I realized that this would lead to the destruction of both body and soul, I prayed God that He would preserve me from this temptation.

Finally, by prayerful reading of the Bible and other Christian books, I began to get more knowledge of God's will, and a desire to do His will with my whole heart. Now I developed an aversion for all sins and talked to others about what I believed, so that different ones began to make fun of me and call me "holy." People said that if I continued to devote so much time to reading, I would lose my mind. I answered that I could not believe that those who meditated upon God's Word would lose their minds, but would rather gain wisdom to practice those things that are pleasing to God.

One day while I was working outside under the open sky I sang from memory the hymn, "Jesus, I Long for Thy Blessed Communion." I had just sung the second verse:

> Strengthen me within by Your mighty power
> That I may discover what Your Spirit can do.
> Capture my mind and my conversation;
> Lead me and guide me, for I am very weak.
> Gladly I surrender to You all that I am, all
>   that I have,
> If You will come and dwell within my soul.
> Then out the door shall depart at last
> All that disturbs my inner peace.

At this point my mind became so exalted that I was not myself aware of, nor can I express, what took place in my soul. For I was beside myself. As soon as I came to my senses, I was filled with regret that I had not served this loving, transcendentally good God. Now it seemed to me that nothing in this world was worthy of any regard. That my soul experienced something supernatural, divine and blessed; that there was a glory that no tongue can utter—that I remember as clearly as if it had happened only a few days ago. And it is now [1817] nearly twenty years since the love of God visited me so abundantly.

Nor can anyone argue this away from me, for I know all the good that followed in my spirit from that hour, especially a deep, burning love to God and my neighbor. I received an entirely changed mind, a sorrow for sin and a desire that other people should become partakers with me of the same grace. I know that I was given a special desire to read the Holy Scriptures, especially Jesus' own teachings.

I wanted very much to serve God, and asked Him to reveal to

me what I should do. The answer echoed in my heart, "You shall confess My name before the people; exhort them to repent and seek Me while I may be found and call upon Me while I am near; and touch their hearts that they may turn from darkness to light."

I spoke first to my own brothers and sisters, with the result that two of them were converted. Eventually the other five members of my family became of the same mind. At every opportunity I sought to confess God's name and spoke to people about His loving desire for their soul's salvation. More and more people became aroused. Many wanted to talk to me. Some said that not all those could be condemned who were not as I was. It was revealed to me that it was not my business to judge other people.

After I had come to this understanding I was strengthened anew and used every opportunity, whether I was in town on business or someone was visiting me, to speak to people about the way of salvation. If I met anyone on the road, I spoke to him about eternal life and how important it is to work out our salvation. Some accepted what I said, others mocked and contradicted me.

* * *

On about St. John's Day, 1796, I went to Christiania [now Oslo] which was located about seventy miles from my birthplace, to arrange for the publishing of an evangelical "Rule for Life." I also delivered to the printer my first book, entitled *Reflections on the Wretchedness of the World*. When I had persuaded the printer to undertake this, I went home again and promptly began work on another book, entitled *An Attempt at a Discussion of God's Wisdom*. I wrote these books for the most part during the time that I was working on the farm, in my lunch hour while my fellow laborers were resting.

Right after New Year's I went to Moss, Christiania and Drammen to become acquainted with some people known to be religiously inclined and dependable, and to promote the distribution of my books. Here and there along the way I talked with people about the things that filled my heart. I had a great desire to speak to others about God's will for us. It was the conviction of my heart, in conformity with God's revealed Word, that we should so pattern our lives and conduct that we might live happily and contentedly here and have a well-founded hope of salvation in the hereafter.

Nor do I wish to conceal that wherever I traveled, I took

careful note of the frame of mind, the speech, the manner of life
and style of dress of every person I met. In this way I could
determine by what means I might most effectively catch their
attention and direct it toward the main goal, that of awakening in
their hearts true esteem for God and His Word.

On the evening of Third Day Christmas [1797] I was visiting
a relative at Fredrikstad. As I was standing talking with him and
several other people, Pastor Feiermann came with a lieutenant and
three soldiers to ask what I was doing. I answered that I had been
speaking about renouncing our wicked nature and worldly plea-
sures. The pastor commanded me to follow him, which I did. I
was taken to Fredrikstad's main guardhouse and placed under
arrest.

As a bailiff's deputy, I expressed surprise at being placed
under military guard. Some said it was done with the hope that
abuse and cursing by the soldiers would cause me to change my
mind. But I engaged the soldiers in conversation. Some of them
began to think so seriously about what I had said that they started
to weep because of their sins. But the others became very angry
and threatened to put a piece of wood in my mouth to make me
keep quiet, and to put me in bonds and beat me. Nothing came of
their threats. Instead they threw me into a dungeon called "the
cage." There I sang and the soldiers listened.

On the second day I was taken out of the dungeon and
conducted ten miles to Sheriff Radich. He charged me in harsh
terms with being a fanatic and leading people astray. I answered
that I had acted in accord with the Christian teaching that people
should mend their ways and renounce their sins; that I did not
think this was to lead people astray. I was returned to Fredrikstad
and placed in the city jail.

The scoffers, the curious, those who were distressed over my
arrest, and others who had a liking for my talks and writings
hurried to this place. For many of my books had already been
published by that time. A great many rumors about my conduct
were circulated. I was shamefully accused of practicing vices and
immoralities, worshiping before wooden images, and the like.
Holding such rumors wholly in contempt, I was indifferent to all
lies, believing that the truth would in the end win the victory. But
later events have taught me that false rumors can do much harm
and greatly hinder the propagation of the good.

I was brought before Magistrate Sivers for a hearing. Pastor
Feiermann and some witnesses were also summoned. The wit-

nesses and I were each particularly asked what we had talked about on the evening of Third Day Christmas. We answered, "About our Christian faith, and about putting off ungodly practices and being diligent in good works."

"Have you pressed anyone for accommodations?"

"Absolutely not."

"Why do you concern yourself with teaching?"

"Because the Bible enjoins us to edify each other."

A copy of this hearing was sent to the county seat. Then orders were given that I should be set free. Five weeks after my arrest, orders came from the sheriff to release me, which was done.

When I had visited my acquaintances, I went to Christiania for the third time and had a short account of these events printed. During the summer of 1798 I [again] went to Christiania, as I was well-known by this time and various people had invited me to visit them. On Second Day Pentecost I attended church and was invited for the evening to the home of an acquaintance on Lake Street. Bailiff Knoph came there and arrested me. I was taken to the city jail, where I remained for three days.

My second day there the diocesan prefect [of the Norwegian state Lutheran Church], Mr. Kaas, came and charged me with vagrancy, saying that I was unwilling to work and wanted only to travel about teaching. He ended by threatening to send me to prison. I replied that I was not a vagrant, as I had worked the whole ploughing season on my father's farm; moreover, I made my home with him. I also said that I had a lawful pass for my trip to Christiania and that I had taught nothing beyond urging people to honor and esteem God's commandments, serve God and learn good from one another. Whereupon I departed.

On the third day I was examined by the town sheriff, Hagerup. He began by asking me what I did for a living. I answered that I was a farmhand on my father's place.

"What errand do you have in Christiania?"

"I am having some books printed."

"Have you made any speeches here?"

"Yes, I have talked with some people during the holidays about our Christian duties."

"Of what does your teaching consist?"

"Just what we have in our [Lutheran] *Little Catechism* and the Bible." Whereupon I recited the third commandment[2] and some Bible passages that enjoin us to live godly lives and edify one another.

"I have nothing against you," he said, "therefore I am speaking with you in a friendly manner."

"Is it the Christian thing," I asked, "that those who get drunk and knock each other down so that they lie in the streets should have their freedom, while I, who go to church every time there is a service, am placed under arrest and threatened with imprisonment just because sometimes, especially during the evenings, I edify my fellowmen with song and word in accord with the accepted religion of our country?"

The town sheriff answered that he did not think it was right and he would tell the governor so. He went to the governor and pleaded my innocence. Then he came into the courtroom again and gave me permission to leave. I asked him to attest my release so that people would not think that I had run away. So he gave a paper to this effect:

"Hans Nielsen Hauge was indeed arrested, but afterward released and found to be not only without guilt but rather upright and well-informed on God's plan for the salvation of souls. He is therefore recommended to all concerned."

I remained in Christiania a week and then was arrested again. According to the orders shown me, I was to be taken home immediately under the guard of bailiff deputies. But they did not escort me very far; instead, they gave me the orders and left me to travel on alone. I brought the papers to the local sheriff, who ordered me to remain at home.

But I had a strong desire to speak with my fellowmen about the matter of our salvation and believed that according to the Bible it was my literal duty to do so. At the same time I did not believe the government was opposed, for I had found that the authorities were of divided opinions, some persecuting me and others helping me. Therefore I could not silence my heart nor quench my spirit.

My personal resources, when I began to travel and print books, were about three hundred dollars. This was now expended except for small amounts received in payment for my books. As I traveled by foot wherever it was possible, my trips did not cost me very much. In most places I had free lodging as I was able to instruct in one thing and another. If I remained in any one place longer than a day, I tried to find work.[3] Besides this I gave away books.

In addition to having experienced three arrests up to this time, I was also beaten on three occasions. The first time no witnesses were present, so the person's name and his position will not be mentioned here. He raged in anger, struck me, and threatened to beat the life out of me. But I remained very calm and when he had raged on for a time, I spoke at length with him about Christianity. Thereupon he became very agreeable and from that day quit persecuting me. God also gave me the grace heartily to forgive him and to pray earnestly for him.

The second time I was beaten by a schoolteacher. With the haughty courage of erroneous opinions and great anger, he broke in upon me with cursing and blasphemy. I said, "One ought not to curse. The commandment does not teach us to behave like this." When he struck me and wanted to throw me out the door, even though we were not in his house, I asked him to wait until I had paid the landlord for my night's lodging. He consented. I took my time, buttoned my coat about me and said, "It is good to be well-clothed when it is cold, just as it is good to be equipped with the love of Christ, so that you can pray for those who attack and persecute you." These words touched his heart so that he, sobbing, was scarcely able to wish me a pleasant journey.

The third time was by a Judge Ziegler who came to his tenant's farm while I was visiting there. He struck me severely with a heavy cane. But after a bit I patted him on the shoulder and told him to calm down. I reminded him that we are all mortal and that an eternity lies before us; that if we are to meet in Heaven, we must be reconciled with God in this world. That quieted him. Despite the fact that I had received some wounds from his blows, I did not lose my desire for travel but became more eager than ever to keep going.

I began my journey to Bergen on St. John's Day, 1798. When I arrived, I reported at once to the chief of police. At this time I was entirely unknown here and the first nights I was inconvenienced by lack of lodging. But it was not long before I became acquainted with several people who invited me to stay in their homes.

I found the printer and had him set up a little pamphlet entitled *The Faith of the Lowly* In this period the wild and irreligious ideas of freethinking Voltaire and his followers had spread everywhere. The number of disciples who, from the godless writings of their teachers, had learned to mock the Bible and everything connected with religion, all too evidently was multiplying.

Blasphemers and haters of religion must have queered me with some of the officials in Bergen. When I had been there a month, I was called before the police court to submit my books for examination. But the hearing was postponed; meanwhile I was threatened with imprisonment if I said prayers, read, or spoke in public. But when the day came and I appeared before the court, this order was revoked.

On the day of the hearing they first looked a little at my books and then asked me some questions about my religious talks. I replied for the most part by quoting passages from the Bible. Then I reminded them of how good it is when people edify one another in the fear of the Lord, put off vice, and live as Christians. With a smile the chief of police answered that it would be fine if I could influence them a little.

When [the chief] expressed the opinion that a legal ordinance prohibited devotional meetings,[4] I stated that I was aware of a legal ordinance stipulating that everyone who cursed and blasphemed God's Word should be placed in stocks. I said I was afraid that if that ordinance was enforced, the town would be full of people in such stocks. Later I was acquitted and have since been free from persecution by the authorities in Bergen County.

In Bergen it seemed the people were less corrupted by luxury and vanity than in other towns in Norway. Most of them were also pleasant—if I exclude a few wild youths who formed a gang and tormented me with their rude behavior, even to the extent of throwing stones at me on the street! (However, I suspect that somebody had put them up to it.) Even so I made a number of friends there. Among them was an unmarried lady, Miss Maren Boes, seventy years old, who willed me one thousand dollars in Danish currency. The king officially sanctioned the will. [Before she died] she sought to persuade me to remain quietly in Bergen by offering me her property, which was considerable. But I answered that I would not be able to remain there even if she should give me the whole of Bergen, since it was contrary to my convictions and desire. It would have meant that I would have to refrain from trying to edify my fellowmen.

I went on to Trondheim, [where] I reported to the chief of police. He signed my pass and I left, only to have a policeman come after me and bring me back to Chief Klingenberg, who in turn brought me to Governor Moltke. The chief maintained that I should be arrested and sent back home, [but] they allowed me to go.

[After I began attending Sunday services,] it was announced at church that those who held devotional meetings should meet with Bishop Schønheyder at Dean Steenbuch's office. I went up there and the bishop asked me various questions. He maintained I should not proclaim God's Word or talk on religious subjects. I answered that it was my conviction, arrived at from a study of Luther's *Catechism* and the Bible, that we were all free to edify one another and to remind one another of our Christian duties.

[Bishop Schønheyder] asserted on the basis of 1 Corinthians 7 that each person should remain in his calling.[5]

I answered, "The next verse explains the [Apostle Paul's] meaning as follows: 'If you are a slave, then remain in your calling as a slave. But if you can become free, use it rather.' "[6]

He said (quoting the Letter of James), "Be not many teachers, that you may not receive the heavier judgment."

I answered (quoting 1 Corinthians 14), "All may teach, all may exhort, all may edify."[7]

Dean Steenbuch then charged me with having in my books accused the clergy of being proud, avaricious, and so forth. I answered that I had never mentioned their names and was not even acquainted with them at the time I wrote.

In the evening a bailiff came and arrested me. He appointed a guard who accompanied me to the next bailiff, Iver Monsen, at Leinstrand. But this bailiff was not willing to accompany me further as he said he thought it was wrong to treat me in such a manner. So I went [back] to Trondheim by myself and reported to the sheriff. He asked me to come again the next day, which I did. I was brought before Deputy Governor Angell, who placed me under arrest for a period of seven weeks. This happened in the early part of the year 1800. I was sentenced as a vagrant to remain in Trondheim prison.

Those in charge of the prison were courteous and treated me well, so I did not actually suffer physically. Nor did I neglect my spiritual pursuits, which bore some fruit. Various acquaintances visited me, even Bishop Schønheyder. He reprimanded me severely for some things, but as usual I used the defense of the Word.

This was now my seventh imprisonment, but my spirit was free, merry, glad and ardent. I had a fairly appropriate word for every type of person with whom I spoke. Feelings of shame over my arrest and the term in prison were like the quick flight of birds over my head. In my heart I felt no burden because of these things. I experienced special strength and comfort in my work and in enduring the afflictions that met me. Often I was filled with gladness instead of the sorrow the world feels under similar circumstances. This gave me the assurance in my heart of God's gracious favor. That many were changed for the better as a result of my conversations with them was my rewarding joy.

When my time in prison was up, a bailiff came to escort me on my way. But before long the bailiff was accompanying me to those who especially desired to consult me. Reports of my coming spread, and people rushed to the places where I was, to such an extent that even though I wanted to speak with them [individually], more came than I had expected. Finally not a single bailiff would go with me any farther. So I traveled as I wished across the mountains [on skis], out through Gusbrandsdal, over Hedemark to Christiania, and from there home to my parents.

While at home in the fall of 1800 I received letters from people in many places in Norway requesting that I come to visit them. I wanted with all my heart to accept these invitations, especially in order to correct one or two errors such as tend to creep in during periods of deep religious feeling and intense emotion. I cannot begin to describe the mingling of sorrow and joy, the hard work and lack of sleep that were mine during this period. Many nights I slept no more than two or three hours. For when I traveled along the road, many people followed me, hoping for a chance to talk. The same thing happened when I stayed in a home. So I was speaking, reading, or writing constantly.

During the winter I traveled about in most of the parishes in the district of Christiania. Many places where I remained for some days I taught my friends to bind books. According to the enlightenment I had received,[8] I also endeavored to give those who asked me the truest understanding of religion. I sought to direct their thoughts, in harmony with the Creator's plan in nature, to their duties to God, themselves, and their neighbor. I encouraged them to such deeds as the New Testament commends.

In various places I found that impetuous and weak-minded individuals who had become filled with self-conceit were neglectful of their normal duties and remiss in their temporal employments. I sought to convince these of their error, urging them to be diligent in their callings and to let their deeds shine for the benefit of their fellowmen. For since we need to eat, we ought to and must work. Sometimes I worked with them at general farm tasks and in the fields. In trying to show the farmers how to make certain implements which I considered the most useful of those I had come across in my travels, I found to be true now more than ever something I had noticed long ago: People willingly exchange superstition for unbelief, and vice versa. With all my might I tried to find and follow the golden mean between these two, and to point it out to everyone who would listen to me.

In 1801 I went from Eger up Hallingdal to Hemsedal mainly because in the latter place some superstitious errors had arisen regarding the imminence of the day of judgment. I promptly sought out those who had propagated such rumors, reproved them for their errant imaginings and showed them the harmful effects such teachings might have upon themselves and others. With Christ's own words[9] I convinced them that no man knows when the day of judgment is to come.

On this trip I talked to two ministers who asked me various questions. One of them posed this one: "Why didn't God send His Spirit upon our forefathers as well as upon you and your fellow believers?"

I responded, "Who is God's counselor, or who has given Him anything that he should demand it back again?"[10]

When the ministers did not reply, a sexton came forward and gave vent to his wrath. He said that I was tearing down everything he had spent forty years in building up.

I asked, "How have you built then, since it can tumble down so quickly? Evidently your building was not founded upon the Rock."

Thereupon they told me to go, even though earlier they had ordered the bailiff to arrest me and to bring me to them! But as I had gone willingly with the bailiff's brother to the clergymen, there had been no need for the use of force. Consequently all charges were dropped.

In the summer of 1801, with the advice of my closest friends, I decided to become a merchant. I thought that by the establishment of more industries and factories, it would be possible to shine before men with good works (Matthew 5:16) and make some money in order to have something to give to others rather than being forced always to receive (Acts 20:35). I established legal residence in Bergen to advance and undergird this aim. I bought a sloop and went with it to Søndfjord to salt down herring. When I had a load, I sailed to Bergen and shipped the herring from there to Christiania. This venture was successful and now I started to deal in various commodities. I made trusted friends and held evangelistic meetings for the fishing people.

But man is always inclined to wander off the right path so that even the most noble aims may end in failure. It was not long before some began to show such diligence in following out [my] plan that they forgot to work out their salvation. In the resulting controversy, my position was that of mediator. I hated laziness and maintained that one could not please God with idleness. It was contrary to my desire to own much in a material way and it was spiritually distasteful to me to be placed in the position of an administrator.

The many tears which a few fellow believers know I shed in Bergen during the year 1804 will testify to the truth of this statement. For I feared that men would exchange a godly mind for love of the world. I saw some go off to one extreme and some to another, while only a few followed the right road. This made the outlook for the future of the church of Christ seem very dark to me.

In the fall of the same year, 1804, I was arrested and arraigned before a royal commission. I was charged with seeking my own advantage, leading many away from their work, and diverting for my personal gain the greatest part of the rightful wages of the simpleminded. Then too, it was said that I taught doctrines harmful to the common welfare and therefore deserved punishment.

Even though my own conscience acquitted me of such charges, since the feelings of my heart and the intent of my actions had been the exact opposite, I was tempted with doubt. Some of my trusted friends now turned against me. Still, what happened? Conscience drove them to tell the truth, yes, even to lament their defection from me and to deplore these false rumors about an innocent person.

As regards my earthly possessions, I had surely given away fifty times as much as I had received in gifts. When what I owed was deducted from the value of my property, I had little riches left. But I wished that I had owned nothing, so that there might not have been any grounds upon which to base these false accusations. For it was a bitter experience to stand before the court and be asked whether this or that person had given me anything. For if I, who had urged such strict denial of love to the world, avarice, and so forth, and who had made known my views to others by tongue and pen on long trips in both kingdoms; if I who had sacrificed everything, even myself, should be revealed as a hypocrite and a deceiver, O eternal misery! Then no witness to God's Word could any longer be trusted.

These thoughts troubled me to the point of bitter anxiety. But after I had considered everything more carefully and had prayed earnestly to God, who can move men's hearts and turn aside the assaults of evil, I became glad instead of distressed. I believed that truth would win the victory and that falsehood would be defeated. It is remarkable what an excellent opportunity a man who is alone, as I was in this prison, has to clarify his thinking regarding many things and to profit by his mistakes.

But many temptations also harass one at such times. Inwardly, I was troubled with evil thoughts and doubts regarding the Christian faith. Outwardly, it bothered me that I was in captivity to strangers. It was a bitter experience to see a brother or a friend without being able to speak a confidential word with him.

Time passed slowly at first, but little by little it went faster, because I occupied myself with knitting mittens. I had done this work as a child. I became so skillful at this craft that I made the finest silk and cotton gloves. Even some of the most important people in town bought them from me. Once when I was twelve years old I had seen this art practiced, but later I discovered a method of my own that was better and faster. I secured and read books dealing with various subjects: religion, science, jurisprudence and drama.

After two years had passed, my health steadily grew worse. The counselor of justice was kind enough to grant me some relief from my suffering and to permit me to come up to visit him from time to time. Especially after the completion of the hearings the third year, I was given more and more freedom. I was also summoned at various times into the presence of Governor Moltke, who enjoyed talking with me. He also gave me different tasks to perform. As a result of the humane attitude of these men, conditions became much more tolerable for me. But the documents in the case had been sent to Copenhagen[11] and remained there a long time.

Meanwhile war had broken out against England and Sweden.[12] Communication between the different nations was interrupted and so too the importation to Norway of various necessities, especially salt. The governmental commission, which had become acquainted with me through my business activities, gave orders that I should be set free. I received a loan of three hundred Danish dollars and a pass permitting me to go to the western part of Norway to establish saltworks; but with this reservation, that I was to return when my errand was completed or whenever I was called back.

[Hauge established several factories that produced salt from seawater, beginning in February 1809. He was then recalled later that year to Christiania as his case was to be brought up again.]

Finally the long-drawn-out case of my arrest and imprisonment reached its conclusion. So much time was spent in summoning and examining witnesses, who were from widely scattered points and numbered between five and six hundred individuals, that oaths on all the testimonies were not taken until the winter of 1813. In December of that year the commission pronounced the sentence "that I should serve a term of two years at hard labor and also pay all the costs of the trial."

I was astonished. In the first place, I was not aware of being guilty of anything beyond this: that I had violated the ordinance of January 13, 1741, by holding devotional meetings without always having informed the [state Lutheran Church] pastors about them. And in the second place, the ordinance in question does not stipulate any punishment in such cases. I was also accused of having used expressions in my writings that were insulting to the leaders of the [state] church.

I appealed the case to the Supreme Criminal Court as the highest tribunal in the country and [one year later] on December 23, 1814, this court pronounced its verdict. It stated that for the aforementioned mistakes I was to pay one thousand dollars in silver to the Fund for the Poor in the city of Christiania and to defray the costs of the trial, which amounted to nearly as much as the fine.

I was acquitted of all other charges.

My friends helped me with loans to pay the fine. I found comfort in this: that the money would be used to help the poor. I have learned to be content in both honor and dishonor.[13] It is not so hard to suffer when one knows that it is for the sake of truth. Whatever I owned in Bergen was taken away from me in 1804, before the trial, by an order of the Danish Board of Justice and the Home Department. Thus far none of it has been returned to me.

During this period I endured ten arrests or imprisonments, besides the final one that lasted eleven years. Several times plots were made against me, but with God's help I avoided the evil intended for me. A great many times my honor, good name, and reputation were slandered. May God give me grace to pray for those who opposed me and to wish them well in return for their ill-will toward me.

Otherwise I am daily content, having joy in my soul and

peace in my heart. I thank God for His special grace that has kept me to this day in His truth. Moreover, with God's help, the good seems to be winning the victory. I live a quiet and unmolested life on a small piece of property close to Christiania. My friends helped me buy it and through improvements in the land and the erection of a mill, I have been able to earn my living. My friends hold me in affection and I flatter myself that I enjoy the respect and friendship of the most enlightened and respected men of our country.

NOTES

1. Bishop Brun's views find a strange parallel in the Apostle Paul's word to the church at Corinth: "God chose the foolish things of the world to shame the strong. He chose the lowly things of this world and the despised things—and the things that are not—to nullify the things that are, so that no one may boast before him" (1 Corinthians 1:27-29 NIV).
2. "Thou shalt not take the name of the Lord thy God in vain" (Exodus 20:7).
3. Hauge showed a remarkable talent for successful business activities. His enterprises included printing and binding plants, fisheries, mills and saltworks. His opponents suspected him of having a huge treasury; actually he gave away much of his earnings, and his industrial holdings were confiscated.
4. The ordinance of January 13, 1741, required that the local state church pastor be informed of the time and place of any religious meetings held within his parish. The pastor was obligated to attend and had authority to forbid them if he felt such meetings were harmful. The gatherings could be held only in daytime, and men and women had to meet separately.
5. "Let every man abide in the same calling wherein he was called" (1 Corinthians 7:20).
6. Cf. 1 Corinthians 7:21.
7. Cf. 1 Corinthians 14:1-5.
8. Hauge dated his conversion on April 5, 1796, when he had just passed his twenty-fifth birthday.
9. Cf. Matthew 25:13; Mark 13:32.
10. Cf. Romans 11:34, 35.
11. Christiania was the Norwegian capital, but at this period of history Norway was under Danish rule, so Hauge's case was decided in Copenhagen. Norway did not establish complete territorial independence from her neighbors until 1906.
12. The war was instigated by Napoleon, who planned to use the Danish fleet in his struggle with England. This resulted in a British blockade of Denmark and Norway.
13. Cf. 2 Corinthians 6:8.

Søren Kierkegaard

Critics' adjectival descriptions of Søren Kierkegaard (1813-1855)— "elusive, enigmatic, mystifying, ambiguous, controversial"—are like the Danish rolls consumed each morning in European and American restaurants—endless. But in the years since his death, certain generally-accepted truths have emerged about the man. For one, he was as brilliant a philosopher as the nineteenth century produced, and it produced many. Too, he shaped twentieth-century thought so distinctly that together with Karl Marx and Feodor Dostoyevski, he is regarded as one of the prophetic voices of his time. Even more significantly, he was a Christian.

To the ordinary believer who looks for spiritual substance to get through the week, a dash of Kierkegaard must seem like a dash of Einstein. One is tempted to ask, why bother? What's more, a study of his life seems singularly unimpressive. Like David Brainerd, Kierkegaard struggled with a melancholy disposition that was continually at war with itself. Relationships with his father, his fiancée, his literary colleagues and his church were all seeming failures. He could not bring himself to take Communion on his deathbed simply because it would be administered by a Lutheran pastor.

Yet the world now reveres the lonely Dane as one of the great minds of his day. Philosophers and theologians in particular—Heidegger, Barth, Unamuno, Sartre—saw in Kierkegaard's existential thinking a clue to what the modern world would and indeed has become. And behind his wide-ranging, satirical attacks on the pretentiousness of human culture, some writers have also discovered a warmhearted disciple of the Lord Jesus Christ and a lover of God's Word in Scripture. Particularly in the closing years of his life, Kierkegaard sought to delineate in his writings the reality of his Christian faith.

Søren Kierkegaard—S.K. as scholars call him—was born in Copenhagen, Denmark of Jutland peasant ancestry. His father, a wealthy draper and a Lutheran, retired early to study theology, but could never erase from memory the fact that as a youth he had cursed God. As for Søren, at the University of Copenhagen he was branded a wit and a dandy. It took him ten years to obtain his academic degree. His engagement to Regine Olsen foundered when he realized that his melancholic frame of mind made him a poor risk for marriage.

He nevertheless became well-known about town for his satire and dazzling conversation. A local novelist made him his principal character. Hans Christian Andersen caricatured S.K. in "The Galoshes of Fortune" as a conceited parrot. But worse was yet to come; in 1846 a comic literary paper, The Corsair, launched a cruel, biting, year-long attack on him.

Kierkegaard's earliest writings, largely on philosophical and aesthetic themes, were followed in time by a preoccupation with religious themes that came to present a definitely Christian point of view. He showed a profound understanding of the redemptive work of Christ and the meaning of the cross. Dropping the pseudonyms that attached to his earlier efforts, he boldly set out (in Works of Love) to defend the heart of the gospel. To some he seemed happier and more calm of spirit, but in 1854 he launched a bitter assault on the Danish state church for its "hypocrisy" and tolerance of nominal Christianity.

As a boy S.K. had fallen from a tree, and it was apparently a spinal problem that shortened his life. When he entered Copenhagen's Frederiks Hospital in October 1855 he said, "I have come here to die," and did so a month later at forty-two years of age. For decades lack of translations of his work kept his fame from spreading, but today Kierkegaard is studied in countless institutions of learning around the world.

The excerpts that follow are taken by permission from Works of Love, Some Christian Reflections in the Form of Discourses, translated from the Danish by Howard and Edna Fong, and published in 1962 by Harper Torch-Books, New York.

THIRTEEN

OUR DUTY TO LOVE
THOSE WE SEE
by Søren Kierkegaard

How deeply the need for love is grounded in the nature of man! The first observation . . . made about man . . . by God . . . expresses just this. For we read in Holy Scriptures: "God said, it is not good that man be alone."[1] Then woman was taken from man's side and given to him for community; for love and companionship first take something from a man before they give.

Everyone who has thought deeply over the nature of man has recognized in him this need for community. How often have men cried woe upon the solitary person or portrayed the pain and misery of loneliness! How often have men, weary of the corrupting, noising, confusing life of society, let their thoughts wander out to a solitary place—only to learn again to long for community! In the busy, teeming crowd which as community is both too much and too little, man becomes weary of society, but the cure is not in making the discovery that God's thought was incorrect. No, the cure is precisely to learn all over again the most important thing, to understand oneself in one's longing for community.

So deeply is this need grounded in the nature of man that since the creation of the first man there has been no change, no new discovery made. This selfsame first observation has only been confirmed in various ways of expression and presentation from generation to generation.

So deeply is this need grounded in the nature of man and so essentially does it belong to a human being that even He who was One with the Father and in the communion of love with the Father and the Spirit, He who loved the whole race, our Lord Jesus Christ, even He felt in a human way this need to love and be loved by an individual human being. Truly He is the God-man and thus eternally different from every human being, but He nevertheless was also a true human being and tried in everything human. The fact that He experienced this need is the very expression of its belonging essentially to man.

He was an actual human being and therefore could participate in everything human. He was not an airy shape who beckoned in the clouds without understanding or wanting to understand what humanly befalls a human being. No, He could have pity on the crowd who lacked food in a purely human way, He who Himself had been hungry in the wilderness. In the same way He could also participate with men in this need to love and be loved, participate in a purely human way.

We read this in the Gospel of John.[2] "Jesus said to Simon Peter, 'Simon, son of John, do you love Me more than these?'

"He said to Him, 'Yes, Lord, You know that I love You.' "

How moving this is! Christ said, "Do you love Me more than these?" It was as if it were a petition for love. Thus speaks One to whom it is important to be the most beloved. Peter himself perceived this and the incongruity of it, as when Christ should be baptized by John; therefore Peter did not merely answer, "Yes," but added, "Lord, You know that I love You." Peter's answer indicates the incongruity. Even if a man knows that he is loved, because he has heard the "Yes" before, he is still eager to hear and wants to hear it again, even though he knows it from things other than this "Yes" to which he still again returns, eager to hear it.

A second time Jesus said to him, "Simon, son of John, do you love Me?"

He said to Him, "Yes, Lord; You know that I love You."

What else was there to answer, since the incongruity became even more perceptible as the question was asked again! Christ then said to him the third time, "Simon, son of John, do you love Me?" Peter was grieved because He said to him the third time, "Do you love Me?" And he said to him, "Lord, You know everything; You know that I love You." Peter did not answer *yes* again; he almost shrank from this incongruity, for a *yes* is like an actual answer to an actual question by which the questioner finds out something, or finds it out more certainly than he knew before. But He who "knows all things," how can He find out anything, or by another's assurances find out something more certainly? And yet, if He cannot do this, then He cannot love in a purely human way either, for this is precisely the enigma of love, that there is no higher certainty than the beloved's renewed assurance.

Dreadful contradiction—that He who is God loves humanly;

for to love humanly is indeed to love a single human being and to desire to be the most beloved of this individual person. That is why Peter was despondent over the third asking of the question. For in love's direct relationship between man and man, there is a new joy in the question's being asked a third time and a new joy in answering a third time; otherwise the too often repeated question makes one despondent because it seems to betray mistrust.

But when He who knows everything finds it necessary to ask a third time, it must be because He knows—since He knows everything—that the love is not strong or heartfelt or ardent enough in the one who is asked, in him who also denied three times. Peter certainly thought this was the reason the Lord found it necessary to ask the question a third time. But how human! He who did not have one word to answer the high priests who condemned Him to death or to Pilate, who held His life in his hands—He asks three times if He is loved; yes, He asks if Peter loves Him "more than these"!

So deeply is love grounded in the nature of man, so essentially does it belong to man—and yet men very often find escapes in order to avoid this happiness. Soon the escape is clothed in the form of sorrow. One grumbles about humanity and over its unhappiness; one finds no one he can love. To grumble about the world and its unhappiness is always easier than to beat one's breast and groan over oneself.

Soon the self-deception sounds out in the form of complaint. One complains about men, that they are not worth loving. One grumbles against mankind,[3] for it is always easier to be a complainer than the one complained about. Soon the self-deception is the proud self-satisfaction which judges it fruitless to seek someone worthy of his love, for it is always easier to prove one's superiority by being fastidious about everyone else rather than by being severe toward himself. And yet they all agree that this is unhappiness and that this relationship is wrong.

And what is it that is wrong, but their seeking and rejecting! Such persons do not notice that their talk sounds like a mockery of themselves, because this [fact]—that one is unable to find among men an object for his love—indicates that one himself is utterly lacking in love. But he who brings love with him when he seeks an object for his love will easily, and to the same degree as love in him is great, very easily find the object and find it to be such that it is lovable. For to be able to love a man in spite of his weaknesses and errors and imperfections is not perfect love; it is rather to be able to *find him lovable* in spite of and together with his weakness and errors and imperfections.

Let us understand each other. It is one thing fastidiously to want to eat only the choicest and most delicate dish when it is exquisitely prepared—or even when thus prepared, fastidiously to find one thing or another wrong with it. It is quite different not merely to eat the plainer foods, but to be able to find these plainer dishes to be the most exquisite. The task does not consist in developing fastidiousness but in educating oneself and his taste.

Or, suppose there were two artists, and one said, "I have traveled much and seen much in the world, but I have sought in vain to find a man worth painting. I have found no face with such perfection of beauty that I could make up my mind to paint it. In every face I have seen one or another little fault." Would this indicate that this artist was a great artist? On the other hand the second one said, "Well, I do not pretend to be a real artist; neither have I traveled in foreign lands. But remaining in the little circle who are closest to me, I have not found a face so insignificant or so full of faults that I still could not discern in it a more beautiful side and discover something glorious. Therefore I am happy in the art I practice. It satisfies me without making any claim to be an artist."

Would not this indicate that precisely this one was the artist, one who by bringing a certain something with him found what the much-traveled artist did not find anywhere in the world? Would it not be sad if what is intended to beautify life could only be a curse upon it, so that art, instead of making life beautiful, only fastidiously discovers that not one of us is beautiful? Would it not be sadder still, and still more confusing, if love also should be only a curse because its demand could only make it evident that none of us is worth loving, instead of love's being recognized precisely by its loving enough to be able to find some lovableness in all of us, consequently loving enough to be able to love all of us?

It is a sad upside-downness, but all too common, to talk on and on about how the object of love should be in order to be lovable enough, instead of talking about how love should be in order that it can love. How often do we not see that even one who calls himself a poet puts all his powers into a refined, effeminate, superior fastidiousness which, as far as loving is concerned, inhumanly knows how to reject and reject, assuming as his task the initiation of men into all the loathsome secrets of fastidiousness! And how many are so minded, are so inclined, are so eager to learn—that is, to get knowledge which really only serves to embitter life for themselves and for others! Is it not true that if one had not learned this kind of thing he would have found much in life to be beautiful or even more beautiful? But when one is first initiated into the contamination of fastidiousness, how difficult it is to win that which is lost, the dowry of good-nature, of love, which God has basically bestowed on every man!

But if no one else can or will, an apostle will always know how to lead us along the right way in this matter, the right way which guides us both to doing what is right to others and to making ourselves happy. Therefore we have chosen a verse from the Apostle John: "If anyone says, 'I love God,' and hates his brother, he is a liar, for he who does not love his brother whom he has seen, cannot love God whom he has not seen."[4] We shall make these words the subject of our consideration in that we, joyful in the task, choose to talk about the duty to love the men we see. It is to be understood that this discussion is about the duty of finding in the world of actuality those we can love in particular, and in loving them to love the men we see. When this is the duty, the task is not to find the lovable object. The task is to find the object already given or chosen to be lovable, and to be able to continue finding him lovable, no matter how he becomes changed.

But first we shall make a little difficulty for ourselves in respect to the apostle's words just read, a difficulty which worldly shrewdness, perhaps even conceited in its acuteness, could manage to make, whether or not it actually does it. When the apostle says, "He who does not love his brother whom he has seen, cannot love God whom he has not seen," a clever person could object that this is a deceptive turning of the idea. Just because one had made certain of the fact that the brother whom he has seen is not lovable, how could it be concluded from this that there was anything to hinder him from loving God, whom he has not seen? And yet the apostle thinks that there is some hindrance for such a person in loving God, although by the phrase "his brother" he assuredly is not talking about one certain individual, but in the larger sense about loving men.

The apostle believes that a divine claim is entered against the credibility of man's assertion about loving the unseen,[5] when it is apparent that this man does not love what is seen, since it would seem just as fanatic to seek to express one's exclusive love of the unseen by not loving anything seen. It is a divine claim entered against human enthusiasm in respect to loving God, for it is fanatical—even if it is not hypocritical—to want to love the unseen in this way.

The matter is quite simple. Man shall begin by loving the unseen, God, for thereby he himself shall learn what it is to love. But the fact that he really loves the unseen shall be indicated precisely by this, that he loves the brother he sees. The more he loves the unseen, the more he will love the men he sees. It is not the opposite, that the more he rejects those he sees, the more he loves the unseen, for when this is the case, God is changed to an unreal something, a fancy. Such a thing can occur only to a hypocrite or to a deceiver in order to find an escape, or to one who misrepresents God, as if God were grasping for His own interest and His being loved, rather than that the holy God is gracious and always points away from Himself, saying as it were, "If you wish to love men, love the men you see. Whatever you do for them you do for Me." God is too exalted to be able to accept a man's love directly, to say nothing of being able to find pleasure in what pleases a fanatic.

If anyone says "Corban"[6] of the gift by which he could help his parents, that is, that he intends it for God, this would not be well-pleasing to God. If you want to show that it is intended for God, then give it away, but with the thought of God. If you want to show that your life is intended as service to God, then let it serve men, yet continually with the thought of God. God is not a part of existence in such a way that He demands His share for Himself. He demands everything, but as you bring it you immediately receive, if I may put it this way, an endorsement designating where it should be forwarded, for God demands nothing for Himself, although He demands everything from you. Thus do the words of the apostle, properly understood, lead right into the subject of the discourse.

When it is a duty to love the men we see, then one must first and foremost give up all fanciful and extravagant ideas about a dream world where the object of love is to be sought and found. That is, one must become sober, win actuality and truth by finding and continuing in the world of actuality as the task assigned to one.

The most dangerous of all escapes as far as love is concerned is wanting to love only the unseen or that which one has not seen. This escape is so high-flying that it flies over actuality completely. It is so intoxicating that it easily tempts and easily fancies itself to be the highest and most perfect kind of love. It scarcely ever occurs to a man to speak evil about loving; more common is the deception whereby men deceive themselves out of really coming to love, simply by talking too enthusiastically about love and what it is to love.

This has a far deeper basis than one thinks; otherwise the confusion could not have taken as firm a hold as it has: the confusion of calling a misfortune that which is a fault—namely, not to find any object of love—whereby they further prevent themselves from finding it. It is commonly thought that love is admiration's opened eye which seeks excellency and perfection. This is why men complain that they seek in vain. We do not wish to contend with this view of love, for this whole conception is a delusion, since love is rather the closed eye of forbearance and gentleness, the closed eye which does not see defects and imperfections.

But the difference between these two conceptions is very essential; there is a world of difference. Only the latter concept is the truth; the former is a delusion. And·a delusion, as you know, never stops by itself. It only leads on into greater and greater delusion so that it becomes more and more difficult to find one's way back to the truth. The way of delusion is easy to find, but it is very difficult to find the way back.

It is told in the legend of the Mount of Voluptuousness, which is supposed to be somewhere on earth, that no one who found his way to it could find his way back. When, then, a man with a wrong conception of love goes out in the world, he seeks to find the object, but in vain. Yet he does not alter his conception. He is convinced within himself that it is not his fault, he who seeks nothing but love. He has not stopped the delusion; quite the contrary, he has now by its help grown quite dizzy in loving the invisible, a phantasm which one cannot see. Tragic delusion! How dreadful! People usually warn piously against wasting God's gifts, but which of God's gifts can be compared to love, which He implanted in man's heart—alas! and then to see it wasted in this way!

The shrewd foolishly think that one wastes his time in loving imperfect, weak men. I should think that this would be making use of one's love, employing it. But to be unable to find an object, to waste love in vainly seeking, to waste it in empty space by loving the invisible—this is truly to waste it.

Be sober, then; come to yourself. Understand that the mis-

take lies in your conception of love. At the very moment when you
have changed your conception of love and have understood that it
is the very reverse of a requirement, that it is a debt to which God
binds you—at this very moment you have found actuality. And this
is precisely the duty, to find actuality with closed eyes (for in love
you indeed close your eyes to weakness and frailty and imperfection), instead of overlooking actuality with open eyes (well, open
or staring like a sleepwalker's). It is the duty, the first condition, in
order that in loving you may eventually reach the point of loving
the men you see. The condition is that of finding a foothold in
actuality.

Delusion is always floating; for that reason it sometimes
appears quite light and spiritual, because it is so airy. Truth takes a
firm step, and for that reason sometimes a difficult one too. It
stands on firm footing, and appears to be very simple. Here is a
significant change: instead of asserting a demand to be fulfilled, to
get a duty to do. Instead of running about in the world, to take the
world as it were upon oneself. Instead of ardently seeking the
delightful fruit of admiration, patiently to have to bear with shortcomings. What a change! And yet it is by this change that love
comes into existence, the love which can in loving, love the men
we see.

When it is [such] a duty, it holds true that in loving actual
individual men, one does not slip in a fanciful idea about how one
thinks or could wish this man should be. He who does this does
not love the man he sees but again something invisible, or his own
imagination.

It is one thing to reject and reject and never find any object
for one's love; it is another thing to love what one himself calls the
object of his love, carefully and honestly fulfilling this duty of
loving what one sees. True, there is always the desire, and a worthy
desire, that the person we are to love may possess endearing
perfections. We wish it not only for our own sake but also for the
sake of the other person. But in God's name let us not forget that it
is not to our credit if he is such [an endearing] person, still less to
our credit to demand it of him.

If a man is going to fulfil the task of love by loving the men
he sees, he must not merely find those he loves among actual
human beings, but he must root out all double-mindedness and
fastidiousness in loving them, so that in earnestness and truth he
loves them as they are. He grasps the task in earnestness and truth,
to find lovable the object which has now been given or chosen. We

do not mean hereby to glorify a childish infatuation for the accidental characteristics of the beloved, still less a misplaced caressing indulgence. Far from it. The earnestness is precisely in this, that the relationship itself wills to strive with integrated powers against imperfection, to conquer deficiencies. This is earnestness [whereas] fastidiousness makes the relationship itself ambiguous.

One does not become alien to the other person because of his weakness or his error, but the union regards the weakness as alien, and to both it is equally important that this be conquered and removed. Because of your beloved's weakness you shall not, as it were, remove yourself from him or make your relationship more remote. On the contrary, the two shall hold together with greater solidarity and inwardness in order to remove the weakness. As soon as the relationship is made ambiguous, you do not love the person you see. It is indeed as if you demanded something else in order to be able to love. On the other hand, when the fault or weakness makes the relationship more inward, not to entrench the fault but to conquer it, then you love the person you see.

Just as there are hypocritical tears, hypocritical sighing and complaining over the world, so is there also hypocritical grief over the beloved's weaknesses and imperfections. It is so easy and sweet to wish the beloved to have all possible perfections, and if something is lacking it is again so easy and sweet to sigh and grieve and become self-important in one's supposedly pure and deep concern. On the whole, it is perhaps a more common form of lasciviousness selfishly to wish to make a show of the beloved or friend and to wish to despair over every trifle. But should this be regarded as loving the men one sees? Ah, no, the men we see (and it is the same when others see us) are not perfect. And yet it is very often the case that one develops within himself this queasy weakness which is good only for loving the complete epitome of perfections. And yet, although we human beings are all imperfect, one very rarely sees the sound, strong, capable love which is good for loving imperfect beings, that is, the men we see.

When it is a duty in loving to love the men we see, there is no limit to love. If the duty is to be fulfilled, love must be limitless. It is unchanged, no matter how the object becomes changed.

Let us think about what we were reminded of in the introduction to this reflection—the relationship between Christ and Peter. I wonder whether Peter, especially in his relationship to Christ, was an epitome of all perfections, and yet Jesus knew his faults very well!

God knows the common run of insignificant and yet pains-takingly hoarded trifles which give us human beings occasion to complain, each one of the other, about self-interest, disloyalty, and treachery. God knows how seldom it usually is that the plaintiff makes even a feeble effort to put himself in the defendant's place so that the judgment might not be overhasty, but might at least be somewhat thoughtful and considered to the extent that it knows precisely of what it judges. God knows how often one sees this sorrowful sight—how passion equips a person, when he presumably is the wronged one, with an amazing acuteness; and on the other hand how an intelligent person, when he presumably is the wronged one, is struck dumb as far as any mitigating, excusing, exonerating concept of the wrong is concerned, for this offended passion takes delight in being blindly acute.

But we will all agree that if things happened between two friends as between Christ and Peter, there would certainly be reason enough to break with such a traitor. Suppose that your life were brought into a most critical situation and you had a friend who on his own initiative loudly and solemnly swore loyalty to you, yes, was willing to risk life and blood for you; and this same person in the moment of danger did not fail to appear. (That would have almost been more forgivable.) No; he came, he was present, but he did not lift a hand. He stood calmly and looked on. But he did not stand unperturbed, for his only thought was to save himself in any way possible. He did not take flight (it would almost have been more forgivable), no, he stood there, like a spectator, a role which he secured for himself by denying you. What then?

We will not even follow up the consequences, but merely sketch vividly the relationship and talk in a purely human way about it. You stood accused by your enemies, condemned by your enemies; it was literally true that you stood surrounded on every side by enemies. The mighty ones, who perhaps could have under-stood you, had hardened themselves against you; they hated you. Therefore you stood while a blinded, raging mob howled insults at you. And this pleased the mighty ones, who themselves usually had deep scorn for the mass. It pleased them because their hate was gratified by the fact that animal wildness and the most wretched meanness had found in you its plunder and prey.

You had reconciled yourself to your fate, understanding that there was not a single word to say, since mockery merely sought an occasion, since a high-spirited word about your innocence would give mockery a new occasion. The clearest proof of your righteousness would embitter the mob and make mockery even more raging. Thus you stood, cast out of human society and yet not cast out, for you stood surrounded by human beings enough, but not one of them saw in you a human being. Yet in another sense they saw a human being in you, for they would not have treated an animal so inhumanly.

O horror, more dreadful than if you had fallen among wild animals! I wonder if the wild, nocturnal howl of beasts of prey is ever so dreadful as the inhumanity of a raging mob. I wonder if one beast of prey in the pack can incite another to a frenzy greater than is natural for the individual beast in the same way as one man among the unrepentant crowd can incite another to a more than animal bloodthirstiness and frenzy. I wonder if even the most bloodthirsty beast's spiteful or flashing glance has this same fire of evil which is kindled in the individual's eye when, incited and inciting, he rages in the frenzied mob!

Thus you stood—accused, condemned, despised. You sought in vain to discover a form which resembled a human being, to say nothing of a kind face which your eye could rest upon. And then you saw him, your friend—but he denied you; and the mockery which had sounded loud enough sounded now as if an echo had intensified it a hundred times! If this were to happen to you, is it not true that you would regard it as too high-minded if, instead of thinking about revenge, you turned your eyes away from him and said to yourself, "I would rather not see the traitor before my eyes!"

How differently Christ acted! He did not turn His eyes away from him in order as it were to become unaware of Peter's existence. He did not say, "I will not look at the traitor." He did not leave him to take care of himself. No, He "looked at him!"[7] He caught him up immediately in a glance. If it had been possible, He surely would not have avoided speaking to him.

And how did Christ look at Peter? Was it a repelling look, a look of dismissal? No, it was as when a mother sees her child endangered through its own indiscretion. Since she cannot approach and snatch the child, she catches him up with a reproachful but also saving look. Was Peter in danger, then? Alas, who cannot understand how serious it is for a man to have denied his friend? But in the passion of anger the injured friend cannot see that the denier is in danger.

Yet He who is called the Savior of the world always saw clearly where the danger was, that it was Peter who was in danger, Peter who should and must be saved. The Savior of the world did not make the mistake of regarding His cause lost if Peter did not hurry to help Him; rather He saw Peter lost if He did not hurry to save Peter. I wonder if there lives a single individual who cannot understand this since it is so clear and self-evident; yet Christ is the only one who saw this at the critical moment, when He Himself was the one accused, condemned, scorned and denied.

Seldom is a man tried in a crisis of life and death, and seldom does a man get opportunity to try the devotion of friendship in such a radical way. But to find only timorousness and prudence where in the power of friendship you were entitled to expect courage and decision; to find duplicity, fickleness, and evasion instead of openness, determination and steadfastness; to find only chatter instead of a thoughtful grasp of the situation—how difficult, then, in the rush of the moment and of passion to be able to understand immediately just where the danger is, to understand which of the friends is more in danger, you or he who thus leaves you in the lurch. How difficult then to love the man one sees, when the man one sees is so changed!

We are now accustomed to praise Christ's relationship to Peter. Let us take care that this praise is not a delusion, a fancy, because we are incapable of thinking or do not wish to tax our minds by thinking of ourselves as contemporary with the event. Consequently we praise Christ in this way and, on the other hand, insofar as we are able to become contemporary with a similar event, we act and think quite differently.

No account is preserved concerning the opinion of [Jesus'] contemporaries, but if you were to meet them, you would hear that on this occasion, as on almost every occasion when Christ did something, it was said, "The fool! However desperately lost His cause might be, yet not to have the power of gathering together all His strength for one single glance which could crush this traitor! What whimpering weakness! Is this acting like a man?"

Thus was his action judged, and mockery got a new expression. Or the influential people who presumed to evaluate the relationship said, "Well, why did He seek company with sinners and publicans, His adherents among the lowest class of people? He should have joined with us, with the foremost men of the synagogue. But now He gets His just reward. It just goes to show how one can depend on this sort of man. Yet up to the very end He was resigned as always; He never once became embittered over such shabby faithlessness." Or the clever people, who even thought they were being good-natured, said, "The fact that the high priests had Him seized and that He, fanatic that He was, finally saw everything lost, must have weakened His mind and broken His courage so that He has collapsed completely into an effeminate and impotent stupor. This explains His forgiving such a traitor, for no man acts in this way!"

Alas, it is all too true—no man acts in this way. It is precisely for that reason that Christ's life is the only instance in which it is seen that a teacher, in the moment His cause together with His life and everything is forfeited because of the denial by His disciple— that a teacher by His glance in this very moment and in this disciple wins His most zealous follower and thus in great part wins His cause, although it is hidden to all.

Christ's love for Peter was so boundless that in loving Peter He accomplished loving the person one sees. He did not say, "Peter must change first and become another man before I can love him again." No, just the opposite, He said, "Peter is Peter and I love him. Love, if anything, will help him to become another man." Therefore He did not break off the friendship in order perhaps to renew it again when Peter had become another man. No, He preserved the friendship unchanged and in this very way helped Peter to become another man. Do you think that Peter would have been won again without this faithful friendship of Christ? But it is so easy to be a friend when it means nothing more than requiring something in particular from the friend, and if he does not respond to the demand, then to let the friendship go— until it perhaps is renewed when he responds to the demand.

Is this the relationship of friendship? Who is closer to helping an erring one than the person who calls himself a friend, even if the offense is committed against the friend! But the friend withdraws and says, when he has turned over a new leaf, he can perhaps become my friend again. And we human beings are not far from regarding even such behavior as high-minded. But truly, one is far from being able to say of such a friend that in loving he loves the person he sees.

Christ's love was boundless, as it must be if this shall be fulfilled: in loving to love the person one sees. This is very easy to perceive. However much and in whatever way a man is changed, he still is not changed so that he becomes invisible. We do indeed see him, and the task is to love the person one sees. Usually one thinks that when a man has changed essentially for the worse, he is changed in such a way that one is exempted from loving him. What a confusion of language: to be exempt from loving, as if it were a matter of compulsion!

But Christianity asks, "Because of this change, can you no longer see him?" The answer to that must be, "Certainly I can see him. As a matter of fact, I see he is no longer worth loving." But if you see this, you do not really see him; you merely see unworthiness, imperfection, and admit thereby that when you loved him, in another sense you did not see *him* but merely his excellence and perfections, which you loved.

But Christianly understood, loving is loving the very person one sees. The emphasis is not on loving the perfections one sees in a person, but on loving the person one sees, whether or not one sees perfections or imperfections in this person—yes, however distressingly he has changed, inasmuch as he certainly has not ceased to be the same man. He who loves the perfections he sees in a person does not see the person and therefore ceases to love when the perfections cease, when change steps in. Even the most distressing change does not mean that the person ceases to be.

Alas, even the wisest and most ingenious purely human conception of love is yet somewhat high-flying and wavering; but Christian love goes from Heaven to earth. The direction is thus an opposite one. Christian love is not supposed to vault into Heaven, for it comes from Heaven and with Heaven. It steps down and thereby accomplishes loving the same person throughout all his changes, because it sees the same person in all his changes.

Purely human love is always about to fly after or fly away with the beloved's perfections. We say that a seducer steals a girl's heart, but one must say of all merely human love, even when it is most beautiful, that there is something thievish about it, that it even steals the beloved's perfections; whereas Christian love grants the beloved all his imperfections and weaknesses and in all his changes remains with him, loving the person it sees.

If this were not so, Christ would never have loved, for where could He have found the perfect man? Remarkable! What was this, after all, which for Christ was an obstacle in finding the perfect person? I wonder if it was not the fact that He Himself was the perfect One, something we recognize by His limitless love toward the person He saw! What a remarkable criss-crossing of conceptions! With respect to love we speak continually about perfection and the perfect person. But we men talk about finding the perfect person in order to love him. Christianity speaks about being the perfect person who limitlessly loves the person he sees. We men want to look upward in order to look for the perfect object (but the direction is always toward the unseen). In Christ perfection looked down to earth and loved the person it saw.

We ought to learn from Christianity, for it is true that no one ascends into Heaven without Him who descends from Heaven.[8] However enthusiastic this talk about swinging oneself up into Heaven may sound, it is sheer fancy if you do not first Christianly descend from Heaven. But Christianly to descend from Heaven means limitlessly to love the person you see just as you see him. If, then, you will become perfect in love, strive to fulfil this duty, in loving to love the person one sees, to love him just as you see him, with all his imperfections and weaknesses. Love him as you see him when he is utterly changed, when he no longer loves you, when he perhaps turns indifferent away or turns to love someone else; love him as you see him when he betrays and denies you.

NOTES

1. Genesis 2:18.
2. John 21:15-17.
3. Cf. James 5:9.
4. 1 John 4:20.
5. Cf. 2 Corinthians 4:18.
6. Mark 7:11.
7. Luke 22:61.
8. Cf. John 3:13.

Christoph Friedrich Blumhardt

The appearance in 1918 of Karl Barth's Commentary on Paul's Letter to the Romans *made a gigantic splash in German liberal theology whose ripples are still felt. Readers of that* Commentary *will note several references to "Bad Boll" and "Blumhardt." That the two Blumhardts, father and son, exercised a strong influence on Barth's revolutionary thinking is known today to only a few. Even fewer know that at Easter, 1915, Barth and Eduard Thurneysen paid a visit to Christoph Blumhardt at Bad Boll.*

Johann Christoph (1805-1880) and Christoph Friedrich Blumhardt (1842-1919) were Lutheran pastors. Both father and son grew up in Württemberg and studied first at Stuttgart and later at Tübingen University. The elder Blumhardt's theology was marked by Swabian pietism derived from J. A. Bengel (1687-1752). He pastored first at Möttlingen, where his prayers were credited with exorcising a demon from a woman suffering convulsions. Subsequent to that remarkable healing a retreat center was established at Bad Boll that ministered to hundreds of Europeans suffering from various melancholic ailments. In time it became an international missionary center, with a strong emphasis on prayer and forgiveness. "Jesus ist Sieger" (Jesus is Victor), words attributed to the original demon, became the watchword of the center.

Young Christoph grew up in this unique atmosphere, and at age thirteen was copying out his father's sermons. He was graduated from Tübingen in 1866, and three years later joined his father, who by then had moved his ministry to Bad Boll. Christoph repudiated the modern theological trend that had taken hold at Tübingen and had stripped the image of Christ of everything miraculous. "I asked God to talk me out of all this stuff that's in my head," he declared. In 1870 Christoph married Emilie Braüninger; they became parents of eleven children.

On the death of his father, Christoph assumed the leadership of the Bad Boll ministry that in time also included pastoring the village church. His preaching attracted wide attention throughout Germany and German-speaking Switzerland, so that he received invitations to preach from many towns and cities. Generous offers were made to him.

In 1888 he was invited to Berlin and preached a series of sermons that attracted thousands of listeners. Blumhardt's final response to such widespread popularity was to reject it. He returned full-time to Bad Boll, where he wrote songs, published occasional papers, and concentrated on ministering to the crowds that continued to come.

Blumhardt's message centered around the wonderful power of victory to be found in Jesus Christ. (Barth called this his "optimism.") Christoph firmly believed that the Kingdom of God was at hand, and he exhorted his followers to await a fresh outpouring of the Holy Spirit. Farmers, laborers, merchants and theologians all came to hear him speak. Attracted by the rising Social Democratic movement, Blumhardt began supporting popular reforms. The Kingdom of God, he said, was justice as well as mercy.

Soon Blumhardt was asked to speak at political rallies, and in 1900 was elected a Social Democrat member of the Württemberg Diet. When his Lutheran superiors censored him for this involvement, Blumhardt resigned from the ministry. After six years in the legislature he refused also to stand for reelection. Blumhardt's basic interests were not political, and he became disillusioned with the workings of his party.

At Bad Boll the load was heavy, and Blumhardt and his wife were often ill. Their large family, the requirements of many patients at the retreat center, and the outbreak of World War I added to his burdens. In 1917 Christoph suffered a stroke, and died two years later. Bad Boll was eventually taken over by the Herrnhut Brotherhood, founded by Count von Zinzendorf (1700-1760).

The following message, with the accompanying devotional thoughts, are taken by permission from Action in Waiting, a collection of the writings of Christoph Friedrich Blumhardt, with commentary by Karl Barth, published by the Plough Publishing House, Hutterian Society of Brothers, Rifton, New York, 1979.

FOURTEEN

JOY IN THE LORD
by *Christoph Friedrich Blumhardt*

Rejoice in the Lord always; again I will say, Rejoice.
(Philippians 4:4)

We should rejoice in the Lord. But why? We must have a reason. We cannot rejoice just in imagination; we also cannot rejoice in pure theory, for all that passes away. We must have something concrete about which to rejoice.

Now it is said that we should rejoice, not in just anything, but in Christ. It is not that all other joys should be taken away from us, but that for now these are not the joys that last. All those things which take place on this earth, making us happy for the moment, are very short-lived. The time has not come in which the moments of joy that the earthly life brings us can continue without interruption. Whatever joys there may be are piecemeal, and joyful moods fill our hearts only fleetingly.

Yet alongside this there is much sorrow, born of all kinds of misery. There is much disquiet, much uncertainty, and much unpeacefulness. We can look where we will, we cannot expect to have constant joy. We must always be prepared for it to pass away. Yet we cannot truly live without a continuous joy, a joy that endures, and we must seek this joy. We look for it in Christ, for in Christ a new future has been opened up for us and a goal placed before our eyes.

That is the meaning of the saying, "He is at hand."[1] It also expresses where the goal lies: namely, on earth. In Christ we may rejoice, for we shall yet experience good times on earth with Him, the Lord of Peace. We have a Kingdom of the future before our eyes, a Kingdom which shall make men happy. This is so firmly established in Christ that we can hold fast to it and always remain joyful in this hope.

This is what our faith consists in, and this faith makes us

firm and hard as steel; this faith makes us defy the whole world as
it is today; this faith is not a "belief" in God, for belief in God
must be changed into a natural, spontaneous awareness of God;
nor a "belief" in Christ either, for this "belief" changes into the
realization—we *know* that Christ is; but faith in *mankind* that men
will become something through God, through Christ, through the
Spirit of Christ, the Holy Spirit: *That* is our faith. Our faith wants
to create something; it wants to create that for which the whole of
human society has been striving for thousands of years.

Who does not want to become happy? Our faith would have
no foundation if our faith in the happiness of men, our faith in the
Kingdom of God on earth, were taken from us. Then it would
rightly be said of our faith that it is false, small, weary, weak,
fainthearted, full of doubt and fear. Then we would become un-
steady and wavering people. But if we dare to believe that we men
can still represent on earth something which is right before God
and men, if we keep our eyes on this, then we are made firm. This
is not only God's will, but is alive in our hearts as well.

This faith makes us firm and turns us into strong people
because it lives in our hearts. Yes, it is true, it is right; man is not
meant to be a miserable creature. He shall not forever perish in
sorrow and in misery; it shall not forever be a disgrace to be called
man. One day it shall be an honor to be a man, to have come out
from the disgrace, out from all the evil and wrong, into justice,
into truth, into joy. This longing lies in our own breasts and is so
much a part of human nature that it cannot be uprooted.

Religious people have tried a different approach. They
sought the future of mankind and wanted to make men happy
with supernatural things. Certainly it is a strength for people in
misery who are utterly at a loss in this world to be able to think,
"One day it will all come to an end, and I will die and my poor
soul will be at rest." Much comfort has been given when this is
firmly bound together with the thought, "Then I am in God's
hand."

But this has never produced strength for men; it has never
led to a truly vigorous life. It is somewhat like the Mohammedans
or other heathen who see death as the end of all misery. When I
think of all the people who have come to me in order that I should
talk with them about God and Christ and all that which is called
the Kingdom of Heaven, I know that this thought concerned each
of them: "Can I not receive any help now, here, in my own life?"
How often have I heard people say, "Is there no God in Heaven?

Not in the sense that I may be blessed at some future time, but that help will be given on this earth one day so that I may be joyful, freed from my sins, and really become a true man?"

This cry reaches us from millions of hearts. It is true that if one man wants God to be God on earth; if one man wants Christ to be born and things to be right on earth; if one man wants truth, life, and the joy of life to play the greatest part—not sorrow and distress, misery and sinful, perverted life—then this cry arises from millions of hearts.

Then we can proclaim: You are right. You can believe this, and because God exists, you believe that the earth exists and mankind too, and that men may attain something. You are right if you do not regard this present society of men as the ultimate one, and if you believe that one day there will be a community upon earth, a society of men in which peace and joy will reign. You are right! Believe it! As truly as God is in Heaven, as truly as Christ was born, as truly as the gospel is preached in Christ, so truly will there be a Kingdom of God on earth! Therefore believe and hope in this Kingdom, even though it still lies in the future.

Yet for those who keep their eyes on this goal, it is not only in the future; it is already coming into being in the present. And it *is* present, for this faith is today shaping a community of men, a society in which people strengthen each other toward this goal. Without such a society it is impossible. In the times of struggle that we will yet go through, the Kingdom of God must be foreshadowed in a human society.

The Apostle Paul calls this human society the body of Jesus Christ, of which He is the Head. He also calls it a building where each stone fits into the next so that the building becomes a complete whole. The Lord Jesus calls it His little flock where all should love one another and all should intercede for one another; where each should answer for the others and all answer for the one; always in the awareness that we are fighters of the future, that we are those through whom the earth must become bright. We know what we believe, and therefore we testify to what we believe, therefore we live what we believe. In this way the Kingdom of God comes into the present; the Kingdom of God comes now to mankind just as it shall be in the future.

In order to form such a society in Christ here on earth, and with our eyes on the goal that we strive for, there must indeed be people who are firm now, people who are free already, people who need not feel anxiety. Right from the beginning, when the apostles appeared in the name of Jesus Christ, this freedom from anxiety was sought.

If it is possible for you to understand it, let me tell you that it is foolish for you to say to your neighbor, "Don't worry!" When a person lives quite alone, isolated in the world, and nobody is concerned about him; when other people kick him around and want nothing to do with him; when a person is excluded from everything that lends human dignity to life; when there is nothing for him to do but earn his bread with much worry, toil and burden, then it is a sin to say to him, "Don't worry!"

Today it is coldly said of millions of wage earners, "They don't have to worry; they get their wages." And people who talk like that can pass by such a man without caring a jot for him. But still the laborers do not get jobs worthy of a human being. They live scattered and isolated in town and country. Millions have not even a friend to whom they can turn confidently and say openly, "Let me live with you. I cannot live alone." What a misery it is to have to beg, and yet how many people have to do it! What an unworthy existence it is for a man who wants to meet his obligations and be a respected person, but who cannot pay his taxes or is unable to serve society in any way. How can I say to such people, "Don't worry!"

No, for the present the whole world lies deep in worries and cares. But within that society and organism which proceeds from Christ, worries should cease. There we should care for one another. When the apostle says, "Do not worry," he takes it for granted that these people live among other people who are united by a bond of solidarity so that no one says any more, "This is mine," but all say, "Our solidarity must take away our worries. All that we share together must help each one of us and so rid us of anxiety."

Thus the Kingdom of Heaven first comes in a small flock free from anxiety. From the beginning, ever since Christ was born, people have sought such a society, a fellowship of the Kingdom of Heaven, free from cares and worries. There is an enormous strength when people stand together, when they stand together in a communal way. This firm and absolute standing together in the common life, where each is responsible for the other, is the society in which you can say to a man, "Don't worry!" Men tried it at the time of the apostles. Later it was attempted in all kinds of ways, but it has always failed. This social order which is to come from

Christ, this community of men loving and sacrificing for one another, has never come into being. And this is the reason why Christianity has become weak among the nations where it has penetrated.

To be sure, men at all times have remembered that this concern about not worrying, this building up of a social order in which one need not worry any more, was originally Christ's will. Christ told us not to seek after riches or the honors of this world only because He took it for granted that "the people who are united in My name will always have what is necessary for life. If you have clothing and enough to eat, let that be sufficient, and this you will have because you have become one in love."[2]

Again and again people have thought: this is the way it should be. But because it did not come about, they gave it up eventually and replaced it by charity where those who have, out of a charitable urge, offer something to those who have not. This is the way it has been throughout the centuries. Many wealthy people, many property owners, have helped many poor here and there. Yet you can see clearly that this was not what Jesus Christ meant. Just the opposite!

What worries are caused by the charitable institutions nowadays! Thousands of poor people have to think how they can get a little here and a little there. Often they are turned away by charity itself. How very hurting that is! Even charitable Christians who are approached say, "I cannot help you." One might have thought that there the poor could surely be freed from their cares, but nothing comes of it. So do not take it amiss if the philanthropists of the world fail to give help. This is not the way. This way people cannot possibly come to the point where they need not worry; and if they have to worry, they cannot work for the Kingdom of God. Therefore we must join together; a united company of Jesus must come about.

How shall this happen? We have lost the feeling for it. One reason why the society of Jesus Christ did not remain organically bound together is that they wanted to draw in too many elements. The members wanted to convert the whole world before they themselves had the inner strength. It is not possible to draw hundreds of thousands of people into the fellowship of this company of Jesus before the members themselves are ready for this. This is especially so if you draw in people who are greedy, people who are envious, people who are not free, who are not willing to be Christians on this condition that they truly are free people now. It would be better if they remained outside and had the cares of the world. Worryers are not fit to be co-fighters.

The freedom of the heart must first be there, a freedom from all that the world plays around with and which attracts us. Then it can happen that we shed all worries, and this gives much strength. How much people are able to do once they are freed from all cares and do not worry about their daily bread! It doesn't take much, only that people must be free from anxiety about their daily bread, and they must be so bound together that they know, "When I get into need, the others will be there." But if they say, "I will amass so much for myself that I never need the others and am the rich man and the other the poor man," this is the ruin of any society in Christ.

I do not think much of such spiritual communities; they do not last. People are friends for a while, but it soon ends. Anything that is to have value must have a very massive foundation. Unless we have community in the body in things material, we will never have it in spiritual matters. We are not spirits; we are men of flesh and blood. Every day we need to eat; we need clothing for every season. We must share our tools, we must work together, we must work communally and not each for himself, otherwise we can never become one in the love of Christ, can never become the flock, the community of Jesus which stands up in the world and says, "Now things must become quite different. Now the individual must stop living for himself all the time. Now a nation of brothers must arise."

This is the way Jesus wants us to get rid of worries, but this way has been thrown out of the world as it were. Yes, people are expected to have faith today in the most impossible situations in life, in conditions where they nearly perish of need and misery, where they exist in wretched huts, hardly knowing how to keep the wolf from the door. And we come along and call out to them, "Simply believe!" To shout into this kind of distress may help some individuals who, dying in the greatest misery, are still able to say, "Praise and thanks be to God, it will soon be over! I will not give up my faith!" Yet we have to admit that generally speaking this way of believing is an agony, and to most people it is an unreasonable demand which cannot be carried out.

For this reason I would like to say that the Kingdom of God must be not only a Kingdom of the future. Certainly for the vast majority it still lies in the future, but in the church community of

Jesus Christ we should seek to become united, and begin to become free, in such a way that at least in the circles where we understand one another, cares cease so that we can thank God and in thanking God, are able to ask and plead. When we ask, we must have a firm foundation. We know where we stand; the ground upon which we are founded is firm. Our community must be stronger than the gates of death and Hell.

There is another thing which should give us joy. This society must be of sterling quality in every aspect, so that no swindle is tolerated. It must not happen that a man be specially honored for being born into a distinguished family. In the society of Jesus Christ it is a matter of virtues, God's virtues, not human ones. Not customs, not people's views, not what a nation happens to believe is right, shall count, but only what is right before God. We ought to think about this.

This is why God's society is so hated. God's society tells the whole world straight to its face, "Your customs are false. Do you suppose we recognize your warlike ways? Do you suppose we are impressed by your hate and envy, your self-love, your whole swindle of being rich? No! We would rather belong to the beggars than go on doing homage to this swindle!" The society of Jesus Christ draws hatred upon itself because it asserts itself in this way. It no longer wants the ways of the world, the ideas of men—what we want is God the Lord!

This causes a violent struggle, which is why the Savior says, "The gate is narrow and the way is hard that leads to life, and those who find it are few."[3] Most people admire this world. They do homage to it. When the Satan of this world comes and offers his goods to them, they do not do what the Savior did. He said, "Be gone! I will not rule by your means."[4] Most people, when Satan comes, bow down before him and say, "Oh, yes, I am sure I can reconcile my relationship to God with the acceptance of worldly honor, praise, and wealth from you. And actually things will go much better afterwards!" This is what most people do, and therefore we now see many Christians who are completely of the world.

Do not deceive yourselves; it is not only the unbelievers. I know unbelievers who have much more faith than the believers. The believers are the very ones who are in danger of shining before men in their piety and saying, "Yes! Yes!" to everything.

It has been preached to us that we are saved only through grace. I believe that. But if I have been saved by grace, then I must achieve something. You may, as a favor, be accepted as a partner in a business; but once in it, you are told to get to work and be a man. Neither in Heaven nor on earth is it possible just to settle down comfortably in something through grace and do nothing and care for nobody else. If I am saved by grace, then I am a worker through grace. If I am justified by grace, then through grace I am a worker for justice. If through grace I am placed within the truth, then through grace I am a servant of truth. If through grace I have been placed within peace, then through grace I am a servant of peace for all men.

To take away for myself something given through grace and to care nothing about others—that is not the right way. Whatever I am through grace makes me a worker, and only the worker counts; the idler, never. Therefore we should always consider in our hearts: What is God's will? This is where the denial of self begins. There is great strength in this, my dear ones. Sacrifice yourself once for the will of God! It will not be in vain. Sacrifice yourself for a truth, for justice! Sacrifice yourself against human reason for something that is truly good. Sacrifice yourself for Christ in all things, for the community of Jesus Christ which through virtue seeks the Kingdom of God. There is a great, great strength in this.

In times past thousands have been driven to their death because of this. They gave their lives joyfully, and even when tortured, they remained strong because they stood in the virtues of God. Nowadays people shun every cross. Nobody dares anything today. Those who once looked kindly upon us turn away as soon as something runs contrary to the ways of men. No one risks anything.

We are often inwardly conscious of wanting to help and share in the work so that God's virtues become truth on earth, but we fear men. Therefore, if we want to have joy in Christ, unending joy, we must learn this self-sacrifice. There is no other way. Things will never be better in the world unless self-sacrificing people offer themselves as workers. A comfortable Christianity will never change the world.

Be bound together in this: rejoice in the Lord, in the hope of His Kingdom. Rejoice in the Lord as resolute members of His church community, that is able to live with others in true self-denial and freedom on earth; the church community that does not condemn, does not judge any more, that has clear eyes for the truth. Rejoice in the Lord, in God's virtues. Stand up for something, and your joy will be lasting. Whoever understands this

Christ will win the fight, and will always have before his eyes the day that shall come over the whole earth, after the battle is won for the glory of God.

* * *

Deep within the heart of the world there is a light now, a light from God, in Jesus Christ, the Savior of the world. And even if they do not know it, He is there! And even if they do not understand it, He is still the Savior of the world. God has created a memorial of His wonders, stronger than all the powers of sin, stronger than all the powers of Hell and of death.

He must rule; that is a must in Jesus Christ, given to Him by God, a blessing to Him from the Almighty. The Almighty says to the Savior: "You shall be victorious; You, with My will, with My compassion, with My love, You shall be victorious on earth." It is just as if He now wants to draw to Himself all the world in its terrible misery, so that He overcomes it. In the surrender of the Lord Jesus, our own death, our misery, and our sin are overcome; it has made a hole, as it were through which many people can squeeze now and emerge from sin, death and Hell.

The Lord Jesus looks out over the whole world: all are divided into stalls—black people, white people, yellow people, the educated and the uneducated; they make their own stalls, and then they are governed by the spirit that rules there. And there the Savior must penetrate everywhere, for He is the Lord, the Shepherd. One cannot be led to pasture by a devil, and false rulers cannot last forever. Therefore the Savior has much work to do from Heaven. He receives His power from the Father's throne, and He goes hither and thither and opens the stalls, and then they hear Him and are led to pasture by Him. In this way there shall be one flock and one Shepherd. It will in the end be fulfilled.

* * *

If it depended on God alone, everything would be good, but the will to be His people is little in evidence among men. God's history on earth is always hidden, as it were, in the history of men. We have not been able to keep God's light burning in us. Darkness was able to enter in, and so it can penetrate into our time and bring wars. Human history always seems to be without God, and yet God's will and rule runs through everything, so that in the end

His will is done. Even if men can often find no explanation for what happens and for the course that history takes—often cruel and horrible—God's plan is still interwoven. Faith presses on over all and sees God's leading as the right motivating force.

* * *

We read in Isaiah 40:26, 27, "Lift your eyes and look to the heavens: Who created all these? He who brings out the starry host one by one, and calls them each by name. Because of his great power and mighty strength, not one of them is missing. Why do you say, O Jacob, and complain, O Israel, 'My way is hidden from the Lord; my cause is disregarded by my God'?" The prophet places himself in the great cosmic movements in Heaven and on earth, all in the same glory of God. And within these mighty outlines lie the little things too, even those concerning the smallest midge, the sparrows, and the flowers. The same great power encompasses them all.

There is a great power always present; the sun runs its course; the earth, the stars, everything makes its mighty circuit. This mighty circuit must come into men's hearts too, so that good will come just as surely as the sun and the rain.

The earth is so beautiful, the earth is so lovely and full of joy, every little midge rejoices, every tree rejoices. All things are arranged delightfully and beautifully by God so that men too can live and move among them in joy and graciousness. We are peculiar people, though; we would rather have melancholy, just as folk songs are mostly melancholic. We often think that our human misery is the only thing that should occupy God. But alongside our weak nature God's power is always present in creation. He is always the life-bringing, wonderful God who touches us also so that we have hope for our own life. Just as God goes up with a merry noise,[5] you should arise too, O man, and let yourself be found strong in the God who has become your Father.

* * *

Sometimes a man is not satisfied with what he is, but he should always remember: with my being, with my nature, with my whole person, something wonderful has been created and that remains and comes to perfection and in the end becomes so wonderful that one cannot understand it in an earthly way. Each one should feel his own worth in what he has and not complain about what he has not.

What is great, living and powerful on earth streams out to us from every land and from each land differently. We have to learn to see the glory and holiness of it all so that we become people of true culture. Coarse people are not proper people; it is the fine-feeling who see in the smallest life on earth the glory and holiness of God.

In every man there lies a seed of the good and the beautiful which should germinate, and all that matters is that a blessing lights on it so that the seed will germinate. From it the praise of God should arise in our spirits. And then it will penetrate also into the body and into the soul so that men become just and understand what the goodness of God is which they should represent on this earth.

* * *

We are involved in two wars. The one on earth is earthly, waged with physical force; the one in Heaven is divine and brings in the end the victory of the Savior over the whole world. Something is being prepared in Heaven and then comes to the earth as well so that we are joyful. That will be a rejoicing throughout the whole of creation! For it does not concern only people but also all the angels, who wait eagerly for God's will to be accomplished and revealed, especially on earth where sin and death rule. Even Heaven has its unclear elements—it must become new.

The earth shall belong to eternity too; but we must cry out against sin, death, and Hell; against all evil we must cry out and plead, as the Savior said about the widow.[6] God seeks those who build on Him. If something new is to arise on earth, God has to do it, but we can sow justice.

The grace of Jesus Christ is justice and truth. It is simple, not complicated or clever. It goes through the world quite simply and grips a few people, and they remain true and help God that His Kingdom comes. In the end, however, God's power will bring justice, and evil must disappear into the mousehole and never show itself again.

* * *

Through Zion will the victory come. There is a heavenly connection with the earth, with only a few people to be sure, but they are more important than everything else. God's people should be exalted, full of spirit and power, and for this there has to be a raising from the dead. An awful lot of effort has been made to help Christianity, in churches and in meetings, but what men do is no help in the end, it peters out.

Where is Zion? That question has to be raised nowadays. It is not so simple, but we say, nevertheless, they are the people who wait for the Lord Jesus. There needs to be a people of faith on whom God can lean, so to speak, and to whom He can give the victory. When God can say, "These people are My children," then comes the blessing. It all depends on this one thing alone, that the people whom God has chosen can remain quite firm. Then we may not be fearful any more for ourselves or for the history of the Kingdom of God.

God wants to be a God of salvation and to be praised among men. It is for this, first of all, that God's people are chosen. Then it shall encompass the whole earth and build up mankind anew. Therefore many must say together: we want to be a little people of God.

*   *   *

We must let God grow in us, not wish to grow ourselves. Reconciliation is already accomplished, yet people do not understand one another. They still want to redeem themselves through their own works, but that is simply not enough.

*   *   *

When we talk—even when praying—we often do not express God's will but our own. Therefore it is good when we are quiet. We must be careful not to speak so much about ordinary things, otherwise joy vanishes. The talking that goes on among people—"I cannot stand this man"—is not light but darkness. Whoever pokes his nose into everything, has a finger in everything, will be caught in the end and attract alien powers to himself which spell disaster. Lord God, make new! Make us new! Make new everyone who calls to You, for otherwise all is in vain!

*   *   *

There must be a difference between those who serve God and those who serve the Devil. One cannot just watch: one has to do something oneself. One has to roll up one's sleeves and do what one can. When a man has his mind on God this redounds also on earthly things. All that is really good in what we do is like a bomb thrown into Satan's kingdom. God's comfort is always an admonition—not flattery, [such as] "O dear little soul, you shall have all the good things too!" Instead He gives man's soul a push: trust in your God! Then that man goes in the way of His commandments.

One has to force oneself: Up with you! Come out! Everything has to come into the light and be revealed. Then God is there again and our sins cannot frighten us. Get up! Do something! Put your hand to something or other in the name of the Lord your God and thank God that you are still able to do so.

[It is our calling] that people can always see the Savior through us as it were, the Savior who brings goodness and wants to dispense love through us now as long as He is prevented from coming to earth. If we do not have faith but turn our backs on God, God's power is hindered and He cannot be as strong in us as He wants to be. He [God] works toward the new creation like a faithful worker, so that what He has in mind to do will be finished. And if the whole world is evil and everywhere only anti-God wants to rule, still in individual people God does rule, in many people.

Behind everything lies a great future of God. It is the deeper bondages of mankind that the Kingdom of God will unloose. The loving-kindness of God penetrates right into the midst of wicked life. It will give the world a new style. Then man himself will become a gold mine again. Then self-will, greed, and all wickedness will not be victorious any more, but only Life.

It shall come to pass that peace shall come to men on earth, in their hearts and in their relationships. There is a great deal still that can be brought forth by God's power. It shall become different among men, and then nature too will be different. Then God can be honored among men. And we are allowed to help Him, in that we keep faith and remain steadfast in hope.

* * *

The day of God radiates faith, the day of God radiates hope, the day of God radiates love in Jesus Christ. In this love we can prove ourselves, and we can be joyful and of good hope in the day of the Lord. We are redeemed, and we are waiting, waiting in redemption.

*   *   *

We must not be silent. The social struggle of millions in our time is not a coincidence. It is related to the struggle of the apostles. The ferment in the nations, the agitation of the poor, the crying out for the right to live—a crying, given into the mouths of even the most miserable of men, which can no longer be silenced—these are signs of our Lord Jesus Christ. They do not know that it is Jesus who wants it. They do not know that they now represent the thoughts of God, however imperfectly. Yet they do believe. They believe in humanity; they believe in a better regime; they believe in better conditions; they believe that one can become a person who is able to live with others. They are a tool of God, and are like the son who says, "I will not obey my father," yet afterward does the father's will.[7]

*   *   *

It is God's honor which we must now exalt in our own persons, both physically and spiritually. Not our own well-being must be in the foreground, but the one desire that God may come into His well-being, into His right on earth. His Kingdom must gain ground in us and in our lives before we can enjoy all the goodness through the miracle-working hand of our Savior Jesus Christ.

Leave for a time your begging before God and first find the way together with us. Let us seek how we can do justice to God in the recognition of guilt and the true striving for God's justice and His Kingdom on earth. Turn your inner being to the opposite direction, and do not look at yourselves and all your suffering. Look at the suffering of God, whose Kingdom has been held up so long because of the lying spirit in men.

*   *   *

We can confidently rely on the fact that God's cause will soon be proclaimed and revealed on the earth. And we can help a bit in this with a living hope for the fulfilment of the Kingdom. But *that* should be something pressing for you! For it is the most important thing that we can work for today. One may simply let everything else lie and be concerned for God's Kingdom. A man who is waiting and praying for the Kingdom of God has to be capable of changing. He must be like a servant who always watches the hands of his master, and never knows what the next hour may bring. When we learn to understand the reality of the new, then we have a firm rock under our feet and we can have trust, even in a time like today.

NOTES

1. Cf. Matthew 26:18.
2. Cf. Matthew 6:31, 32.
3. Matthew 7:14.
4. Cf. Mark 8:33.
5. Cf. Psalm 47:5—"God is gone up with a shout."
6. Cf. Isaiah 1:17; Mark 12:40.
7. Cf. Matthew 21:28, 29.